D1610682

The Laughtermakers

DAVID NATHAN

The Laughtermakers

A Quest for Comedy

PETER OWEN | LONDON

ISBN 0 7206 0361 7

PETER OWEN LIMITED
12 Kendrick Mews Kendrick Place London SW7

First British Commonwealth edition 1971
Reprinted 1971
© 1971 David Nathan

Printed in Great Britain by
Lowe & Brydone (Printers) Ltd London

To Ernie Burrington

Contents

Illustrations

The photographs of Tony Hancock and Warren Mitchell are reproduced by courtesy of Odhams Newspapers Ltd, and that of Wilfrid Brambell and Harry H. Corbett by courtesy of Central Press Photos Ltd. Other illustrations listed above are reproduced with the permission of the British Broadcasting Corporation.

Acknowledgements

I am heavily indebted to all the comedians, writers, producers and directors who have provided so much of the basic material for this book. They have been more than generous with their time, their patience and their scripts, and I am deeply grateful to them all. I have also received much help from others whose contributions have had to be cut or altogether omitted through space limitations. All the same, their knowledge of their peculiar craft has contributed to whatever glimmers and insights may be found in this book. My sincere thanks, therefore, to Arthur Askey, Charlie Chester, Roy Douglas, Dennis Jones, Michael Pertwee, Sandy Powell, Brian Rix, Peter Rogers, Talbot Rothwell and Dick Vosburgh.

Others, too, have helped and among them are Dr Sidney Crown, a psychoanalyst who has studied the springs and motivations of the urge to create comedy and who made his conclusions freely available to me; and Michael Levien who brought to his job of editing an invaluable tact and skill.

There is also Deborah Sher, my niece, who, when my own house was uninhabitable, provided the haven of her room in which most of the writing was done.

Lastly and mostly I acknowledge a debt to my wife Norma, who, in hazardous times, gave me unfailing and steadfast support.

D.N.

Introduction

Laughter is part of the human survival kit, a sticking-plaster on the wounds of existence. It will not ward off a bee-sting but it has helped people to endure wars, pestilence, persecution and politicians.

As anxieties increase, the demand for comedy seems to grow greater. Every new advance in communications has always been seized by the laughtermakers to extend their trade. If television had existed in Shakespeare's day, Gobbo and Son would have been a series and Hamlet would have recalled Yorick's great farewell performance at the London Palladium.

Given enough distance in time or space no subject is too grim or morbid for laughter and death itself has a special corner. The fall of past heroes provides material for today's sketch writers and there are even jokes about the death camps of Europe while the survivors are still suffering from nightmares.

'Mention death with the right twist and it gets a hell of a laugh,' said the late Bud Flanagan who was not noted for gallows' humour. That aggression and pain are close relations of comedy is a commonplace. Tony Hancock used to make one of his stooges stamp on his foot so fiercely that he once had to go to hospital. 'How did this happen?' inquired the nurse brightly. And Hancock baffled her by saying, 'A feller stamps on it twice nightly.' He told his reluctant assistant, 'If there is no pain, they don't laugh.'

But pain and aggression are the last things uppermost in the minds of the comedian's audience unless they happen to be the butt of a fusillade of racial jokes. This kind of humour invites the harsh laughter of bigotry as it welcomes confirmation. It seems to me that the offensiveness of racial material, on the increase in clubs and pubs, lies first in the degree of affirmation it gives to an unpleasant aspect of the stereotype (i.e. Jews are mean; Negroes and Pakistanis are idle and lazy) and second in the degree of real threat that exists in the world outside the joke (i.e. Scots are mean; the rich are idle and lazy). Remove the consequences of the audiences' attitudes outside the escapist atmosphere of the place where

11

the joke is told, and there is little offence. The Scots have not suffered recent persecution and the rich are not affected by social or occupational discrimination. For the most part it is enough to the laugher that he is laughing and, for the comedian, that he is the cause of laughter. The physical and psychological humps that may have driven him to his peculiar occupation may be of interest to the curious and those who are fascinated by the mysterious mechanisms that create and recognise laughter. But the comedian, like any artist, should leave his neuroses alone, for they are the very causes of laughter in those of us who share them but who are more successful at covering them up.

Those comedians who play Pagliacci and insist on revealing their woes and miseries to the world have no more reason to command the public's sympathy than the plumber has the right to bore the housewife with his sorrows. As Frankie Howerd, one of the finest solo performers in the business, says, he is there to provide a service and he gets well paid for it.

All the same, in the course of the long interviews on which much of this book is based, some of the humps and bumps have been disclosed, however reluctantly. It is not my job—nor have I the equipment—to evaluate them in relation to the comedian's or the writer's development. For the most part they, like their possessors, speak for themselves. In that respect this book does not set out to maintain some general theory of comedy such as propounded by Freud, Bergson, Koestler and several hundred others. Their ideas are frequently fascinating and I have not hesitated to pillage them whenever I have thought them apt or illustrative. In fact, the gap between theory and practice is often astonishingly narrow, but it seems to me that what the performers, the writers and the directors themselves have to say is more enlightening.

Koestler, for instance, tells a joke in order to illustrate a point.*

'Two women (he writes) meet while shopping at a supermarket in the Bronx. One looks cheerful, the other depressed. The cheerful one inquires:

" What's eating you?"
" Nothing's eating me."
" Death in the family?"
" No, God forbid."
" Worried about money?"
"No . . . nothing like that."
"Trouble with the kids?"
"Well, if you must know, it's my little Jimmy."

* *The Act of Creation* (Hutchinson, 1947).

" What's wrong with him then?"

"Nothing is wrong. His teacher said he must see a psychiatrist."
(Pause) "Well, well, what's wrong with seeing a psychiatrist?"
"Nothing is wrong. The psychiatrist said he's got an Oedipus complex."
(Pause) "Well, well, Oedipus or Shmoedipus, I wouldn't worry so long as he's a good boy and loves his mamma." '

Koestler can, perhaps, be forgiven for the clumsy build-up full of unnecessary detail (supermarket, Bronx, death, money—who needs them?), the punchline swollen with the words 'He's a good boy' and the absence of the essential information that the women are Jewish. But 'Oedipus *or* Shmoedipus'?

Leo Rosten in *The Joys of Yiddish** deals with the 'sh' and 'shm' sounds. 'Not words,' he says, 'but prefatory sounds of mockery or dismissal that pooh-pooh the word they prefix. To negate or deride the meaning of a word, the word is repeated—but with *shm* prefixed to the repetition. "The doctor says she has a serious virus? Virus-shmirus, as long as she's O.K. (This is, of course a variation of the classic "Cancer-shmancer, as long as you're healthy"). . . .'
And Rosten, a professional humorist, tells the joke as it should be told :

'Mrs Siegel confided to her neighbour that her son had gone through so miserable a phase that he was now seeing a psychoanalyst. "And the doctor says my Marvin is suffering from an Oedipus complex!"

"Oedipus-Shmoedipus," scoffed her neighbour, "so long as he loves his mother." '

All right, so in the theory of comedy, Koestler's an expert. Expert-shmexpert, he still tells the joke like no comedian would have done. If you want to know about comedy, go to the comics.

This is a time when there is a greater output of comedy than there has ever been before in the whole laughter-seeking history of the human race. Television has virtually invented a new form—the half-hour situation comedy, and in one random summer week there were, on the three British television channels, $6\frac{1}{2}$ hours of it in the London area alone. Other kinds of comedy totalled another $7\frac{1}{2}$ hours, and light entertainment, primarily devoted to singers, seems to feel obliged to include segments of comedy if it is only provided, for the most part ineptly, by the singers themselves. There are also the chat programmes to which comedians are frequently summoned scriptless and which, on the whole, they would be wise to avoid.

* W. H. Allen, 1970.

Some of this colossal output is boring and stale. But a great deal of it is funny and inventive and some of it is truly creative, leaving the viewer in a state of satisfaction that is matched by hardly any other televisual experience.

It seems to me that there are four main sources of modern humour. Undoubtedly, these sources had their sources, but there is little point in writing about past comedy glimpsed only fitfully through other people's books. For, it is a slippery thing to get hold of at the best of times. Timing, inflexion, emphasis, the raising of an eyebrow, the flicker of an eyelid—-the eyes are always the most important feature of a comedian's face—a slight hesitancy in the utterance of a word, these are all difficult to pin down when the only equipment is a handful of punctuation marks. These are the things the reader will have to remember for himself, helped by the deep imprint that the best comedians make on the minds of their audiences. For the most part, the comedians' styles will be familiar; for the most part they are also the comedians who make me laugh.

The four influences are all post-war. In *Take It From Here*, created by Frank Muir and Denis Norden, lies the origin of the situation comedy and much else. The awful Glums are the ancestors of the terrible Garnetts; and Mr Glum and his son, Ron, have something of the trapped relationship of Steptoe and Son.

The Goon Show on radio, through its presiding genius Spike Milligan, the most gifted creative comedian of all, tapped the wild fantasies of our dreamworld and opened up a channel to the unconscious. On another plane it celebrated the disintegration of the British Empire for, like all good comedy, it was the product of its time. More permanently, it deeply influenced the following generation of comedy writers and its echoes are still reverberating. Milligan himself is still to be seen capering in pursuit of his fantasies through a landscape of staid English figures and institutions. He, Michael Bentine, a walking illustration of the Koestlerian theory of the relationship of comedy to science,* Peter Sellers and Harry Secombe created a countrywide and class-defying cult that, as Jonathan Miller once wrote, was 'crucially and quintessentially English'.

---

* 'The boundaries between discovery and comic invention are fluid. That the Jester should be brother to the Sage may sound like blasphemy, yet our language reflects the close relationship; the word "witticism" is derived from wit in its original sense of ingenuity, inventiveness. Jester and savant must both "live on their wits" . . . the Jester's riddles provide a useful back-door entry, as it were, into the inner workshop of creative originality.'—Koestler, op. cit.

Without the Goons and the impact they made on the national consciousness it is doubtful if the bizarre and puckish Marty Feldman would have been welcomed so heartily when, ten years later, he came grinning and anarchic out of the screen, a Jack-in-the-Telly-Box who, a few hundred years ago, would have had the milkmaids swearing that he had kicked over the pails.

But comedy cannot be neatly ticketed and tagged and put into clearly defined, separate compartments. The influences mingle and coalesce, weaving together the most unlikely strands. The ancestry of *Monty Python's Flying Circus* lies deep in Goon humour though it came eleven years later which, in the chronology of entertainment, is almost a lifetime. But equally, its creators were the product of the wave of university and intellectual humour which started with *Beyond the Fringe*, the third of the major sources, and went on to liberate whole areas of experience which, until then, had been taboo to radio and television, and were still emasculated in the theatre by the Lord Chamberlain's powers of censorship. It was not *what* was said in *That Was the Week That Was*, the *Fringe*'s television spin-off, that was so shocking or exciting. It was the fact that it was being said on television which had hitherto confined its comedy either to domestic cosiness or fantasy and had left political and social comment severely alone. Certainly, there had been serious programmes like *Free Speech*, in which politicians were allowed to fight their battles in public, but the BBC itself stood aloof, shifting any responsibility for controversy on to the participants.

For *That Was the Week* and subsequent Saturday night programmes such as *Not So Much a Programme, More a Way of Life*, *BBC 3* and *At the 11th Hour*, the BBC itself had to take full responsibility. The actual effect of all this in terms of social change is hard to gauge but probably it was not much. 'Laughter,' says Henri Bergson in his essay, 'indicates a *slight* (my italics) revolt on the surface of social life.' He also says, 'By laughter, society avenges itself for the liberties taken with it.'

The opponents and/or victims of these displays of hostility succeeded in imprinting disreputable overtones on to the word 'satire' and, with changing circumstances, chief of which was a new government, the fashion waned. It will no doubt return when conditions are right, unless the BBC continues to regress into its former foetal crouch. The great wind that blew through its corridors is now reduced to a few fitful gusts and most doors are safely locked and bolted against the respectable Shavian notion that it is proper to treat the most serious subjects with the utmost levity. Certainly, the formula of quip, sketch and song was worked out, but that does not explain the present situation where the only controversy in comedy is to do with how many times the words 'bleeding', 'bloody' or 'bum' are used.

'Satire', in fact, was always a word strongly resisted by those connected with the Saturday night programmes, though it was apt enough for some of the material.

The general impression persists that these programmes were wholly the work of waspish young men from Oxbridge whereas, in fact, a good many of those involved were journalists whose university background, if it existed at all, was distant or irrelevant. Like *Beyond the Fringe* many of the items had little in common with undergraduate humour—another devaluating epithet that was frequently hurled. Traditional university humour, as Jonathan Miller says, is based on the proposition, 'Wouldn't it be funny if . . .' and is obsessed with parody—that is, style rather than content. The basic premise of *Beyond the Fringe*, Miller points out, was 'Isn't it funny that . . .' and the television shows took it a little further by saying, 'Isn't it absurd that . . .'.

Using one institution to attack other institutions and their hitherto impregnable supporters was great fun while it lasted. Part of the fun was that Ned Sherrin, the producer who pioneered Saturday night satire, clothed everything in the trappings of show-biz. He gleefully recruited performers as unalike as Sir Michael Redgrave and Frankie Howerd, Peter O'Toole and Tommy Trinder whenever it was appropriate and sometimes when it was not. However serious the subject, however virulent the venom, the knockabout atmosphere of music-hall was never far distant.

Music-hall has been proclaimed dead and buried on innumerable occasions. The reports have been grossly exaggerated. The bricks and mortar may have been pulled down or put to other uses and the jugglers, tumblers and unicyclists all conjured away. But the music-hall itself has not died. It is to be found, debased perhaps, in the provincial pubs and clubs, it exists in the *Carry On* films and, above all, it is alive in the lonely figure of the stand-up comic who can be despairing or cocky, who can parade his inadequacies or his wit, who tells of disasters or of triumphs, who battles his way through a world in which everything—even, sometimes, the audience—is against him. He may or may not employ writers, but that hardly matters. What comes over is an individual and usually wry view of an imperfect world where humiliation lurks around every corner. When these men are in full flower they turn the best writers into— to use Denis Norden's words—'comedian's labourers'. They are usually far funnier than their scripts because what we laugh at is not the joke but the joker. The one factor common to stand-up comedians is the gift of painting verbal pictures and the most illiterate of them have the enviable knack of choosing exactly the right word at precisely the right moment. Apart from this, they come in all shapes and sizes and are all kinds of men. Some of them go on stage and are able to magnify themselves like the frog in the fairy tale, projecting their natural contours to twice the size of life. Others seem to adopt a totally different personality from their normal selves by flourishing one comic and extrovert factor in an otherwise deeply serious and reserved character. Many are insecure and are themselves baffled at their choice of such an insecure profession. Others appear to have more self-possession than is decent.

They go back a long way. They were the jesters kept by kings as mnemonics of mortality, the contrast needed by heroes as proof of their heroism and the means by which the ordinary man became reconciled to his humiliations and took revenge on those who inflicted them. They are the fourth source, commonly called the music-hall. But they existed long before music-halls were built, long before there were theatres of any kind and, if ever we emigrate to other planets, one or two of them will be among the passengers. The clowns may not be the spirit of mankind, but mankind would have little spirit without them.

I | *Take It From Here*

It was audacious. It was the first radio comedy to comment, however obliquely, on the values of its audience. It took the film, the staple entertainment of its day, and subjected it to mercilessly accurate parody. It threw out the sacred family, backbone of radio situation comedy in which scatter-brained wife and good-hearted hubby faced life's little middle-class upheavals with a barrage of quickfire quips, and came up with the atrocious Glums in which mother was relegated to a dark corner of a dusty bedroom from which an occasional strangulated cry emerged, and father was a shifty, dirty and unctuous boozer sunk deep in ignorance and lechery.

It took the respectable state of being engaged and dwelt on its frustrations, scouring the women's magazines for the right social aspirations and derisively foisting them on the hapless, ill-equipped Ron and Eth.

It also went in for heavily plotted puns, so diabolically tortuous that they rattled the listener's teeth.

'Thou art spending all the Royal coffers on this female person,' says the Puritan, Silas, remonstrating with the profligate King Charles in a Nell Gwynn sketch. 'But yesterday you sold the Crown Jewels. And what for? To buy her a sedan chair with a sunshine roof.'

'So I blued a couple of baubles,' says the King. "Tis of no account.'

'But,' says Silas reproachfully, 'you're forever blueing baubles.'*

Take It From Here was the first radio show to emerge from the post-war comedy explosion when, it now seems, all the physical and mental restraints of the years of trial and hardship culminated in a mad scramble to seek and provide laughter. Certainly, it was the first show to have no connection with the war, either in real terms

---

* 'A pun is two strings of thought tied together by an acoustic knot.'—Koestler

'Words are plastic and may be moulded into almost any shape.'—Freud

or through association. Its writers, Frank Muir and Denis Norden, its principal comedians, the booming, bustling Jimmy Edwards and Dick Bentley, a gifted Australian who, as the moronic Ron, could make stupidity irresistibly comic, the girls, Joy Nichols, later succeeded by June Whitfield and Alma Cogan, all bore names unconnected by the public with blood, sweat, toil, tears and forces entertainments.

Muir and Norden became the *gurus* of British comedy, achieving, before they eventually dissolved their partnership, the distinction of becoming advisers and consultants on comedy to the BBC. 'You mean,' said the American humorist Mel Brookes when he met them, 'You mean you know?'

They know, in fact, as much as it is seemly for creators to know about their own creative processes. This is frequently a mystery to the people most concerned. When someone wrote an erudite book about ITMA (*It's That Man Again*), the wartime show that teemed with fantasy characters who could have stepped straight out of the looking-glass, its writer, Ted Kavanagh, looked at it, shook his head and said, 'I suppose he knows what he is talking about. All I know is that I write fourteen pages of jokes every week.'

It was with ITMA, *Band Wagon*, which preceded it, and the wartime services gang shows that radio took its first step away from almost total reliance on the music-hall and concert party. Pre-war, variety bills were the norm, though there were occasional desperate attempts to disguise them. For *Whoopee Paris*, for instance, the listener was invited to 'Come to Paris with a jolly party which includes Clapham and Dwyer, Stainless Stephen, Yvette Darnac and Gerry Fitzgerald. Tommy Handley will be your guide.' It sounds an unlikely excursion now and could not have carried much conviction even then. The comedy event of the pre-war week was *Music Hall* or *Palace of Varieties* on Saturday nights. At their most glittering they had George Robey or the Mills Brothers, but a more typical bill would be : Georgie Harris (Small, but Full of Vitality), Rupert Hazell and Elsie Day (the Bright, Breezy Couple), Suzette Tarri (Character Comedienne), Abe and Mawrus (In Arguments and Contradictions) and Paulo (The Singing Clown). In the winter there were excerpts from pantomimes and in the summer excerpts from concert parties. There were hundreds of comedians and variety acts to choose from and the aim seemed to be to re-create, through radio, the atmosphere of the theatre rather than to create a specific radio comedy. The exception was *Band Wagon*, in which Richard Murdoch and Arthur

Askey were supposedly the inhabitants of a flat at the top of Broadcasting House.

Sid Colin, creator of *The Army Game*, commercial television's first successful comedy series, is probably the only scriptwriter today who was active before the war. Colin was a jazz musician who started writing comedy for band shows. 'You'd come home about 2.30 in the morning after playing in some hotel,' he recalls, 'and tune in to Radio Schenectady in America to pick up their shows—Jack Benny, Burns and Allen, Fred Allen, Charlie McCarthy and Edgar Bergen. What they were doing in the way of material and jokes was a revelation. One realised that there were people other than Stainless Stephen. People forget that there was nowhere else to look except to America. It was the golden light of the West. British films were beneath contempt, were ludicrous. If one went to see them it was to send them up. This was being part of the in-crowd of the time. The Marx Brothers and, more specifically, Groucho, introduced us to the idea of the wisecrack, the quick, destructive line. What was fascinating about Benny's show in particular was the architecture. We had nothing like it. We had variety, music-hall; the American shows were entities. Characters were invented and exploited. They were incredibly good. I didn't see how anybody could be that good so consistently. You tore home to listen through waves of terrible static which usually came on the punchlines of the jokes. Often you had to guess them. But the important thing was that they were built like plays, with plots. The writers didn't go in for one-line he-and-she jokes. They banked on effects which came later. It was an extremely complicated and sophisticated technique. We pinched stuff for the band show and at the same time tried to discover what the trick was, how it worked technically. Eventually, one could invent for oneself. I started to get the hang of it.'

Like all comedy writers then and since who try to inject a touch of realism into their characters' speech patterns, Colin came up against the BBC's little black book of taboo subjects.

'I can remember,' he says, 'being outraged at having the word "strewth" cut from a radio script. I was told, "Surely you know that it is a corruption of God's truth?" But every now and then somebody pushed the frontier on and a new norm is set.'

When the BBC realised that the epithet 'burke' was derived through Cockney rhyming slang from Berkeley Hunt/cunt, it was banned.* But later when somebody used it there were no protests.

* The hidden semi-obscenity was used deliberately in *The Goon Show* with the occasional reference to a character called Hugh Jampton (huge hampton/Hampton Wick/prick).

Now it is so commonplace that it is used on children's shows in the mouth of the fox puppet, Basil Brush.

Denis Norden recalls that among the taboos still in force after the war were biblical references, no matter how indirect (i.e. B.C./ Before Crosby), or any mention of underwear (i.e. winter draw(er)s on). Royalty, religion, speech impediments, physical handicaps, colour, were all absolutely forbidden. Muir and Norden once sent a script to a producer friend convalescing after an illness. It began, 'C-c-c-christ,' said the king to the one-armed nigger. . . .'

Terry-Thomas recalled recently that he was not allowed to use the phrase 'poke his eyes out' because the producer, a woman, was reminded of the sexual connotation of the word 'poke'. It was all nonsense, of course, and still is—now that the debate has progressed to how *many* times (not *if*) the word 'bloody' can be used in a programme.* All the same, it is a curious experience to read what John Watt, Head of BBC Variety, had to say about censorship in a foreword to a book he compiled in the 'thirties.† 'Negroes,' he wrote, 'must not be referred to as "niggers", though many spirituals continually being sung by coloured gentlemen contain this apparently offensive word. Chinese, also, must not be referred to as "Chinks", so I presume we must have a larger Chinese audience than one would anticipate. Jews, apparently, resent being referred to as "Shenies" even in fun.'

Mourned the then most powerful figure in radio comedy : 'There are not very many things left about which to be funny on the radio.'

All the same, Muir and Norden succeeded in being quite funny without one mention of Niggers, Chinks or Shenies, even in fun.

Denis Norden was born in Hackney in 1922, son of a gown manufacturer who still does not understand why the boy did not go into business and is still not quite reconciled to the fact that he didn't.

When Norden was asked by the London *Evening Standard* to review a book called *The Rationale of the Dirty Joke*, he was, he says, highly conscious of the literary honour, nothing of its nature having come his way before. 'I was,' says Norden, 'thrilled to bits and I worked for six days to produce 600 words. When the review was published I was inordinately proud. I popped down to see my parents and they were sitting there with the *Evening Standard* and their faces were rather bleak. My mother said, "So this is what it's all come to—you're the expert on dirty jokes." '

He doubts if there is any specifically Jewish strain in his humour, though when he was writing the screenplay for the film *Buona Sera,*

* See the Cook and Moore skit, pp. 113-16.
† *Radio Variety* (Dent, 1939).

Mrs Campbell with Mel Frank, they decided that the Italian characters had to have a different idiomatic sound from the Americans.

'We didn't want to use Italian stage dialogue,' says Norden, 'and Mel said, "I've always had the theory that Italians are Mediterranean Jews, so let's write them Jewish East Side or East End without any of the phrases but with the inversions like 'so now he tells me' and maybe with the Italian accent grafted on it will come out Italian." ' It seemed to work.

'My parents were—are—very Orthodox but I'm not at all. Still, I suppose you can't help being affected. Marty Feldman believes we were forced up like Jewish boxers were and that comedy was our kind of escape-hatch. But I think that's romanticising it tremendously. I was never conscious of that kind of pressure. To be Jewish in Stamford Hill in the 1930s was nothing like being a Puerto Rican in New York in the 1960s or 70s. I was beaten up by the Mosleyites and things like that, but it might as well have been Celtic and Rangers.'

He won a scholarship from primary school to the City of London School and then had a chance, because he spoke French and Spanish, to go to the Spanish Civil War with a journalist and train with him.

'My parents put their foot down, so, more or less in pique, I refused to do any more schooling and went to see the Hyams Brothers who controlled a chain of cinemas—the Trocadero, Elephant and Castle, the Troxy in the Commercial Road and, later, the State, Kilburn. I asked to join them in some capacity where I could write. They said they would eventually employ me on the publicity side but first I had to learn every branch of the entertainment business.'

Norden started by cleaning out the boilers, became an usher, a stage electrician, a stagehand and a projectionist. He also worked in the drawing department of the cinema architects and wound up as assistant manager of the Trocadero, Elephant and Castle. An evening's entertainment at the Trocadero usually comprised two films and a variety bill. One that Norden remembers featured Flanagan and Allen, Sophie Tucker and Larry Adler. There were four hundred seats at sixpence each. It was an experience that has made him acutely aware of the audience, especially in the cinema. These days Norden is concentrating on writing films. 'I will cling desperately with my finger-nails to stay in films as long as I can,' he says. 'My idea is that if a person pays 4/-6 for a seat to see a film I've written I want to give him at least 6/-3 worth of entertainment. And you can call entertainment whatever you like—

whether it makes him laugh or whether he is simply distracted. I've had a lot of experience with audiences and you know when they are interested. You know when they're not coughing, when they're not looking around for the ice-cream girl, when they're not thinking of something else. It's not just the sheer volume of laughter—you can easily be fooled by that. If you happen to get an audience who are in a mood to laugh you get marvellous laughs and you think that what you did was great. It was simply that the audience were in a good mood and were ready for distraction. The best moments are when you start with an audience in a bad mood. Hot weather audiences are very difficult to make laugh. If you can break them down and make them forget the hot weather and the sweat, then you can say you have given them a good half-hour, that it's been worth their while *schlepping** all the way out to wherever it is and having to go all the way back again.'

Norden plunged almost immediately into a screenwriting career. The cinema circuit employed a number of organists whose musical interludes were illustrated by slides. Norden wrote the text for these slides.

'They were,' he recalls, 'the equivalent of writing very small television programmes today. You had to pick a subject like "Rhapsody in Colour" and the organist then played "The Lady in Red", "Deep Purple" and "Mood Indigo". The slides cost nine-pence each to make and the number of words on each was limited, otherwise the price went up. You had to be cogent. The work involved writing parodies of popular songs of the day. If it was a good organ interlude it would, as it were, get networked in the sense that the rest of the organists on the circuit would pick it up and play it. Sometimes I was playing seven theatres at once with organ interludes.'

The war broke out and shortly afterwards the Holborn Empire was bombed. At the time, Norden was managing both a cinema and a variety theatre in Watford, and Sidney Caplan, who had been Musical Director at the Holborn Empire for years, moved to Watford.

'I had lots of chats with Sidney about the great days of variety at the Holborn which was the number one family variety house in England, the Palladium being the place for special occasions. So I wrote to the BBC and suggested that they do a series called *Memories of the Holborn Empire* and illustrate it with records from the BBC files. I did the research from Sidney Caplan's memories.'

---

* *Schlepping*: a Yiddishism. When you have dragged yourself from point A to point B and your body feels like a heavy suitcase, then you have *schlepped*.

Norden was called up by the R.A.F. He is a bit vague about the date, it was probably 1941. He became a wireless operator and found that if he wrote service shows on message-pads it not only whiled away the boring night hours but exempted him from day-time guard duties. He landed in France on D-Day and organised and wrote for revue groups all through France, Belgium, Holland and Germany, finishing up with a show that included Bill Fraser and Eric Sykes.

When he left the R.A.F., Norden started writing for comedians, the arrangement being that his fee would come from the plug money the artist got for singing the song to which his patter routine was the preamble.

'It was,' says Norden, 'slightly dodgy because the smaller the comic, the less the music publishing house would pay. If you got Issy Bonn you got a very good fee. It entailed travelling to all the provincial and London suburban theatres and hanging round the bar asking comics if they wanted any stuff.

'One doesn't realise now how many comedians there used to be. It was mandatory to change one's style of writing for each of them. Each comedian was striving to be individual. There were things like brother acts and man-and-woman acts—you'd be hard put to it to find a man-and-woman comedy act today. I wrote for Nat Mills and Bobby and Billy Carlyle and Hilda Mundy and each of them carefully explained their style—you'd call it their gimmick now. Some of them were very clever and very individual. It's a tragedy that there's no place for such people now.

'I think of myself as somebody who supplies comedy material for other people, not as a writer in the sense of a novelist. Even in films I don't feel that I have any sort of individuality or any sort of personal statement to make. Or that I have any message for the ages.

'I have a theory about anybody who wants to do comedy or, as it were, thrust his opinions on other people—either as a politician or anything else. I think we may get into a half-arsed area of psychology here, but when I was at school I was good at English and I used to get my English essays returned with $\frac{10}{10}$ written on the top in red ink with V.G.—Very Good. Sometimes they used to be read out to the class. I was six feet tall at thirteen and some-thing of an oddity, very skinny, all wrists and ankles and a pair of braces, and I wasn't very good with girls. If we danced—you remember in those days dancing was cheek-to-cheek—I used to have to bend myself to the shape of a question-mark in order to get into the right position. But the moment of glory was when I was singled out because of my essays, and I think that every form of writing I have done during the rest of my life was done because I wanted to get $\frac{9}{10}$ V.G.

'This can mean insecurity, a seeking for reassurance, a seeking for approval. You can rationalise it how you like, but it's in that area somewhere.'

'I too,' says Frank Muir, 'was tall at school. But beautifully proportioned.'

Ted Kavanagh, the ITMA writer, had started a kind of writer's commune or co-operative called Kavanagh Associates and on the strength of six ideas for radio shows which Norden sent him, Kavanagh invited him to join his stable.

A similar invitation was extended to Muir, another ex-R.A.F. man.

For a time they contributed separately to various radio programmes, then producer Charles Maxwell suggested that they should get together to write a new series called *Take It From Here*.

'There was,' says Norden, 'a certain amount of fear. We had both written for series but only as contributors. You could be lousy and still be redeemed by the rest of the show. You didn't bear the brunt. Now we were offered the chance of writing a whole half-hour and there was no cop-out. If it failed it was because of us.

'I can remember the day I met Frank who was, and is, rather impressive-looking. He looks rather like an eighteenth-century gentleman and when he was younger he was even more willowy—not my style at all. As it happens, he's not far off in his background. That evening I went to a cinema in Lower Regent Street near Ted Kavanagh's office. There was a second feature about the French Revolution, starring, I think, Cornel Wilde. The hero had lost his girl and was talking to a very wise old man in a café and the wise old man said, "It doesn't matter, you will forget her. Time will heal the wound. She will find happiness elsewhere." And the hero said, "Ah, maybe, but men are different from women." And the old man said, "Ah, monsieur is a philosopher." I laughed and I heard one other laugh and I looked round and it was Frank.'

Frank Muir is the son of a marine engineer who came from New Zealand. His grandfather had gone there from Scotland to build a bridge. 'I think,' says Muir, 'it fell down or something.'

Muir is indeed willowy, languid even, looking more as if he has uncurled himself from a Max Beerbohm caricature of elegant Edwardian undergraduates than from a long line of craggy Scots engineers. But there were hard times when he was young, though his father still managed to send him to a private school. 'It was,' says Muir, 'a tremendously efficient educational machine. There was no time for much else in the way of character building. It was all fairly hard work.

'Anybody who has this comedy thing has a power and uses it to compensate for other deficiences in his make-up, his un-averageness. I think everybody in comedy is un-average in that they need this power to make people laugh or to get something out of their system. They have a hump or a depression of some kind. It need not necessarily be physical. I'm quite a shy person actually, still uncomfortable with strangers and not very ebullient. I'm either saggy and wet or else I perform. I think it's the discovery that one can perform that readjusts one. It compensates for this sagging business. It's the same now at parties. I've either got to go into top gear or the eyes go glazed and I lean up against the wall hoping everybody will go away.

'I detected quite early on that I had a facility for amusing people, not in a performing kind of way, but I could make them laugh a little when I was quite small by generally seeing the ludicrous side of things.'

Muir's education veered between Chatham House—where Edward Heath was, but earlier—and Leyton County High School. But it all came to a stop when Muir was fifteen and his father died. From 1934 until the war broke out he worked for a carbon paper firm.

'The war,' says Muir, 'had the marvellous effect—for the survivors—of stirring up everything and cutting them away from their predestined lives. You could make a fresh start. That's why those of us who are a kind of post-war wave probably wouldn't have gone into it at all had it not been for this cataclysmic upheaval. I had a very soft war, though quite a long one. I had a white flash in my cap—which meant that I was air crew under training—for almost all of the six years. I never actually got as far as training. I was interviewed and accepted quite early on and this wretched flash got greyer and greyer as the troubled years rolled slowly by. I was a photographer and after becoming an aircraftsman 1st class was sent to Iceland in 1941. A man called Bickerstaffe should have gone, but he went on leave and fell down a bomb-hole and sent a cable back when he was recalled saying : CANNOT COME. BEST BLUE AT CLEANERS. It was apparently the only uniform he had with him and you weren't allowed to walk around in civvies.

'So I was sent to Iceland in his place. It probably saved my life. The camp I left was heavily bombed a few days later and I might have been posted to a much hotter theatre of operations. Iceland, on the whole, was a pretty quiet front. It was a typical British invasion. They invaded Iceland and then hired the radio station at God knows how much per day to broadcast to the victorious troops. I never actually photographed anything for years but I wrote some radio stuff in Iceland. It was more jolly than funny.'

After the war Muir sent some sketches to Ted Kavanagh, who asked him to try to write an act for a comedian. 'It was pretty awful,' says Muir, 'and was never used, but Ted sent me a cheque for ten quid out of his own account, just for encouragement. Then I wrote something for a comedian at the Windmill called Peter Waring, who was offered a BBC radio series. I did eight, then he was arrested for fraud and hanged himself.'

Muir became friendly with Jimmy Edwards who also worked at the Windmill about that time, and when Edwards went into a radio show called *Navy Mixture* Muir supplied his material. Also in the show were Joy Nichols and Dick Bentley for whom Norden was writing. The *Take It From Here* team was formed.

'We've had a very funny career,' muses Muir. 'A year after starting, our press cuttings said, "Without question, Britain's leading comedy writers". We had one year of the exhilaration of climbing and twenty-three years' experience of slipping. It's a most curious graph.'

The comedy cascaded out of them in those early years of the partnership. Apart from *Take It From Here* they wrote radio programmes for Bernard Braden and revue sketches for Jimmy Edwards and Tony Hancock.

'*Take It From Here*,' says Norden, 'was due to run for six shows and we received a bit of a bashing. Everybody hated it. If we had written all the six before they started to broadcast, then I think we would have been on a loser. But after the first couple we saw there were ways to go which had never . . . which we couldn't find a precedent for. We saw that some of the things we did worked and we decided to get more adventurous. We were working on pure audience reaction. We heard people laughing and we got drunk with it, so we thought we'd go a bit further. By the time the sixth one was out there was a generally favourable audience reaction.

'There were other, funnier shows, like *Much Binding in the Marsh*, the Eric Barker and Charlie Chester shows, all going at the same time. But they were really wartime shows which had survived. *Take It From Here* was completely post-war in its attitudes and it recognised the literacy of the listener.'

There were arguments with the BBC, who objected to some of the material they wrote on the grounds that listeners would not understand it.

'Certainly,' says Norden, 'it's no good writing on a subject that people are not conversant with but, in one case I remember, we wrote a line about Picasso and the BBC said the public wouldn't know who Picasso was. They were looking in the rear-view mirror. They ignored the fact that people were buying more newspapers than ever before and there were television and radio. It was quite possible that the listeners had never seen any of Picasso's works, but at least they would know, we argued, that he was a modern painter. It would not be the same as referring to, say Kierkegaard. Picasso was within the general knowledge. The thing to do is to keep up with what people are aware of, even if they are not aware that they know it. This entails reading ahead of people, seeing the underground papers and watching for the first signs to appear in the overground. And then seeing if there is a funny side to it. I have no academic qualifications and I am not in any way in advance of other people intellectually. It's simply that my job pushes me ahead sometimes. Once I know that they are in on something, have caught up, then I consider I can write about it.

'*Take It From Here* seems very unrevolutionary now and it's very difficult to say what distinguished it from anything else. One of the things was sending up Hollywood films which, strangely, as far as one knows, hadn't been done. I suppose we got near to it because we were both film fans and I had been a cinema manager. We could get the flavour of the dialogue and start from there for the comedy.'

JIM : Well, listeners, there's a spate of rather turgid films around now, dealing with the American occupation troops in Japan.

DICK : You know—the complications that crop up when the handsome G.I. falls in love with the pretty Japanese girl but regulations forbid them to see each other.

JIM : Well, it occurred to us that this basic situation—how does a soldier in an occupied country solve his romantic problems?— can be no *New* thing. Why, it probably cropped up as far back as the Roman occupation of Britain.

DICK : Shall we see if it did?

And they do, with Jimmy Edwards as Caesar forbidding any 'Latin frattin' with the local Anglo-Saxon girls.

'You know Caesar,' says Dick Bentley as Cato Lascivius to his woad-covered Ethelfreda (June Whitfield), 'You can argue with him until you're blue in the face.'

'But I *am* blue in the face,' answers Ethelfreda.

'What we also did,' continues Norden, 'was to send up relationships between people, family relationships, things that were fairly sacrosanct at the time. Ron and Eth started from a sketch we did about an engaged couple. We suddenly realised that one of the most hilarious and ludicrous positions to be in was this state of being engaged. It doesn't apply now. We described it in one of the programmes as driving with one foot on the accelerator and the other on the brake. Nowadays it is driving with both feet on the accelerator. Strangely, there was something very sexual lurking behind it, though it could never be made explicit in those days. But that was what we were on about, that was what we found funny, that state of having to hold back all the time. Frustration. It was possibly the very first glimmer of the permissive society struggling to be born. People sort of recognised that if you were engaged the question was why don't you go to bed together. But one never dared say it, never mentioned it. It was just simply this blind groping, this aching state, the tension. Of course we weren't allowed to indicate any of this for a second, but I think it just caught the public at a time when they were becoming aware of sexuality.

'Ron's voice was funny, grotesque, June's voice was absolutely true—we knew who she was founded on. There were a lot of cosy family serials and soap operas on the radio, so it was a slight send-up of them too. We wanted to make the father ghastly, an insensitive pig. It was a reaction against the non-Alf Garnettism of the BBC at that time.'

GLUM : I'm sending Mrs Glum off to the pictures and it'll take her a good hour and a half to walk back. She can't move very fast at the moment, poor sweetheart—she's breaking in me new boots.

Glum reveals his idea of a proper home : 'You couldn't have a finer front room for a social evening. Put the telly up on the sideboard and there's room for eight people to pass out in comfort.'

A picture of the room is given by Eth : 'Oh Mr Glum, look at it. Pair of braces hanging from the mirror and a lace runner stuffed all anyhow into the biscuit barrel.'

But it's not a lace runner; it's Ron's vest.

Mr Glum protests that she is seeing the room under the worst circumstances—with the light on.

Eth yearns for a respectable bourgeois existence. 'It's a social life that we lack,' she complains. 'I feel it must be more satisfactory to find oneself part of a large circle of people . . . after all, we are members of the Young Engaged Set.'

She is ambitious: 'If Ron doesn't mix with better-class people, how's he going to get on in life? In this world it's not what you know, it's who you know, isn't it Ron?"

Ron : 'Yes, Eth. And I don't know either of them.'

Insofar as he is aware of anything, Ron knows he is not the stuff executives are made of, but it is far too much bother for him to try to puncture Eth's illusions. Besides, she needs them; they protect her from full realisation of her inevitable defeats. The combination of Ron's incredible stupidity and Mr Glum's beery shiftiness will always win. She seizes on the superficial deficiencies* and declares that if Mr Glum had done his duty as a father and spent a bit of money on some new furniture, curtains and carpets, Ron would be a managing director. Mr Glum is deeply wounded by this aspersion. He is not a man who goes in for material things. Hasn't he always spent his money on his friends and relatives? He appeals to Ron : 'Isn't it true that none of our family's wanted for anything?'

Ron : 'Except Uncle Charlie, Dad. He's wanted for bigamy.'

Ron is totally honest, undeluded, ready to admit his ignorance. When, discussing a holiday overseas, Eth asks him, 'Ron, what do you think of Shanklin?' Ron says, 'I can't really offer an opinion, Eth. I don't think I've ever shankled.'

Mr Glum, however, cannot abide being thought ignorant. La Zoute is mentioned.

'La Zoute . . . La Zoute . . . that's South France, isn't it?'

'North Belgium,' corrects Eth.

'Oh yes,' agrees Mr Glum, 'you're quite right. I was thinking of *before* the war.'

Alf Garnett himself couldn't have got out of it better.

'We always used to say,' says Norden, 'that Eth was the sort of girl for whom women's papers published photographs of ideal kitchens. She was completely brought up and conditioned by women's papers. We used to read them just to get the picture of Eth. Ron was a complete grotesque. What was extraordinary though was the number of letters we got from girls asking how we knew that when two people were alone they talked like Ron and Eth, because that was exactly how their fiancés talked. And the letters were couched most affectionately. The obvious answer was that your fiancé is a moron, but they didn't see him like that. They saw him as the ideal fiancé, completely infatuated and dominated

* Peter Cook was to use the same device with his coal-miner who would have been a judge if only he had had the Latin (see pp. 82-4).

both by parents and girl. That was how a fiancé should be. 'The Glums weren't really as complicated a set of figures as, say, the Steptoes are. They were much more comic strip. They had characteristics rather than character. But we tried to slip in recognisable phrases, things we had heard ourselves or other people say. The most exciting part of comedy is when a non-funny line gets a laugh because people recognise that either they or their Aunty Gertie have said it. I tend to use my relations a lot in this way. I remember one phrase we gave Jimmy—"It's not fit for 'uman 'abitation to live in". That was the kind of thing we strove for because you could think of your uncle saying it.'

But the social content of the work was never uppermost in their minds.

'No writer,' says Frank Muir, 'is ever conscious at the time that something significant is happening. The intellectuality comes after and is usually something of a shock to him. Ray Galton and Alan Simpson didn't write *Steptoe* as a penetrating illumination of the human condition in a trapped relationship. They thought they had got a few giggles. It started off with one of them saying, "How about writing a story about two junk men?" And in order to get the jokes they had to create a relationship. The more dramatic and real the relationship is, the easier and funnier are the jokes. By technique they have set up something which gives them their lines. But because of their talent they are in fact responding to and illuminating a very real and deep family problem. So on the surface they are just writing jokes, but when there's talent present there's all sorts of stuff going on underneath the surface. What is wrong is to try and dig for the underneath stuff and reckon that that is what their intention is. If they wrote a story about trapped relationships without the funny surface it wouldn't work at all. Galton and Simpson do have terrible consciences. They worry about the world; they care very deeply about things. It's the other face of comedy in a sense.

'It was the same with Johnny Speight and the Garnetts. He thought he was writing about someone he thought very funny. I can't think of any effective broadcast comedy which was written with a sociological aim. Garnett may have turned out that way, but it started off as an attempt to write funnies. God knows, it's desperately difficult enough to get a titter as it is. The danger is when the writers start believing the intellectuals. If you try to sit down and write something penetrating and illuminating about the human condition you don't come up with the Steptoes; you come up with some boot-faced piece with inserted jokes.

'Weekly comedy writing to a deadline is something like 95 per cent experience and technique and 5 per cent creativity. This may sound as though the 5 per cent is hardly worth it, but unless it is there you are on a dying fall. It is the vital bit. The trouble is that there is an effect like an optical illusion and it can look as though the 95 per cent is enough. The amount of creative talent around is very small, the amount of professionalism is huge. Television tends to move away from creative areas and into areas where technique is a substitute. American comedy is very rarely creative. It's much more technique comedy where skills replace talent and everything is in episodes because episode writing is maximum technique and minimum creativity. The creative elements come right at the start, in the concept. After that, it is reproductive. Creative comedy people may occasionally pinch a bit to get themselves out of trouble but they don't want to go in directions that other people have already taken. Creative comedy doesn't lie in the joke field. Gags are easy to write. It lies in character. Character requires insight into human nature, an understanding of the way people behave and pretend. The great power of character comedy is that the audience identify with the people and are in sympathy with them.

'A few years ago we used to say we were comedians' labourers. There was a rather inflationary attitude towards comedy writers— that if the script was good you had nothing else to worry about. We adopted our attitude to balance things out. It's wrong when you come up against work that is not primarily a vehicle for a comedian. *Steptoe and Son* was a good idea, but when Harry H. Corbett and Wilfrid Brambell—both interesting actors but not world class—were cast, they fitted so beautifully that the sum total was greater than the parts. But Galton and Simpson could not be called comedians' labourers when they were writing it. When they were writing *Hancock's Half Hour* they were servicing a unique talent and to that extent they were working towards a talent other than their own. All the same, the creative qualities they brought to the servicing of a comedian were not less than when they were writing for actors. It is irrelevant to say that one thing is more important than the other. In one, the unique talent of a comedian brought out creative writing of the very highest order; in the other there was no unique talent to bring it out but it happened anyway and they, in fact, were serviced by the performers and the performers were the scriptwriters' labourers.

'A comedian is one who has a unique view of life, a unique way of interpreting it. A performer is somebody whose technique and charm is what he is about. W. C. Fields was a comedian, Bob Hope is a performer. Performers are interchangeable. It's only a question

B

of quality, not kind. If you write a show for Bob Monkhouse and you can't get him, Dickie Henderson could do it just as well. But if you write a picture for Frankie Howerd and he is not available, you cannot find anyone else. The comedian can transcend poor material, the performer is almost entirely dependent on material. These divisions are fluid and woolly. They aren't value judgments. It's not a matter of one being better than the other.'

Take It From Here ran on radio for twelve years and then Muir and Norden moved over to television with a number of half-hour comedy series. Eventually came their appointment as consultants and advisers on comedy to the BBC.

'I loathed it and was very bad at it,' says Norden. 'Frank loved it and was very good at it.'

But not at first.

'We didn't want to go on the staff,' says Muir. 'The sort of money we were earning as free-lance writers was way above any staff scale. So eventually we agreed on a formula whereby we continued writing series for a guaranteed minimum and, in the interstices, gave them the benefit of our experience. It didn't work, of course, because adviserships don't. For one thing we used to have to go into purdah when we were writing, so for six months of the year the advisers were no help to anybody. The other thing was that advice isn't any use. Whoever is responsible has to do it on his tod. When I went back in control, when I became Assistant Head of Light Entertainment and was no longer advising, it was fine.'

But before that there was another spell of free-lance writing during which they did a show for Rediffusion—'a flop show with enormous influence' is how Muir puts it. This was *How to Be an Alien,* the first non-fiction comedy series, the first about real things. 'Without it,' says Muir, '*The Frost Report* couldn't have happened.' Then came another series with Bob Monkhouse and, finally, the split.

Norden had come to think of his name as 'and Denis Norden' and Muir says : 'After seventeen years sitting on opposite sides of a desk we both felt very lonely when we split up, but we had a strong feeling that the view had improved. It was a traumatic thing. It was like a marriage without the more obvious advantages of a marriage. We saw more of each other than we did of our wives. We wrote everything together. But how long can you go on doing that? How long can you go on being half an entity with no real development? When you have done all the technique stuff, the joke writing and the setting up of series, people only want you to do the same thing. The only forward step is to dig deeper into yourself and produce more of yourself on paper. And you can't do that in harness. We yearned for our own identity after all those years. It was a very amicable splitting up.'

Muir went into his executive position with the BBC; Norden went into film writing and worked with Mel Frank.

'I'm aware,' says Norden, 'that I've a hell of a long way to go with film writing possibly because I started writing in radio and I'm hung up verbally. I verbalise, I don't visualise. People tell you that television is visual, but it's only just started. The mere fact that you could issue the best of the Hancock and Steptoe shows as LPs tells you how verbal the best television has been and still is, except for a very few exceptions like *Monty Python's Flying Circus*.'

Muir was happy in his executive role. 'I could do something,' he says. 'Because I was there other people did better things than they would have done if I wasn't there. I liked the companionship of working in a department, of working with producers. I think producers liked having me to talk to. It's marvellous to find you have a sort of tiny aptitude which you didn't realise was there—that of creating an atmosphere of work.'

Muir moved to a similar position with London Weekend Television where he stayed until 1969, when his was among the first wave of spectacular resignations over policy differences.

'A group of us,' he says, 'had gone into London Weekend with a sort of forlorn hope of doing something a little bit different. It wasn't possible in that set-up and we lost; we were defeated. I had complete freedom within limits—you can't have all the money you want, can't get all the people you want, but no one ever stopped me doing anything. I think I did fourteen comedy series in the first year, which was twice as much as any other company had ever done. There were a couple of healthy flops but most of them did very well, extremely well.'

One show was *We Have Ways of Making You Laugh*, in which Muir himself performed. It was taken off. 'I was in an awkward position because I was talking both as Head of Entertainment and as star of the show. But I thought it was a great mistake to take it off. I felt we were getting close to what we were trying to do and it was very cheap. But there were all sorts of politics behind that decision; I never knew why it was taken off.

'The desire to perform is very strong in me. It is part of the drug, part of the need. Ego is the spur with me and performing is a tremendous sop to the ego.'

'Performing,' says Norden, 'we owe a lot to our physical appearance. We got a lot of publicity and 90 per cent of the reason they wrote about us was because I'm six feet three and Frank's six feet six, and so every piece started with "Radio's tallest writers" or "Television's tallest writers". Not the best, but the tallest. You got more for your money in terms of sheer length, sheer flesh. So we were invited to go on to television programmes before we went on radio simply because of this rather ludicrous picture we presented. Frank is a very good performer. He is an extrovert and he likes it. I get screwed up. My stomach contracts to a walnut before and it takes four hours to recover. But it was the team. We had no separate identity in those days. There was no point in putting one on without the other.

'I don't want to perform, except that there is some stuff I can't sell to anybody because nobody does that sort of thing. It's tentative, not a belly-laugh—annotations, marginalia. "My Word", for example, is a kind of writer's joke. If a performer did it you'd have to have much bigger jokes. It's offered very tentatively. I will only go on chat programmes if there is a subject on which I have a little sort of line. If there isn't one I refuse. I'm not going on to be a comic and do jokes. I've refused to go on *Any Questions?* six times. There are certain things I will talk on and offer facetious comments, but there are other subjects where I would consider it an impertinence for me to sound off. I have a rooted objection to show-business people sounding off about subjects outside their field. And, in any case, I would be rude to politicians. My nightmare is being on *Any Questions?* with Gerald Nabarro and having to observe the civilities.'

Muir came out of London Weekend Television feeling 'extremely apprehensive'. 'A lot of people,' he says, 'say, "Well, of course, you'll be all right", but you never know. What you do know is that reputation in this sort of thing is a bubble and you never know when the tide is swinging in another direction and you will no longer be of much interest.'

While Muir was still an executive he tried to get playwrights to turn to comedy. 'They wanted to, because the money's better and it is fun, but it's a terrific chasm to jump—though it looks quite narrow. The starting-point is so different. A playwright cannot sit down to knock up a few giggles. He's got to get the thought that he is writing about clear in his head. As soon as you do that it becomes a different thing—a light drama. And light drama isn't the weird stuff that we do. There's nothing funny on paper. All you are playing with is a bagful of potential. Even when the show's written you haven't got anything. Comedy is like a torch battery—there is no point in it until the circuit is complete and the bulb, which is the audience, lights up. It is how strongly the bulb lights up which determines how well you have done your job. If you have done a play it exists, it stands four-square, good or rotten. It is there.'

But sometimes the comedy is there too, coming ready-made and polished out of life, needing no invention, no embellishment. All the writer has to do is to pick the right time and place to use it. One such story came to Muir.

'My brother-in-law came back from a caravanning holiday on the Continent and, at one of the caravan parks, some English friends next to him had had a marvellous experience. You can actually travel in a caravan on the Continent and this chap had pressonitis to get down to the south. His wife wanted a nice long lie-in. He woke up with the dawn sun on his face, crept out, hitched up the caravan and got going. He spun along happily for a couple of hours and was then stopped by traffic-lights in a little market town. It was about 9.30 a.m. with everybody out shopping. His wife woke up, put on her dressing-gown and stumbled out of the caravan to go for a pee. As her foot touched the pavement the lights changed and there she is, in her nightdress and her Marks and Spencer's quilted blue dressing-gown with her hair undone and no face on in a French shopping centre.

'The husband drove along merrily until suddenly a Vespa shot in front of him with a woman in her night-clothes on the back. "Funny lot, these French," he thought to himself. . . .

'We put it in as the finish of a camping episode in *Never a Cross Word* and it worked beautifully.'

But mostly, ideas come from within the writer. His sense of humour is not the kind that distinguishes between what is funny and what is not funny; the true comedy writer sees the funny side of everything and many a script has been fashioned out of domestic incidents which would be considered good evidence in a divorce court and frequently have.

'One is self-censoring,' says Norden. 'There are things I don't find funny myself, but this isn't to say that they shouldn't be subjects for humour. You can make jokes about cancer, atomic explosions, Hitler, Dachau and Belsen and they can be very funny and I might laugh at them. I just don't find an impulse to see a funny side of certain subjects. They don't inspire me.'

But he has sometimes found himself writing something he did not think was particularly funny on the assumption that other people would.

'This,' he says, 'is what happens when you are a professional comedy writer. There come moments when you have got to get by on what you loosely call technique. You don't have an idea but you have enough experience in the technicalities of writing comedy to get by. You're ashamed of it; you know that it's a cheat. It's very easy to do it with a domestic sketch, and you get a response about anything in a doctor's surgery because people have been conditioned to find it funny in the context of other funny things. You know there's nothing funny there and you're simply coasting.

'There isn't to my knowledge any theory that covers all the situations in which you laugh, but the best overgeneralisation is that in a majority of so-called jokes the laughter is generated by an unexpected withholding of sympathy.* You'd be surprised how many jokes can be covered by this—most sex jokes, most relationship jokes, most jokes about authority—doctors, teachers, policemen. It happens when your sense of humanity demands that there should be sympathy and sympathy is unexpectedly withheld.

'Of all forms of communication there are only two that evoke a physical response from the audience. One is comedy, the other pornography. Each only succeeds to the extent that it gets a physical response. The audience has to change its physical posture. In a sense you could say that the laughtermakers and the pornographers are the most neurotic because they are the most power-hungry. A novelist, a journalist or any other purveyor of information receives no physical response. They can watch someone reading what they have written and, though it could be changing the reader's life and converting him to new opinions, they will not necessarily see anything on his face which indicates that they have power over him. But when the comedian tells a joke it transforms the hearer from passive to active.

'From there you can go into all sorts of Cloud-cuckoo-land about sexuality and power. The life and soul of the party who is effecting physical changes on everybody around him is practising a sort of rape, a kind of assault.'

Norden is now less concerned with jokes than he ever was. 'In films, I like the sort of plot where the audience asks, "How's he going to get out of this?" And when he does, it is in a way that they should have realised. That's the point at which they laugh. It's a laugh that's with you, for, having given them all the evidence, they should have seen it for themselves. To an extent that sort of plot is based on predicament. Comedy doesn't change over the years; what changes is the element of predicament. You could write—and they did write—films in the 'forties which depended on, say, a husband thinking that his wife had been to bed with another man. That was the predicament and it had its own built-in penalties. If it was true, it was the end for both of them. What the

* ' Laughter is a momentary anaesthesia of the heart.'—Bergson

permissive society has done is to make this cease to be a predicament because it is now not necessarily the end of the marriage. It isn't for me a question of what people laugh at, it's a question of predicaments. Losing a job was a tremendous menace at one time, today it isn't. I can only work first of all with the main character. How is he different at the end from what he was at the beginning? Then what is threatening him, what price has he got to pay if it goes wrong? What's difficult today is to find the price.'

For Muir too—although 'I don't think any areas of life are uncomedic,' he says, 'any more than there are any areas which are untragic or undramatic. What varies is the public acceptance of what is dramatic and comedic. I remember when the Battle of Britain was a kind of Holy Grail. Since *Beyond the Fringe* it has become fair game. It may seem inconceivable now but it is possible that Dachau could be a source of comedy. I'm absolutely certain comedy was there among the people in Dachau because the extremities of human suffering do produce it. It is a question of timing and audience attitudes.

'It is the audience who dictate the kind of comedy we get, not the writers. In the early 'sixties with the red-necked Texas colonel's finger on the H-Bomb button and the Conservatives in power for the previous 140 years, the audience needed the kind of malicious comedy which was called satire. Now things have changed. The world has changed and the need for comedy has changed. Now malicious entertainment just looks old-hat. It isn't, it's just that we don't need it any more—for the moment. Now it seems to be the wild, gleeful, fantastic comedy, the *Monty Python* type, that's wanted. If *Monty Python* had been written eight years ago it wouldn't have worked because we wouldn't have responded to it.

'It is possible to create a need, but you have to be a genius to do it. Generally speaking, most stuff is run-of-the-mill. One stream will take an audience's fancy, and if it happens that at the same time the potential of writers and cast is up to it you can get a great show. But it's the audience that make it into a great show. It starts off as a terrifying step into the darkness.

'If you could pin it down the computers would be on to it. You can replace it with a synthetic product, which the Americans have done. You replace humour with good humour and it's all beautifully planned, but there's no individual attitude towards life because people might not like it. You have charm and love and soft-heartedness instead, and it's half an hour's pap which sells rather well. Good comedy is relevant and local and pinned to a time. It's the froth on top of the beer, the fag-end in the gutter. ITMA needed the war. It was nothing before the war, fantastically good during the war and awful after the war. *Take It From Here* could only have happened after the last war which explains its temporariness. The best post-war show was the Goons, because they brought a new dimension into comedy. The thing about *The Goon Show* was that it could have happened after any war. It was not the product of anything apart from Spike Milligan's near-genius—if not complete genius. It came about through Spike's—everybody's—reaction against regimentation. It happened with Lewis Carroll when he threw off the mathematician's logic. But it's not only the writing end, it's the receiving end as well. If Spike had written *The Goon Show* at any other time it wouldn't have worked. The audience's receptivity has to be right for that sort of show, or it doesn't get off the ground. All the same, the Goons was a far more permanent sort of humour than *Take It From Here*. It was a far more positive creation. It influenced the whole world of humour.'

2 | *The Goons*

The announcer said, 'This is the BBC Home Service.' There was the sound of zooming aeroplanes, chants of *Sieg Heil*, the noise of a cattle stampede and the vroom-vroom of a motor race. It was May 28th, 1951, and *The Goon Show*—then called *Crazy People* —had begun.

'What,' cried Harry Secombe in his wild Welsh tenor, 'What is the zaniest comedy show on the air today?'

Spike Milligan made a hesitant guess, 'Da,' he said, '*Today in Parliament*?'

'No,' corrected Secombe. 'It's those Crazy People, the Goons.'

It started in the days of austerity when, six years after the war, the sweets (and meats) of victory were still on ration and the word 'goon' was used by returned prisoners of war to describe their German guards. It ended nine years later, in March 1960, when Britain had been told for three years that she had never had it so good and four young men were about to cast doubt on this premise in an Edinburgh Festival entertainment called *Beyond the Fringe*.

It took time for *The Goon Show* to develop the characters and characteristics that turned it into a cult. The derisory view of the rapidly disintegrating British Empire was present from the beginning, but such officer-class figures as Grytpype Thynne and Major Bloodnok were yet to come. So were Henry and Minnie Crun, Moriarty and Bluebottle, though Eccles was to appear within the first few weeks. There was, however, Sir Harold Porridge, forever in search of the East Pole or Tutankhamen's tomb. (His assistant, Harold Vest, is given its location in a dream by a voice which arranges to meet him there. 'But how will I know you?' asks Harold. 'I will be wearing a reincarnation,' says the voice.) There were also Arnold and Mrs Fringe, Ernie Splutmuscle, Phillip String and a couple called Hershell and Jones. And the effects or, as they are marked in BBC scripts, F/X. They were an integral part of the image-building, image-shattering technique that is the basic tool of radio comedy. In Milligan's hands the method leapt to stratospheric heights and the listeners' imaginations joyfully abandoned all restraint and followed him.

When one of the characters is offered a cocktail, Milligan's instructions read : 'Make with the effects of eight jet planes, a police siren, the victim of a maniacal strangler, the San Francisco earthquake and the Hydrogen Bomb. It dies away in a strangled sob and hiss.' The verdict on the cocktail then follows. It is : 'Quite nice.'

Milligan, with some assistance from Larry Stevens, an ex-commando whose early death robbed comedy of a major creative force, and Jimmy Grafton, a publican and scriptwriter, created the Goons in his own image. Eric Sykes, both in collaboration with Milligan and on his own, wrote a number of scripts but stepped down because friction developed. Suggestions also came from the three major performers, Secombe, Peter Sellers and Michael Bentine. Bentine contributed a lot but his ideas were in a rhythm different from Milligan's and, after a couple of series, he left the Goons to pursue his own fantasies and capture them for the television screen, a place which, despite some attempts, was largely inaccessible to Goon-type humour until technical developments were able to provide the visual equivalent of F/X.

Milligan is a clown whose full range of fantasy is not yet tapped. He is an anarchist with a contradictory passion for conservation, an exhibitionist performer so sensitive that he seems to lack a protective layer of skin. His nerve-ends are acutely receptive to pain and cruelty yet give him access to experiences and worlds most other people only reach through dreams. Much of his comedy comes from seeing things from a totally unexpected and highly sophisticated viewpoint, or so simply and directly that the purity of the vision is childlike—or idiotlike. He remembers the first joke he ever wrote. It was about a man who visits a psychiatrist, removes his hat and there, perched on his head, is a duck. The psychiatrist goes 'Shoo' to the bird which stands up. He sees that it is attached to the man's head. 'When did this start?' asks the psychiatrist, and the duck says, 'Well, I first noticed two little lumps on my feet. . . .'

An early *Goon Show* had Sir Isaac Newton (Harry Secombe) demonstrating his Law of Gravity in the manner of a stage magician.

SECOMBE : Would any gentleman care to come on to the stage? Ah, you sir, thank you.
MILLIGAN (as Eccles) : Da, that's O.K.

SECOMBE : Now just jump into the air.
MILLIGAN : Da, O.K. (*F/X jump effect.*)
SECOMBE : There, you see what happened? You jumped up in the air but you came back down to earth again. Now why?
MILLIGAN : Da—'cos I live there.

The *Goon Shows* were not all fantasy. A very recognisable picture of the times emerges from one of the early sketches. It was done during the Festival of Britain in 1951 when the South Bank of the Thames flowered with strange architectural structures and a government-sponsored circus tried to distract people's minds from the quality of the bread. At the same time the Festival attempted to blow away some of the national self-doubt with a few blasts on the national trumpet. The Goons were not having any. They sounded a derisory note. Their 'Salute to Britain' opened with a couple of radio tributes from far-off places. From Australia came : 'We are divided from you by fifty thousand miles of land and sea. Let's keep it that way.' From America came : 'Yes, indeed, without doubt Britain *can* take it. Every dollar that we have sent to Britain, Britain has taken.'

ANNOUNCER : Food! Despite rationing, a special effort is to be made in this Festival Year to make British restaurants attractive to visitors.
BENTINE : Stimulated by shortages, British culinary arts have risen to new heights of invention.
SELLERS : This is what a famous French chef said after sampling one of our traditional meals.
SECOMBE (*agonized*): ! ! ! ! Ooooooooooooooh ! ! ! !
ANNOUNCER : Hygiene. In the department of sanitation Britain stands ... alone. Despite the fuel shortage and the exhortations of Cabinet ministers, the average Briton remains wedded to his weekly bath-night.

(*F/X bathwater running and splashing. Secombe sings.*)

WOMAN (*off*) : You in the barf, Fred?
SECOMBE : Yerst, why?
WOMAN : Well I want to clean your boots.
SECOMBE : 'Old on—I'll take 'em orf.

(*The orchestra plays* Land of Hope and Glory *softly under the next speech.*)

BENTINE : And so Britain has struggled valiantly on through the post-war years, fighting for a better standard of life, for the pursuit of happiness, for freedom . . . fighting for her very existence. Until today, the Motherland can still raise her proud face to the skies and say . . .

SECOMBE : Heeeeeellllllllllpppppppppp ! ! ! ! !

As a picture of life in Britain in 1951, as a guide to a general feeling of disenchantment, it would not be without value to the historian.

The Goons looked upon the then rapidly disappearing Empire with a mixture of affection and derision. Each week they plunged into an Empire-type adventure. They were trapped in forts while the Dervishes encircled them, they climbed Mount Everest (from the inside) and they trekked across every trackless waste from the Kalahari Desert to Hackney Marshes. Above all they roamed around India, a crowd of battered not-so-pukka-sahibs watching the sun set on a Raj which they peopled with upper- and middle-class failures and idiots. Phillip String (Harry Secombe), whose saga went on for several weeks, is a bank clerk who has absconded with £1 million in gold. He entrusts it to the purser of the ship on which he is fleeing and the purser goes off with it in a rowing-boat. String is stranded penniless in India and joins the Indian Army. He is immediately given a commission in the 3rd Bengal Cheroots, a fine body of men who have only one thought in mind—mutiny. He becomes a fearless soldier, taking daredevil risks in the line of duty.

'Have you seen String, sir?'
'No. What wild foolhardy risk is he taking this time?'
'He's walking about with his bootlaces undone.'

Milligan was born in 1918 in Poona, son of a sergeant-major in the Royal Artillery. 'I wasn't consciously aware of it,' says Milligan, 'but I had had enough of the British Empire. The Goons gave me a chance to knock people who my father and I as a boy had to call "sir". Colonels. Chaps like Grytpype Thynne with educated voices who were really bloody scoundrels. They'd con and marry rich old ladies. It was cowards charging everywhere with guns.'

Milligan's father must have been a rare kind of sergeant-major. 'Really,' says Milligan, 'he was a frustrated entertainer. He actually won a talent contest at Collins Music Hall when he was home on leave by doing an impression of G. H. Elliott. He influenced me greatly in that he was a superb professional—a fantastic tap-dancer and a very good actor. But he didn't have the courage or my mother's backing to take it up professionally. Life in the army in

India was entirely different from army life in England. My father organised lots of shows and I really was in the wings in a pram in India. My mother played the piano. When he got leave he went to the Grand Hotel, Bombay, changed his name to Leo Gan and did a week's cabaret. He did a toffed-up dandy act with a yellow silk suit and gold bowler—very posh. He became a regimental sergeant-major in the end and, being working class, was too frightened to go beyond that.

'I grew up in the atmosphere of entertainment. The first chance I had was when I was about seven at the Convent of Jesus and Mary in Poona. It was a girls' school. My mother, I think, was a bit overprotective and was trying to keep me from getting hit. They asked me to play the part of a clown in a nativity play. I've been a clown ever since. The Mother Superior wanted to make me black but only had some dark blue paint, so they made me a blue clown with red lips. I remember getting laughs and liking it. The first thing I did was to jump up in the air and mouth the word "Oh". It got lots of laughs from the audience. Then the Mother Superior said I mustn't go near the crib where Jesus was, because it wouldn't be nice. This hurt me and I did go on despite that and I took my hat off and I remember them clapping.'

In 1929, Milligan's father was posted to Rangoon where they stayed until 1934. 'We came back to England then, and lived an impoverished life. I had shown a liking towards music and learned to play the ukulele when I was about seven. When we came to England I found I liked jazz and bit by bit I learned to play the guitar, then the double bass, then the trumpet. I won a Bing Crosby crooning competition at the Lewisham Hippodrome.

'The Government cut the army by 10 per cent and my father, who was still a young man, disappeared into the back streets of Fleet Street and sold photographs.'

Milligan himself started playing in dance bands and when the war started he joined the army—the Royal Artillery—and formed a band. 'We were the only entertainment in Bexhill so we did some concerts there. We used to get dressed up in rags and tell jokes. People used to laugh at me, but I didn't think of myself as being particularly funny.'

Milligan had a fairly active war, serving in North Africa (where he met Harry Secombe) and getting wounded in Italy.

'I went to the Central Pool of Artists where they had collected all the wounded, bomb-happy, crippled and cowards—everybody who had finished with the fighting—into an entertainment unit. Among them were Harry Secombe and Norman Vaughan. I played in the band which backed Harry when he did his act. Then they wanted a musical act to go round in a touring concert party. I used to play in the barrack-room with a couple of other musicians and I was very good on guitar by then. Someone heard us and asked if we could fill in with an ENSA concert for a week. We said sure, anything to get out of barracks. So we got dressed in rags and we paralysed them. I did a few funny announcements in between numbers. We couldn't believe it but we knew we were on to a good thing. We became the rage of the Central Mediterranean Forces. Gracie Fields saw us and insisted on the trio appearing in Rome on the Allied Forces Victory Night. We stopped the show. There was a theatre owner in the audience and he sent us a note saying that when we returned to England he could give us a straight run of fifty-two weeks. There was a lot of funny comedy in the act. We did non-stop gags but the music was good. If you can play and be funny like Victor Borge it's an absolute winner. When we got demobbed the Central Pool of Artists took us on as civilians and we got £10 a week each, which was knock-out money in those days. Finally, we thought we must get back to England and really make a go of it.

'Leslie Macdonnell (recently retired Managing Director of Moss Empires) had seen us and got Val Parnell to come down to the Hackney Empire first house Monday night in that terrible winter when there was no coal (1946-7). There were about eighteen people in the place. Ghastly silence! We never heard from Val Parnell. Or anybody else. We started the dreary round of variety theatres, round and round. I realised that the two boys with me were not adventurous. They wanted to stick to the same act for ever and ever. I thought this was wrong. You've got to change your act all the time, be different every time. Finally, terrified out of my life, I turned it in. They said, "You're a bloody fool, you'll end up in the gutter."

'That's more or less what happened. I didn't work at all, just sort of wandered around. I'd meet Harry and then I'd meet Peter Sellers who was at the Windmill Theatre. They were successful. Somehow or other I ended up at Jimmy Grafton's pub in Westminster and I used to tell jokes. Harry Secombe was there and I'd play the piano a bit and Harry would sing and Peter would come in and do a few impressions of Kenneth Horne and others. Michael Bentine was there. We all used to laugh a lot. We had a strange sense of humour.

'Jimmy was writing for Derek Roy and asked me if I would like to write with him. He gave me a quid or two. I used to graft like bloody mad. I'd never written before in my life but I wrote and wrote and bloody wrote. There must have been reams of the stuff. Some of it was very funny—for its day. Stuff like : "I taught him to play the grand piano." "How?" "I just hit him till he did." "Where is he today?" "Today, that man is Eileen Joyce. Tomorrow, he could be. . . ."

'They were mad jokes. I used to do nothing but write bloody jokes. "Dear Sir, my wife has just made a pancacke ten feet in circumference. Is this a record?" "I don't know, try playing it on the gramophone." "Dear Sir, when a girl goes out walking with two boys should she walk in the middle?" "No, the two boys should walk in the middle." "Dear Sir, I have difficulty in making my wife understand me." "Why?" "She's a Bulgarian." "Can't she even write?" "No." "She sounds like an ignorant Bulgar to me." "Hello, is that Park 3429?" "No, it's Hampstead 3841." "Sorry, it's the wrong number." "That's all right, I had to come down to answer the phone."

'Harry and Peter used to use them and lots of them still keep coming round.

'I was a great picturegoer as a boy in Poona—Charlie Chaplin, Chester Conklin, the Keystone Cops, Charlie Chase. The Indians laugh much easier than the English do, so I was helped along. I got a great feeling for that kind of comedy, that wonderful *ideas* comedy. On top of that I used to see my dad doing his sketches. He tried to write some stuff for me when *The Goon Show* started but, of course, it was just a try-on to get some loot. He didn't really make the scene.

'I had a grandmother, Margaret Burnside, whose laughter invoked laughter. She used to cry with laughter. I can remember it even now. My father was always banging his head on something. He couldn't help doing it at least once a day. My mother and my grandmother knew he would get angry if they laughed so they used to run out of the back of the house and cry with laughter. We used to hear a bang from the other room, a cry of pain and "Oh, Christ!" and they would be out of the back door like a shot.'

Milligan wrote continually but did little performing. He wrote for Bill Kerr, Alfred Marks, Harry Secombe and Peter Sellers. He wrote a little for Frankie Howerd, though Eric Sykes was providing most of Howerd's material at this time. He wrote jokes like the one about the old lady who was taken to the seaside for the first time in her life. She looked at the sea for a long time and then said, 'Is that all it does?'

There was also the man who complained to British Railways, 'I saw a sign saying, "Book a third class ticket to Epping Forest and get the smell of the pine trees." So I booked a third class ticket to Epping Forest and I've been sniffing it for three days now and I can't smell any pine trees.'

'I don't know where the ideas come from, says Milligan, 'and sometimes you just switch off inside like a time-bomb that suddenly stops working.

'*The Goon Show* had a bigger effect than I ever dreamed. There was an immediate reaction from young people who had come out of the war and found a new world after a restricted period of life. It seemed silly to go on being serious after having had five very serious years. I suppose the idea was to get as far away as possible from what was normal. It was a reaction to the stringencies of war.

'Peter Sellers was instrumental in getting the show on the air. He was doing very well on radio and went to Pat Dixon (a BBC producer) and said that we four would like to be together in a show. Harry had already made his mark, Michael Bentine was doing *Starlight Roof*. They were all on the scene but I wasn't. I don't think Michael thought I had any talent. I think he said so to Peter. I was feeling very inferior at the time because I hadn't got any work. I heard a joke on the radio and I did it and they laughed and then Michael found out it wasn't mine and he never forgave me for it. I felt terrible about that and I went on to prove that I was a writer—as I have proved substantially since.

'Anyhow, we got together and sent the first script to Pat Dixon and he said, "Yes, but I'm not going to handle it" and gave it to Dennis Main Wilson. It exploded. "You're Harry Secombe of five feet two fame?" "Yes." "Haven't you been declared a danger to shipping?" "Yes, I make my living on the stage." "Have you ever played the Palladium?" "Yes." "I can bear that out, I've never heard it played better."

'It was one-liners all the time.'

Then Eccles came along.

'Eccles,' says Milligan, 'represented the permanency of man, his ability to go through anything and survive. They are trying to get off a ship in the Amazon and lower a boat. When they get to shore, Eccles is already there. "How did you get ashore?" "Oh hum, I came across on that log." "Log? That's an alligator." "Ooh. I wondered why I kept getting shorter."

'Peter did Bloodnok and Grytpype Thynne and Henry Crun, Harry was mostly himself—Neddie Seagoon. Michael, while he was there for the first two or three years, did Osric Pureheart, the man who invented the solid lead violin for deaf musicians. Nobody was sitting down for the writing except me. Ideas were tossed in but not on a major scale. Michael provided most of them, but I found his ideas were contrary to the speed of the show. He would have one joke which took four minutes to build up. It's his style, he needs room to work.

'Prisoners of war called their German guards goons but I got it from Popeye. There was a creature called the Goon which had nothing in the face at all except hair. It had huge talk-bubbles with one little word in them like "Eeek!" It was very kind and gentle. I liked the word and we called it *The Goons*. When the show was well established there was a prisoner-of-war play on and the chaps in it were digging a tunnel and one of them had to say, "Quick, the goons!" The first night the place exploded and they had to cut it out of the play.

'Pat Dixon was a great back-room rebel at the BBC and I think they were all very frightened of him. If you condemned one of his shows he went insane and wrote memos in all directions and they don't like that. He and, I believe, Michael Standing in the background, said the show should be given its head.

'I wasn't performing much at the beginning. I used to say "Yes" and "Shut that window" and do odd voices. I didn't think I could compete with Harry and Peter. I was frightened. They all had good egos, they were young. I was always in their lee as a performer and I never really reversed that until I did Oblomov on the stage. It was not my own writing and I managed to become a real clown.

'It was the chemistry of us all together. Split up it doesn't happen. I knew that if I wrote a line that could make Harry Secombe, Peter Sellers and Michael Bentine laugh, that was all that mattered. Of course, we became aware that we were doing something very extraordinary. We were becoming a cult and it gave us more confidence to go further and further out. In fact, the last six *Goon Shows* which I wrote, but which were never performed, are incredibly abstract—absolutely mad. There was one more throw of the dice to go, but I think that if we had thrown it we would have gone down and been forgotten. We got out while we were right on the top.

'There were twenty-six shows a year for nine years. This was the crucifying part of it. They got better, they became story lines and each story had to be unique. There were things like the attempt to capture Napoleon's piano that he had played at Waterloo. They had to get it across the Channel—in the key of C. They're in the Louvre trying to get the piano out and they discover it's got four legs. So they say, "That's no good, they'll call it a table with a keyboard. We can't sell that; it's got to have three legs like every other piano." There's a sawing sound, a breaking wood sound. Silence. Then Eccles, puzzled: "Hey, I keep falling over."

'Radio's the great mind medium. They couldn't do a joke like that on television with puppets. If you did, it would be just a puppet's leg. You've got to have flesh and blood to make it work.'

When the series was over Milligan went to Australia, where he did thirteen radio shows similar to the Goons but with Australian characters. 'They loved it in Australia,' he recalls. 'It's extraordinary that a sense of humour exists exactly like ours right across the other side of the world.

'I was developing as a performer without realising it. I was a natural clown but I didn't know it really. When the Goons finally finished and the whole thing had broken up I was out of work. I didn't know that you could disappear from the scene like nothing.

'My marriage broke up because I'd had a terrible nervous break-down—two, three, four, five nervous breakdowns one after the other. Overwork. *The Goon Show* did it. That's why they were so good. Eight in the morning till twelve at night, that was the slog. So the end of it was disaster.'

But the beginning of it was great.

> VOICE : Bad eyesight can also be responsible for the loss of perfectly good teeth, as this dentist will testify.
>
> SECOMBE : Yes, one of my patients came to me with a violent toothache. I had to extract eighteen teeth before it stopped. This would never have happened if I'd had good eyesight.

The Emergency Service has had a call from the circus to say that the india-rubber man has his head caught in the bars of a cage.

> 'Have you tried to get him out?'
>
> 'Yerse, the strong man's been pulling on 'is feet for the last 'alf hour.'
>
> 'O.K. We'll send an ambulance with a stretcher.'
>
> 'Stretcher? Blimey, he's eighteen feet long already.'

It was a show which, as they put it, catered for people of all ages—especially the Ice, Stone and Dark.

For five years it was produced by Peter Eton who later produced *The Army Game* for Granada TV and thought up its sequel, *Bootsie and Snudge*. Eton, now a film producer, says: 'The Goons were a strong reaction against the pomposity we all shared during the war. When you see old wartime films on television you realise how incredibly pompous and artificial we were. People like Spike and Larry Stevens tried to cut through this, and it so happens that Spike has this marvellous Irish imagination and is able to transplant

things from one area to another and make them even more
ridiculous than they are.

'Michael Bentine has the same type of mind as Spike but is
much more articulate. With Spike it's all inside. It's an awful job
for Spike to bring anything out. I have great sympathy for him.

'The first year we worked together I gave Spike a copy of
Rabelais for a Christmas present. It was and is my Bible. As far as
I knew, Spike had never heard of Rabelais. I love it. I can quote
passages of it. It's a vulgar, lavatorial thing and Spike was absolutely fascinated by Rabelais's use of words. He started to build up
names and descriptions in the Rabelais manner—wry-necked,
upstart, wizened gulper of mists, seller of eggshells, broker of
chambermaids. Spike wrote brilliant little sketches. Sometimes they
were brilliant, other times they were bloody awful, so puerile it
wasn't true. In the early days of *The Goon Show* they were either
absolutely brilliant or rubbish. But I tried to get him to write a
more dramatic story. Occasionally we did a topical show and when
Westminster Pier sank I suggested it as a subject. I think Henry
and Minnie were born then. Henry was called something else
before—Quagmire Vest. This is how Fred, the Oyster, was born
too. This old oyster-sexer goes down with the pier and is brought
up from the river-bed with an oyster in his hand. He puts the
oyster on a table and we built up the tension and you heard the
oyster creak open slowly and then came the most frightful raspberry. Actually, it was a donkey farting. It was a fiendish noise
and it brought the house down. This raspberry noise is now called
Fred the Oyster. It was made up for me out of three or four donkey
farts played slowly and speedily, then edited. It's the most revolting noise you ever heard. And it was the most brilliant thing we
ever did. We used it for four or five years. There was the announce-
ment, "This is the BBC Home Service", then came Fred.

'At the same time I was doing bread-and-butter comedies like
Meet the Huggetts and quizzes, but I loved *The Goon Show* and I
lived for it.

'Fundamentally, I love the lowest things in life. I love dustbins
and lavatories. I love anything connected with dustbins. Spike used
to write show after show with references to dustbins, because he
knew I would laugh. He actually rewrote one of my favourite
songs of the time—"Laura". I loved the film, loved the sugary,
sentimental quality of "Laura". I thought it was marvellous. Spike
knew this and wrote a new lyric—"Laura, just a name on a dustbin
lid"—and from then on it got filthier and filthier and even when
I think of it now I still laugh. He knew I had this low, lavatorial
sense of humour. I love belching and farting. The other thing I

love is old age. Old people like the Cruns always made me fall
about. I love doddering old fools. I'm sorry for them but I love
them.

'We used to have frightful rows on *The Goon Show*. I actually
fired Peter once in the middle of a programme. I went backstage
and said, "Get out of the studio and never come back. You did
not do as I said." And he went. Then he came back and was as
good as gold after that. I reminded him of this recently when he
was saying that some directors are very difficult. I said, "You were
the awkward one." I think it probably did me the world of good.
Once you could cope with those three you could manage anything.

'Spike invented a voice called Miss Throat which was very low.
He started doing it during rehearsals and I thought he was belching. I said, "Spike, I'm trying to hear what you are saying, for
God's sake shut up and just read the line." He did this belch again
and I went down and said something like, "Get out of the bloody
studio till you can do what you're told." Spike lost his temper. He
went round the Aeolian Hall, ripping out all the electric-light fit-
tings. He did ninety quid's worth of damage. After it was all over
the studio was a wreck and we were as happy as sandboys.'

The unperformed *Goon Shows,* the last that Milligan wrote,
were macabre and doom-laden.

'This is the BBC Home Service, therefore will clients please
use handkerchiefs when coughing. If a listener suffers such
spasms, signal a BBC attendant who will be only too willing to
destroy you with a humane killer. . . .'

That was how the last one opened. It ended with starvation,
incarceration and cannibalism. The spirits are more wild than high
and the laughter is chill. It presents the story of the Luminous
Plastic Piano with Built-in Oven. Moriarty is starving and he and
Grytpype Thynne are looking for a booking in Blackpool for the
summer season. They contact Bert Swirn—theatrical Blackpool
agents, bread extra.

THYNNE : Any work there Bert?
SECOMBE : No, there's a waiting list as long as my arm.
THYNNE : Quick, the chopper.

(F/X chopper, chopping through meat.)

SECOMBE : Scream!
THYNNE : Now what's the excuse?
SECOMBE : There's a waiting list as long as my short arm.

Moriarty and Grytpype Thynne see an advertisement for 'two comedy duettists, must supply own piano'.

SECOMBE : Wait a minute, are you lads qualified to do comedy duettist at the piano?
THYNNE : Are we? Moriarty, tell him who your mother was.
MORIARTY : Morecambe and Wise.

They are booked on the Harry Stenchcombe bill. Ned Seagoon is singing insanely when there is a knock on his dressing-room door. He shouts : 'Come in.'

(F/X splintering door and car pulls up in a scream of brakes.)

THYNNE : Car park was full.

He is told that the job is already taken by Bannerjee and Sons, the Singing Wogs. There is the sound of shots and screams.

SEAGOON : Gad, an unexpected vacancy, the job's yours.

Moriarty and Grytpype Thynne have no piano and are given three weeks to get one. Grytpype Thynne has an uncle and aunt who make trick pianos for the variety profession. There is the sound of a tinny piano being tuned and Henry Crun's voice : 'The damp is getting into the green felts, Min. The sunny Blackpool air is bad for pianos.'
But there is one piano that is not suffering from the damp. It is made of brown plastic and has a built-in Regulo gas oven. It is an ideal piano for touring comics called Moriarty and Thynne, says Minnie. Neddie calls on the Cruns and they wish him Merry Christmas.

SECOMBE : Stip stip stop . . . Christmas was six months ago.
MIN : We've only just heard of it, Ned . . . the wireless was late.

There is a fade-out on the piano-tuning and the chat and in comes Mate (Sellers) as an old Cockney.

MATE : My name is Doris Hare and I've had a rough time of it. This last thirty years I been stage doorman, man and boy for the past forty years. I seen 'em come and I seen 'em go. There was Grytpype Thynne and Moriarty.

(*Pause.*) 'Ere, I never saw them go.
MORIARTY : Hello stage doorman of old England.
MATE : 'Ello a little twit boy.
MORIARTY : I'm not a little twit boy.
MATE : Oh, a little twit of a girl.
MORIARTY : No.
MATE (*aside*) : He's not a boy and he's not a girl . . . the back-bone of the theatre!

Moriarty and Grytpype Thynne go to their dressing-room and find their plastic piano. Mate is immediately involved in a car crash and a funeral service starts. 'Cor blimey,' he says, 'you aren't arf in in a 'urry to see me orf . . . I mean, I'd like to let a bit of *rigor mortis* set in first.'

Grytpype Thynne and Moriarty discover that their piano is luminous. The oven, he tells Neddie, is for the encore.

NEDDIE : You're going to cook for an encore?
MORIARTY : Only if there's hunger in the stalls.

These lads, muses Ned, will be the rage of sunny Blackpool. That luminous piano with the built-in oven could break the iron heel of television and bring back the countless dozens who at one time packed the first three seats at the Empire, Bootle. Moriarty and Thynne flop and the audience start sharpening swords.

Fifty years later when Neddie Seagoon has reached the top, he is driving along when he sees two men in the gutter. They are Moriarty and Thynne. Moriarty has not eaten for thirty-three years. Thynne says they have saved a fortune this way and are willing to sell the secret. 'Gad,' says Neddie, 'If I could give up eating I'd be a millionaire.'

He takes them home with him. Ten years later he is begging for food. Moriarty and Grytpype Thynne have turned him into a sideshow.

MORIARTY : Roll up, roll up. Sixpence to see the living Welsh skeleton.
THYNNE : Still not cured of eating Ned of Body? Yours is a tough case Ned . . . but thirty more years should do the trick.

Ned calls for help and faints. He is put under the floorboards and Moriarty and Grytpype Thynne leave.

NED (*stifled*) : Let me out . . . let me out . . . Ohhhhhh . . .

ohhhhh, buried alive by floorboards . . . I'll write to the Minister of Floors about this.

There is a knock on the door. It is Bluebottle. 'Anybody for a bob a job?' he asks. Ned shouts for him to come in but Bluebottle can't find him. He is joined by Eccles who has come from the Ministry of Drains in response to complaints from neighbours about the smell under the floorboards. They find Ned.

'Ah lads,' he says, 'you've saved me from a face worse than dead. Have you seen two unscrupulous men called Moriarty and Thynne? No.'

NED : Thank heaven, they're gone. At last I can eat . . . (*gulp*).
ECCLES : I . . . Ohhh.
BLUEBOTTLE : Here, where's Eccles gone . . . you . . .
ECCLES (*muffled*) : Helppp . . .
BLUEBOTTLE : Hey . . .

(F/X thumping on inside of Neddie's belly.)

BLUEBOTTLE : Here . . . what's all those fist lumps keep coming out on your belly?
ECCLES : It's me, throw down my glasses.
BLUEBOTTLE : Why?
ECCLES : If this is the end I want to see it.
NED : I'm sorry I had to do it, I was hungry . . . you're a well-built lad . . . (*gulps*).
BLUEBOTTLE : Cor, it's dark in Ned's Welsh belly . . . Eccles?
ECCLES : Hello . . .
BLUEBOTTLE : Where are you?
ECCLES : Here I am trying to get out the back.

(F/X door opens.)

ECCLES : I'm out.
NED : Ah, that's better.

There follows a note in Milligan's hand : 'Here ended incompleted and unperformed—the last Goon Show, No. 227.'

Waiting in the wings were Peter Cook, Dudley Moore, Jonathan Miller and Alan Bennett. But before we come to them there are further adventures to record of the four intrepid Goon travellers as they journeyed through the catacombs of comedy.

3 | *The Goons Go On*

'So the end of it was disaster,' says Milligan. 'Anyhow, I had no work at all and I was going round begging, really. Then Bernard Miles asked me to play Ben Gunn in *Treasure Island* (at the Mermaid Theatre) and while I was doing it John Antrobus and I wrote *The Bed Sitting Room*.'

In fact, *The Goon Show* ended in March 1960, and it was not until December 1961 that Milligan worked at the Mermaid.

The Bed Sitting Room was offered to the Mermaid but could not be taken at the time. It was first staged by a group of students at the Marlowe Theatre, Canterbury, where it contained the memorable line 'The world is full of fog and chickens,' which has to be said very quickly for its hidden meaning to be realised. It is a play about events after the Third World War which lasted two minutes, twenty-eight seconds. Radioactivity is rife among the survivors and Lord Fortnum of Alamein fears that he is turning into a bed sitting-room, which he is. This is not as strange as it sounds, for other survivors are being turned into cupboards, chests of drawers or birds through the mutation effect. 'It is,' I wrote at the time, 'a painful joke, frothing at the edges with agony.'

A year later it turned up at the Mermaid, this time with Milligan himself playing the part of Mate, a one-man 'chorus' in dirty old raincoat, railway cap and stubble beard. 'Every now and then,' I wrote, reviewing it a second time, 'it forces the audience into horrified shock at the realisation of the deep and sane anguish lying underneath the lunacy.'

A month later, the play transferred to the Duke of York's Theatre and, relating its history, I recalled that what had started as a brief one-acter in Canterbury was now a full-length work. This time, I said, 'Beneath all the lunacy lie the horrors of the Bomb and the play somehow brings off the double miracle of ramming them home while purging them with laughter,' which is what I meant to say in the first place.

In July it transferred to the Comedy Theatre and I managed to suppress the feeling that somehow I had a duty to write about it again. In 1970 it was made into a film. It is clear that not everyone finds Spike Milligan funny. 'I am deeply allergic to the quirky Mr Spike Milligan,' wrote novelist Penelope Mortimer wearing her film critic's hat in *The Observer*. She thought the film was brilliant but revolting. That, on reflection, does not seem to me to be a bad thing, considering Milligan's theme.

Oblomov opened on October 6th, 1964, at the Lyric Theatre, Hammersmith. It was a night to remember. *Oblomov* is a serious play based on a celebrated Russian classic by Ivan Goncharov. Oblomov himself is totally incapable of action and spends most of his time in bed, living on the income from some distant, crumbling estates. He is briefly moved to activity by falling in love with the beautiful Olga but, proving himself equally incapable in that direction, he takes to his bed again.

The opening night was, to say the least, something of a shambles. Milligan muttered, mumbled and ad-libbed furiously. After the interval he came on stage to find that most of the audience were still in the bars. He interrupted his co-star, Joan Greenwood, to say, 'Let's start again when they come back', and sat in the wings occasionally shouting out to those members of the audience who had reclaimed their seats, 'Are they back yet?' The audience shouted 'No' until they were.

'This,' said the director Frank Dunlop shortly afterwards, 'gave him confidence. He was in his element and even spoke up and was heard. It's a big breakthrough for him. Spike was very worried about overacting. He doesn't like being loud on the stage.'

'He's a marvellous fellow,' commented Miss Greenwood, 'but not exactly blissful to act with.'

'Originally,' says Milligan, 'Oblomov was going to be a straight performance. I'm a dedicated person and I like to know my lines properly from beginning to end. But we never seemed to get round to proper rehearsal and Frank Dunlop, a very nice lad, didn't crack the whip at all. There was fresh dialogue all the time and when the opening night came there was not a hope in hell. So I thought, what do I have to lose? It was a great breakthrough for audiences. It was the first time an audience was considered part of the plot. Afterwards we often used to say, "Look, shall we have an early interval or two intervals and get more drinks in?" The manager came round and said, "You can't do that", so I told him to leave the keys and I would lock up.

'I can't actually remember much about that first night. I was white with fear. I thought, "Goodbye Milligan, that's the end of it." That's when I thought, "I haven't got anything, I've been kidding myself."

But Oblomov did well at the Lyric and subsequently transferred to the Comedy Theatre under the title *Son of Oblomov* where it ran for a year.

Milligan's mind is restless, obsessive about comedy. Sometimes he sets himself little tasks of writing something funny within sixty seconds. His incessant search for new ideas can lead him unerringly to triumph or disaster. He will never be accused of mediocrity. In the late 'sixties he did two television series, in one of which he partly submerged his own personality to emerge, chuckling gently, as Beachcomber, and the other Q5 in which he pushed hard at the boundaries of television comedy and sometimes slipped flat on his face.

'I was trying to do something new,' he reflects, 'some new patterns of technique. One was the film. I discovered you could get cartoon speed without making the people rush about, by cutting the film. You show, for instance, a piano on stage. The pianist comes in and there is applause. He sits down, puts his hand on the keyboard and disappears. This you do very simply by cutting the camera, getting him off and then starting the camera again. Then he suddenly reappears and you can see that he's wondering where he's been. He gets back to the piano to play again and disappears again. Then you put an old grandmother sitting on the stool, fast asleep with her head on the keyboard, and when the pianist gets back he looks at her and she disappears. He goes to sit down and we stop the camera, pick up the stool and when we restart the film it is right upstage so that when he brings his hands down with a crash there is no piano there. Next time he puts his hands on the keyboard there is a basin of water there and he goes splash. He looks at his hands, puzzled. The next thing you see is a plumber lying under a sink mending it. As the plumber goes to put his spanner up to mend the basin we put the piano back so the plumber is now underneath the piano. He gets up, looks at the pianist, there is applause from the audience and they both bow and go off.'

In Q5 Milligan also broke the tyranny of the traditional sketch form by spreading one, serial-like, all through the show. There are certain subjects such as smoking and boots that Milligan returns to again and again. A pair of smoking boots—that is, boots that have exploded and have wisps of smoke wafting away from them—is a favourite image with both him and Bentine. In Q5 Milligan created at least two classic smoking gags. In one he produced a very tall man and solemnly announced : 'This man took up smoking. If he hadn't taken up smoking, this man today would be eighteen feet nine.' And in another he asked : 'Is it true what they say about smoking?' There was an immediate cut to a pair of shoes with a head immediately over them saying angrily through a cloud of cigarette smoke, 'It's all rubbish. You don't get any shorter because of smoking.'

There were elaborate jokes with long-delayed pay-offs.

'I sang "September Song" dead straight so that it wasn't wasted,' Milligan recalls. 'It was sung outside a bistro and autumn leaves were falling and I was dressed beautifully in a lovely grey suit, just like Adolphe Menjou. At the end I stood up and walked away and from the back I looked as if I had been hit by an explosion. It was all shattered and smoking and in rags from top to bottom. It was my favourite joke of the whole show; I couldn't wait to turn round.'

The ideas come, but just how, Milligan neither knows nor cares. 'It's chemistry. It's like the shape of your nose, you're stuck with it. I can't explain it. But sometimes you switch off inside.'

Some of the humour is not yet acceptable, perhaps never will be. 'I once wrote a straining contest with what Michael Mills (Head of BBC comedy) called anal implications. It had nothing to do with shit really. It was a straining competition at Worslem Fair and these four swede-bashers were all sitting on chairs and straining. There was a straining meter and the man who strained most won the golden cauliflower. One chap says to the other, "You've won the prize for two years running. I wonder what you'll get this year." The answer is "Hernia". They didn't do it on the BBC. The other one they didn't laugh at was the Grandmother Hurling Contest off Beachy Head. They were hurling these grandmothers out to sea and they had to swim back to the rocks within three minutes. The grandmothers were all very happy about it, but it was a bit sadistic and they didn't laugh much in the studio at all. There are some things, I suppose, you can't laugh at. There's no comedy, for instance, in having it off, except in the mind. Though getting to it is funny.'

Milligan is a frequent 'guest on shows hosted by people such as David Frost, Eamonn Andrews and others. The host usually introduces him with a mixture of anticipation and acute apprehension.

'What happens,' says Milligan, 'is that you have a few drinks and get very worked up. It depends upon how much you can inflate your ego until you think yourself brilliant. Or you are so frightened that you can't help but try and do funny things all the time to hide your fear.'

Harry Secombe is a fat, beaming man who walks enveloped in warmth and affection, not only of the massed fans but of the people who actually know him. He is preserved from an unbearably lovable puppiness by a gleeful sense of mischief and an occasional tart astringency. In Secombe there is a real compulsion to clown which seems, at times, to be almost uncontrollable. I remember a Royal Variety Show rehearsal some years ago at the Coliseum Theatre where he nearly drove the producer, Robert Nesbitt, out of his mind. Nesbitt has a difficult job in licking a vast show into some kind of shape in less than two days. The stalls, during rehearsals, are filled with performers, agents, managers and newspapermen, and discreet signs of appreciation such as short bursts of laughter or a spattering of applause are permitted. Secombe, on stage and awaiting instructions to begin his performance, was held up by some complicated business over the lighting or tabs. He fidgeted, then beamed at the audience who giggled. Encouraged, he did things with his eyebrows and made some Goon noises. The audience laughed louder. Mr Nesbitt, sitting half-way up the stalls, powerful behind his little table with its telephones, masses of notes, and bottle of champagne, tried to make himself understood to the technicians. The laughter was by now coming in waves and Secombe gained strength from it like Popeye gulping down huge helpings of spinach. Mr Nesbitt asked Mr Secombe to desist; Mr Nesbitt, like a High Court judge, warned that if any more of this levity went on he would have no hesitation in clearing the stalls. A Royal Variety Show rehearsal, he indicated, was no place for laughter. Mr Secombe did his best to obey Mr Nesbitt's instructions to stop clowning. He stood rigidly to attention, thumbs down in line with the seams of his trousers, face immobile, half-witted. Then he raised his eyebrows a fraction and the theatre exploded. Mr Nesbitt tried to be angry but was seen to smile.

'Oh, Bob's all right,' remarks Secombe, 'we get on very well together. At things like the Royal Variety Show rehearsals though, he now keeps me off the stage until he can't go any further without me. That kind of situation is ideal for me—an audience out there and someone trying to get something done. I suppose I'm a destructive element really. I'd rather be in the chorus as an idiot than standing in front without laughs.'

Secombe is not just a natural performer; he is only natural when he is performing.

'I find that I really come alive when I'm on stage,' he says. 'If I'm not well I'll go on and feel great. No one ever dies on stage—they always collapse in the wings. Some alchemy takes over and pumps the adrenalin out. I'm lucky inasmuch as my stage or television personality is an extension of me anyway, so I haven't got to put on an act. If you are essentially anti-social it is very difficult to work in public, I should think, because you're exposing yourself all the time. The instinct Spike has when he gets nervous is to hide.

For all this zest for performing, it may be significant that Secombe who is so short-sighted that, as he puts it, he has to wear braille socks, never works with his spectacles on. 'The first time I began to make any headway as an entertainer was when I took my glasses off. That way I can't see anybody. I think most comics would say that if they see one person in the audience not laughing they are instinctively drawn towards him and want to explain (he put on a joky voice) "What I really meant was. . . ." '

Secombe was born on a council estate in Swansea in 1921, son of a commercial traveller. His neighbours were mainly sailors and dock-workers. 'You were part of a community, and there was a wonderful feeling of fellowship and fun.'

He was a thin boy and often sickly. The laughter he aroused at church socials was, he says, 'like manna'. He has a fine Welsh tenor voice which at one time he used, half-apologetically, as an adjunct to his clowning. Now it is a central and straight part of his performance.

Secombe was seventeen when war broke out and, falsifying his age, he joined the Royal Artillery. He showed an early talent as an impressionist.

'The C.O., a chap called Carstairs,'* he says, 'was very Sandhurst. He had a batman called Probert who was servile, cringy and smarmy when Carstairs was there and called him all sorts of horrible names when he wasn't. One day they all went off on an exercise leaving me behind to watch the battery office and Probert, who was supposed to make the fires and help me sort things out. By 8.30 they had all gone and I called up the stairs to Probert who was in Carstairs' room. "Fack orf," he said. So I thought I'd put on Carstairs' voice and said, "Probert!"

' "Coming, sir," he shouted and dashed down the stairs and saw me. "You facking bastard," he said and went back upstairs thinking he was set for the day. It started to rain and about ten minutes later Carstairs came back for his mac. He stood at the foot of the stairs and shouted, "Probert!"

' "Bollocks," said Probert.

'Carstairs couldn't believe his ears. He looked at me and shouted again : "Probert!"

* I have changed the names in case the story is true.

' "I'll beat your bleedin' ears in," shouted Probert.

'Carstairs rushed upstairs and found Probert lying on his bed smoking his fags. He couldn't understand why Probert tried to put the blame on me.'

Secombe had a distinguished army career, rising to the rank of Lance-Bombadier after several years.

'He looked as though he personally might put two years on the war,' comments Milligan, recalling their chance desert meeting.

'I was the regimental idiot,' says Secombe. 'I remember getting laughs as a kid in school, but it is more difficult when you're in action. I suppose I did make people laugh. Natural vanity, I suppose, and it helps to take away your own fear. It's something that's expected of you, I think.'

Secombe's active war ended when he suffered exposure after being lost in a snowstorm in Italy. He joined an army concert party where he entertained by tap-dancing in boots and doing impressions of Stainless Stephen and Sandy Powell. One morning he was larking about while shaving and his companion in the tent started to laugh. Secombe worked up the routine into an act and it became the basis of his peacetime variety performance.

He and Milligan were brought together for the second time and became close friends. 'We had the same off-beat humour,' says Secombe, 'which was against the average run of humour at the time. I was doing this mad shaving act and singing a Jeanette MacDonald-Nelson Eddy duet with myself. Spike had this crazy way of thinking, this illogically sane thing that goes beyond the gag. He's got a tremendous ability to evoke crazy mental pictures. He thinks visually, which is most unusual for a comic. Eric Sykes has it and Keaton and Chaplin had it.

'I speak too quickly to be good at gags. (If Secombe does tell a joke it is virtually in inverted commas—"This is a joke, folks.") Most of my material comes from observation, but if you're working regularly in a show, comedy evolves from an ad-lib. You retain the core of a sketch, and the rest is built up around it. I'm far better after I've been working with something for a couple of weeks than when I begin. With *The Four Musketeers* at Drury Lane we had a few tryouts and previews before we opened, but we didn't go on tour so one didn't know the real strength of the comedy or how it was going to evolve. If we had been on tour I would have had a chance to work on it and find out what worked and what didn't. By the time we finished *Musketeers* (it ran for a year) it was a riot. It was a bit restricting at first but eventually I think I did what Spike did with *Oblomov*. You have to turn it into a vehicle for yourself if it's not strong enough to stand up on its own.

'*The Goon Show* gave me the strength to resolve to carry on as I was, rather than to try and fall back on telling gags. It was young men's humour, servicemen's humour. Sometimes we used the pay-offs of dirty army gags. If you could slip something in for a giggle it was worth while, because if no one knew what it meant it couldn't offend them, and if they did know they had a good laugh. *The Goon Show* was essentially a team thing as far as performing went. Spike had tremendously soaring ideas but he was a bit diffident as a performer at first because he wasn't quite sure of himself—a bit amateur in his approach to it. Peter and I had been out working in the variety second spots and were a bit more hardened.'

Working second spot in variety you had either to harden or fall apart. Once a man came up to Secombe and said, 'You've got a good act there, lad. You nearly made me laugh twice.' And in Bolton the audience sat through his shaving act in silence save for a low, threatening mumble. Afterwards the theatre owner sacked him on the spot with : 'You shave in your own time, not mine.'

At Leeds City of Varieties they have a long bar which performers are allowed to visit in make-up during the intervals.

'It was just before Saturday night second house,' says Secombe, 'and I only had one clean shirt left. I thought I'd go to the bar for a Guinness—I was trying to build myself up in those days. The place was crowded and I fought my way through and got the drink. Right at the other end of the bar a big fat man waved me over. I didn't want to be impolite so I struggled through with this Guinness clutched to my chest. Somebody jogged my arm and it went all down my shirt leaving a huge brown stain. When I got to this fat feller, he said, "You Harry Secombe?" I said, "Yes." He said, "My wife can't stand you on bloody wireless" and turned away to his friends.'

What is extraordinary are the proprietorial rights audiences assume in comedians and the furious indignation they can suffer if they feel let down by one bad broadcast or television show. 'They believe they own you,' comments Secombe, 'and, in effect, you can't be rude to them because they genuinely believe that you're part of their lives, especially since television when you're in their parlours. You *are* part of the family in a way. I said "bloody" once in a sketch and the number of letters I got ! How dare I say bloody in front of children ! When you think of all the other things that go on television ! I've never said it since. You suddenly become aware of the fact that people do watch a tremendous amount, and, I suppose, look to you—look at you—in a certain way. It's a sort of trust and you mustn't betray it. They can get very angry.

If I get really upset I go quiet. Being angry is a useless thing.

'You've got to be likeable to be a comic, otherwise you don't succeed at all, that's for sure. You're in the business to be liked. And if you like them in return, then you get something back. It's a reciprocal thing—it's got to be both ways otherwise it doesn't work at all. Even if you've got a bad audience you go out there and love them.

'I get generally apprehensive but never frightened. Anyone who goes on and says he's not nervous, especially on opening nights, is telling a lie. Or he's an insensitive burke who shouldn't be in the business. It's a strange thing, you go out and you send out tentative waves, like a sonic thing, to see whether they come back. You offer something and wait to see whether they accept it. You offer yourself; expose yourself—decently.

'I do like people, genuinely. I'm interested in people. You can't shut yourself off. Comics especially have to be aware of how the average bloke carries on, otherwise you become so removed that you cut yourself off. You must make friends with the company as well, must know them all by name. You can't go about it consciously but it must happen. I've got to like them before I can go out on stage. You spend so much time in the theatre that unless you enjoy going there you might as well stay at home. It could be agony, torture. I was in a show years ago when I was a second comic and the atmosphere was murder. I used to dread going to the theatre.

'Never underestimate an audience. Sometimes you get carried away with a bit of ad-libbery, especially in a show like *The Four Musketeers* and you do go too far and you've lost them. But you're aware of it before it actually happens. You think, "Ah, they're going" and you pull 'em back. You must never relax too much on stage. Even the most relaxed comedians are aware of what's going on. You're listening all the time. It's like watching the needle on a sound machine. If it goes right over too soon it's going to come back all the quicker. You mustn't give all you've got to start with. You build up to something.'

Secombe builds up his act on chat and a highly professional throat-clearing gawkiness. A lot of it is talk about his family.

'It's not an "I love my family thing", but a giggle. I talk about the baby, say she's knee-high and teething and is biting everything in sight. When she gets a bit taller I'm leaving home. It's throwing myself on the audience, not for sympathy but as "This is me, folks, let's enjoy ourselves". It's a lot different on television. Television is more impersonal and there is a constriction of time. In the theatre you can expand and relax. In some cases I think I've been a bit big for the screen. You have to try to scale yourself down and you lose something in the process. You get an innate sense of what the audience will accept from you as being funny. I like doing different things. Bumble in *Oliver!* (the film) was a straight part and so is the role in *The Song of Norway*. If you rest on your laurels they tend to become wreaths. It's a very restrictive profession. People want you to do the same thing all the time and you can be put into a niche, as I was at the very beginning. I was a good second spot comic and that was me, mate. If you tried to do something else there was always someone saying, "Well, I don't know, Harry. . . ." To get out of the rut I had to think of something different, had to prove myself to be different. The same thing applies even when you are successful.'

Michael Bentine burst on to the public consciousness shortly after the war, a wild, black-haired, black-bearded young man who did strange and funny things with sink-plungers and kitchen chairs. A mime, a man whose appeal was almost entirely visual, it was odd that he should be one of the early Goons, a voice on radio, though the right limitless experimental sense of humour was—is—there. He is the mad scientist who wants to fool the world, a Frankenstein who would have created his monster in the image of Punch. He is a Peruvian who was born in Watford and went to Eton and he is convinced that he is partly Jewish through descendance from Spanish armourers who accompanied the expeditions that conquered South America. Armoury, he says, was a Jewish trade. He spends a lot of time messing about with old guns and restoring with great skill opulent Victorian paintings.

His father was a scientist and Bentine might have been one too but for some nasty wartime experiences which put him off doing anything, however seemingly harmless, which might be used by politicians for an anti-social purpose. But his mind still works in a scientific way, not in a methodical examination of known facts but with that leap of the imagination that Koestler believes links creative humour and scientific discovery.

'I'm always sparked off,' Bentine says, 'by a visual idea which I have to find words for. Spike is usually sparked off by an idea which is essentially non-visual and which he then makes visual. I think that as we've got older, Spike and I have formed a mutual admiration society but we've also got a slight feeling that if we do work together again we will in some way irritate each other. I've got a lot of affection for him. It's an odd sort of affection, for it is two minds with utterly different backgrounds which yet think tremendously alike. Our humour is based on the assumption that the

C

audience have had the same sort of education that we've had—that is, off the back of cigarette cards. In other words, they have a large number of references to past events like the Siege of Sidney Street, the South Sea Bubble, the sinking of the *Titanic*. These are images in the mind which become situations for comedy. That orchestra playing on the *Titanic* as the ship sank is a very grim thought. But when you call it *The Great Crossing Disaster* and set the scene on the Woolwich Ferry which is trying to get the Blue Riband for the crossing of the Thames and there are emigrants taking a last look at Woolwich before starting a new life in Silvertown and the ferry goes down in the mud, one automatically assumes that people know about the *Titanic*, know about the emigrants on board, about the Blue Riband for the fastest Atlantic crossing. It is the basis of *Goon Show* humour with its stuff about the building of the *Brabagoon* and the digging of the Suez Canal.

'But few people laugh at the same thing. Tell fifty people a sad story and you'll get approximately the same reaction from them all, though you may get the oddball who will fall about laughing at it. Tell the same fifty people a funny story and you'll get fifty different reactions. One bloke will say, "And then . . . ?" Another will say, "Oh, yes" and not really understand. Another will stop you half-way and give you the wrong tag. . . . If you actually get 65 per cent of an audience screaming with laughter at you then you are about the world's greatest comedian. I shouldn't think I have ever hit more than about 30 per cent. Even when you've got an audience absolutely flat on their backs, most of them are probably laughing in sympathy with their companions or so that they're not left out. They are not genuinely laughing at the image you have evoked. The comedian must be either liked or loathed by the audience. There mustn't be anything in between. I mean the audience who are going to respond to him. No matter what you do, 20 per cent of the people are going to hate you as soon as you walk on the stage, possibly because you remind them of somebody they don't like. They haven't necessarily paid to see you. If you take a cross-section of a club audience, some people have come in to get drunk, some because they were lonely, some because they had nothing else to do. Reluctant husbands are brought by wives and reluctant wives by husbands. Some look round and say, "Oh, Christ, he's not on is he?" Even when they have paid to see you it's no guarantee that they want to. When I was playing in Yorkshire once a man came up to me and said, "I've sat in the same seat every Friday night for twenty years and I've never laughed once." And he was desperately proud of it too.'

Bentine does a lot of work in Midland and northern clubs and, like Sellers and Milligan, commands a masterly Indo-Pakistani accent. Racial jokes in clubs in areas where racial tension is high range from the crude and malevolently clever to a head-patting benignity. Bentine is intensely against racialism of any kind and, being no fool, knows that many members of his audience do not share his view.

'That is the reason I do coloured jokes,' he says. 'But if you look at them, there's no sting in them. If you clamp down and say nobody must ever tell a coloured joke you are screwing down the last safety valve. Racialism is based on fear and if you make people laugh at something you dispel their fear of it. I do a whole routine in which I say, "I was talking to the Pakistani High Commissioner, an awfully nice chap, and we were discussing the Pakistani population explosion. He said, 'It's what we people of Pakistan call the big bang. I believe that this population explosion in Pakistan is mainly caused by a large number of Pakistani people, both men and women, all having a bang. I believe the only way to stop the Pakistani population explosion is for the Pakistani people to remind themselves to use more control—either self or birth—and that the way to remind them to use this control is for the Pakistani men to tie a knot in their turbans. And that is what I think Mr Enoch Powell meant when he told the Pakistani people to get knotted.' "

'In this way you're taking the sting out of Enoch Powell. It's no good trying to fight Powell and everything he stands for on the basis of what we fought the last war on, because too many people are for him. I think he's a menace and if you're going to fight him you don't tell jokes in which Powell is aggrandised in any way. If you ridicule him you alienate your audience and they won't listen to you.

'I do very little racial stuff, but you stand up there for an hour and you can't ignore a whole segment of your audience's experience. I would sooner dismiss it with a couple of references which are funny without being bitter than ignore it altogether. Long before the immigration question I had done a lot of Pakistanis and Indians in my shows, not because I was agin 'em but because it's a funny thing when they speak English. I've told Yorkshire stories and I've been castigated by Yorkshire newspapers for it. They have asked, "What right has Michael Bentine when he's not a Yorkshireman to tell a Yorkshire story?" But the Yorkshire audience had fallen about laughing at it. I've actually had people say, "What right has a Peruvian to criticise the British?" and I've said, "Five years hard work in a war." I do honestly believe that if you start to censor humour you're going to be in deadly trouble.'

But racialism is only partly based on fear; contempt and the need to support a sense of superiority are also ingredients and there are many jokes which bolster and confirm these attitudes. The funniest of the racial jokes are the ones that go against the stereo-type—like stories about Negroes who have no sense of rhythm.

'The British have a contempt for everything in the world which isn't British,' says Bentine. 'You'll never alter that. The English are prejudiced and bloody-minded. One town is prejudiced against another. Paris doesn't speak contemptuously of Marseilles, but Manchester does of London and vice-versa. Leeds doesn't really dig Bradford.'

Bentine's club work is a minor aspect of his life; his real contribution to comedy has been through television, principally by his series, *It's a Square World.*

He was always raiding the BBC Television Centre at White City for the programme and once, during a mock attack by Indians—Red, not immigrant—he set part of it alight and a brick was scorched. He was, he swears, sent a memo which read, 'Under no circumstances is the BBC Television Centre to be used for purposes of entertainment.'

'We would usually film our stuff at the Centre from late Friday afternoon and through Saturday and Sunday because the building was pretty empty then,' recalls Bentine. 'We were always rushing around blowing it up or sinking it or digging our way out of it as escaping prisoners while Gestapo types with BBC armbands shot at us.

'Apparently, about eighteen months after I'd left the BBC, a Jaguar car pulled up one Friday afternoon and four men got out with stocking masks over their faces and carrying pick handles. As they stood there, irresolute for a moment before rushing into the cashier's office, one of the security men said, "Nice to see you back Mr Bentine." The men then ran into the office, took the money and, as they dashed out to the waiting car, the same security man shouted after them, "When's it on?" I don't know whether it is true or not but it could be.'

It could be because Bentine and his crew did, in fact, get up to the most extraordinarily lunatic things in and around London while the public averted its collective eye and pretended that they were not there. For one programme he took a Chinese junk on to the Thames and fired plastic cannon-balls at the Houses of Parliament which were sitting at the time. In the background of the film you can see chaps in bowler hats striding purposefully over Westminster Bridge and deliberately not looking at the martial scene.

'After all,' says Bentine reasonably, 'if you are walking over

Westminster Bridge and you see a Chinese junk firing cannon-balls at the Houses of Parliament you are not going to turn round to your companion and say, "Look at that Chinese junk firing cannon-balls at the Houses of Parliament", in case there isn't a Chinese junk firing cannon-balls at the Houses of Parliament.

'We'd been firing for two hours and nobody was taking a blind bit of notice. A patient came out on the balcony of St Thomas's Hospital on the other side of the river, took one look and hurried back inside. After two hours a police launch, which had been nosing in and out of the bridge for some time, approached and a policeman shouted through a loud hailer, "Do any of you gentlemen speak English?"

'No other country in the world would accept this. My other country, Peru, would have thought it was a revolution. We used polythene cannon-balls and they floated. The river was filled with them, but that didn't seem to surprise anybody either. The final shot was of forty bowler hats floating down-river after Parliament had been sunk. Nobody ever investigated.'

The ideas for scenes like this come in a surprisingly direct fashion which has nothing to do with waking up in the middle of the night and shouting 'Eureka!'

'I was going up the Thames in my boat,' says Bentine, 'when I saw a beautiful Chinese junk. I pulled alongside and said what a beautiful boat it was and the owner said he had bought it off Garfield Weston, the biscuit manufacturer. Later I was in a Chinese restaurant in Limehouse and was talking to a Chinaman who was furious with the authorities for knocking down all the old buildings in Limehouse and erecting blocks of flats without consulting the Chinese "lesidents". I said, "Well, what are you going to do about it?" And he said, "If I had a war junk I would fire on the Houses of ——" and I thought, "Yes, what a marvellous idea." So in the sketch I had a local G.P. in Limehouse—we called him Dr Fu Manchu, of course—who was furious about this and actually set out and did it. There was one bit in it which, I feel, was a beautifully creative piece of comedy. I was playing the part of a radio interviewer talking to Dr Fu Manchu and he says, "Silence him!" So his Chinese henchmen draw knives and cut the microphone lead.

'It's odd how the images come. I was doing a series up North with Dick Lester (who graduated from directing television into films) and we had a first-class band and wanted an idea on how to introduce them each week. I was walking through Hyde Park and I saw a bandstand with a sign saying, "Next Week : The Band of the Royal Army Medical Corps". Instantly, I visualised them playing in white smocks with the conductor using a giant thermometer as a baton. So each week we presented the band differently. Once it was as the band of MI5 and another time as the Band of the Foreign Legion inside a fort and, as the Arabs go round and kill them off, the arrangement went down, instrument by instrument, with the "dead" bandsmen propped up in the embrasures and the leader rushing round playing a toot on each instrument to give the impression that they are all alive.

'In the U-boat band we had this periscope cutting through the water with sheet music attached to it on the surface. We then cut to a British destroyer, then to a binocular mask, and as the British officer spots the periscope and music he says, "It's the dreaded Rudolf Friml." It was a bit grim really. There was a depth-charge attack and the orchestra made their escape through a hatch, clutching their instruments. The last shot was of a 'cello, bass drum, double bass and other instruments floating in the water.'

Probably Bentine's most successful creation is his flea machine in which tiny, unseen fleas walk across sand leaving footprints, climb a ladder, depressing each rung as they go up and then dive, plop, into a teacup.

'I was doodling and I drew the little ladder and a springboard and a cup and a flea and I thought—wait a minute, what if the rungs of the ladder move and the flea dives and supposing the sand jumps up? I suppose it evolved from the oldest mime act in the world—the flea jumping from hand to hand. But with me I automatically added a mechanical process which made the sand jump and did all the other little things.

'I used another model in which I was a television producer showing Count Dracula how we were going to do his life story. As I moved the cameras over the model, little panels shot up and hands came out and kidnapped the cameras. One camera fell out of a cupboard with a knife in its back. I got the idea from watching a producer who preferred to move model cameras around a model set rather than actually get on with the show.'

Many comedians are terrified of new material. 'For me,' says Bentine, 'it's the breath of life. It's pointless scrapping old material when it is new to the audience you are performing to, but the fascination is the creation of new stuff. It's one's reason for survival. The comedian who has decided ideas about comedy will eventually cease to create. You must be flexible or else you become a comedic dinosaur. It's too easy to say, "They laughed at that twenty years ago and they'll laugh at it now." Because they won't, not necessarily, anyway.'

His favourite gag is one he wrote for Sellers. Sellers was a suffragette chained to the railings of 10 Downing Street. Two coppers come and 'she' starts hitting them with her brolly crying, 'Take your hands off me you filthy beasts' and words to that effect. The policemen pick her up and pull her away. This causes the whole façade of Number 10 to fall down, revealing Disraeli in his bath. He turns round with a look of extreme surprise and says, 'My life!'

Of all the Goons, Peter Sellers is the one who has achieved the greatest success; of all the Goons he is the one who looks back with most nostalgia on those golden Goon days.

'They really were my happiest days,' he says, 'those Sundays when we did *The Goon Show.*'

Sellers has become a character actor of such power that, like Olivier, like Paul Scofield, he turns interpretation into creation. His immersion in whatever role he is playing is so complete that some people, including his unofficial and unassisted biographer, Peter Evans,* suggest that his own personality is almost non-existent. Certainly, it is complex, elusive, perhaps even fragmented in the sense that his rate of change seems faster than most people's and he carries private role-playing to exceptional lengths. But he shows an astonishing understanding both of types and individuals, and whatever insecurities he has in his personal life are matched by his cast-iron confidence in his professional abilities.

He was born in 1925 and two weeks later carried on stage at the King's Theatre, Portsmouth, where his parents were appearing. His mother was Jewish, but not his father. His mother was dominant and protective. If these are crucial factors then the world is full of unsung, unknown Sellers, which is both an improbable thought and a contradiction in terms.

The necessary prelude to extraordinary powers of impersonation is the gift of extraordinary powers of observation. Sellers is able to look and listen to a person and gain an experience of him as Van Gogh was able to look and listen to a cornfield and gain an experience of it. Any part that heredity plays in the process is more to do with chemistry than circumstances. The *desire* to perform, to gain approval, to exercise power, is a different matter and many comedians—and actors—have had either an intense or insufficiently satisfying maternal relationship. As, indeed, many clerks or bus-drivers have had.

Sellers, records Peter Evans, frequently impersonated officers while serving as an aircraftsman in the R.A.F. during the war, not jokily, as Secombe once did, but with a daring that could have

* Evans, *The Mask Behind the Mask* (Leslie Frewin, 1969).

earned him severe punishment. When he was demobbed he hung around Archer Street looking for work as a drummer. Then he auditioned at the Windmill Theatre and became a comedian. He was introduced to Secombe, Milligan and Bentine by Jimmy Grafton, who thought they all shared a similar sense of surrealistic humour.

'We hit it off from the word go,' says Sellers. 'We were brimming over with ideas and we had sessions where we sat around and built mad, lightning sketches. The only way I can describe the form of humour we enjoyed is that we took any given situation and carried it to an illogical conclusion. That's where I find my comedy. You take a situation and think what would happen if you didn't do what you would normally do but something else. It's the runaway idea. You take an idea and just let your mind wander. I became saturated with it.'

Sellers started in radio through a typical stroke of audacity.

'I had an aptitude for dialects, and I'd studied them. I figured that the more dialects I could do and the more precise they were, the more chance there was of getting a job on the BBC. That's what I was after—to be a BBC voice man like Jon Pertwee, Maurice Denham and Kenneth Connor. Dennis Main Wilson had seen me at the Windmill and asked if I'd like an audition. I jumped at the chance. I was shown into a room with a microphone. No one else was there and I did my piece. I was told afterwards that I'd be hearing soon. But I didn't.

'There was a radio programme at the time called *Showtime*, introduced by Dick Bentley, and I wanted to get on it. The producer, Roy Speer, was a very senior man and I thought he must know Kenneth Horne and Richard Murdoch whose *Much Binding in the Marsh* was one of the biggest things on radio. So I telephoned Roy Speer's secretary and said, "This is Kenneth Horne." I thought I'd be able to tell from her voice whether Speer knew him well or not. Anyway, he came on and said, "Hello, Ken."

'In Horne's voice I said I was calling because "Dicky and I saw a young feller the other evening—extremely good." "What's the name of your show, old chap?" Then I did Dicky Murdoch's voice hissing urgently in the background, *"Showtime, Showtime."*

' "What? Oh yes, *Showtime*. He would be marvellous on your *Showtime*, this boy."

'So Roy Speer said, "Who is he, what's his name?"

' "His name? Oh Peter, Peter—er . . ." Dicky hissed "Sellers". "That's right, Peter Sellers."

' "Well, it's very kind of you chaps to take the trouble," said Roy Speer.

' "Oh, not at all. We're always on the lookout. Matter of fact we thought we might use him in our show."

' "Oh, did you? Will you be seeing him again?"

' "Yes, we can see him right now."

' "Oh, I wouldn't go to all that trouble."

' "Trouble? No trouble at all, Mr Speer, because I am Peter Sellers."

' "What? What's that? What did you say Ken?"

' "I am Peter Sellers and I've been impersonating Kenneth Horne because I couldn't get in to see you."

' "You cheeky young bugger. You've got the nerve of the devil. All right. Come up and see me."

' "I got three and a half minutes on *Showtime*. I was twenty-three and I was introduced by Dick Bentley as "a new, young talent. . . ." '

Sellers impersonated all the well-known radio voices of the time —Tommy Handley, Jimmy Jewell and Ben Warris, Jon Pertwee, Claude Dampier, Robert Moreton.*

'You have to have an ear to be able to copy a person's voice,' remarks Sellers. 'It's like music. Then, when you can do it, you've got to do something funny with it.'†

As a result of *Showtime* and other radio engagements Sellers achieved his ambition and became a regular radio voice man on *Ray's a Laugh*.

'I find,' says Sellers, 'that I get most of my ideas through watching people and listening to them. I know I'm a constant disappointment socially unless I'm with people I know. Most comedians are very serious people when they're not actually on. They are not at all funny privately.' He assumed an upper-class drawl. 'I hear you are frightfully funny, please do one of your funny things. . . .

'You close up when you hear things like that. So normally I don't want to be the one who leads in company. Sometimes, though, I spot someone who is potentially good material for some later occasion and I try to feed him, bring him out so that he will talk more.'

Sellers revels in Goonlike stories about the show, slipping into his quavering Henry Crun voice at every opportunity.

'In the early days, we had a very small listening figure, but it soon got up to huge proportions. There used to be weekly meetings

* 'The Bumper Fun Book' man who was later to die in a gas-filled room in Australia.

† 'It (imitation) accords the hearer an extraordinary amount of pleasure and makes its subject comic even if it still keeps away from the exaggerations of caricature.'—Freud

of the programme planners and, one week, one of the old boys looked at the agenda and asked an executive, "Tell me about this 'go on' show."

' "No sir, it's not 'go on', it's actually 'goon'." '

' "Coon? G. H. Elliott d'ye mean?" '

' "No sir, that's chocolate-coloured. It's goon, not coon." '

' "Goon? What is a goon?" '

' "I don't quite know sir, but they have very big listening figures." '

' "Well then, they must go on." ' '

Sellers never quite discards an idea. After use, it lies quietly in some compartment of his brain until it is reactivated by a connection. In this way, a skit on Sooty, the puppet, in *A Show Called Fred*, had its effect on his portrait of Dr Strangelove, the mad scientist, years later.

'In one of the Fred shows,' recalls Sellers, 'we decided to see what we could do with the puppet idea. Harry Corbett and Sooty were very popular, so a shot was set up of someone who, to all intents and purposes, was Harry Corbett with Sooty. Sooty kept hitting him and "Corbett" was saying, "Stop that little Sooty! Stop it!" But little Sooty wouldn't stop, so suddenly he gets a slap and becomes stiff. He drops out of sight while the man says, "He is a naughty little Sooty doing that, isn't he? What a naughty Sooty! Sooty mustn't do that again." Then Sooty comes up with a gun in its hands and fires and the man slumps forward. Then the camera crabs round and you see that "Corbett" himself was being worked by someone else with his hand up the back of his jacket. He looks round, startled, and says, "Oh!" It was a very weird moment.'

Years later Sellers made the film *Dr Strangelove, or How I Came to Love the Bomb*, directed by Stanley Kubrick.

'One day,' says Sellers, 'Stanley suggested that I should wear a black glove which would look rather sinister on a man in a wheel-chair. "Maybe he had some injury in a nuclear experiment of some sort," Kubrick said. So I put on the black glove and looked at the arm and I suddenly thought, "Hey, that's a storm-trooper's arm." So instead of leaving it there looking malignant I gave the arm a life of its own. That arm hated the rest of the body for having made a compromise; that arm was a Nazi. When it tried to choke Dr Strangelove the other arm had to hit it.

'It was the same thing as the Sooty sketch—the arm or hand having a life of its own, hating the rest of the body.'

Peter Evans records Kubrick as saying that Sellers 'is receptive to comic ideas most of his contemporaries would think unfunny and meaningless'. And Sellers himself once said: 'Some forms of reality are so horrible we refuse to face them unless we are trapped into it by comedy. Anyway, to label any subject unsuitable for comedy is to admit defeat.'

Sellers needs strong-minded directors when he makes a film, for the most difficult lesson for all performers with powerful creative urges is to learn how to place a curb on invention. It seems to be a trait common to all ex-Goons. 'It must have been difficult for any producer to try and control us,' comments Sellers.

He no longer has any need for the isolated comic idea that would have filled a minute of radio time or could be built into a sketch. But the fountain is not dependent upon the thirst and they still come pouring out. 'I write them down and file them,' he says. 'I have a mine of material.'

Eric Sykes is a figure peripheral to the Goons but central to the general business of comedy writing, and no mean performer either. He struggles against partial deafness and tends towards bouts of melancholy, gratefully clinging to comedy as the only sane and safe thing in a storm-swept world.

'If you understand comedy, you understand life,' he says. 'Drama, death, tragedy—everybody has these. But with humour you've got all these and the antidote. You have found the answer. It doesn't follow that because you're a good comedy writer you're a happy fellow. I've got one of the most miserable faces in the world. I am only happy when I'm working. If I'm not working I get screwed up because my time is going, my life is slipping by. Sometimes I get so miserable that I have to shut myself away from people and tell the children, "Kids, it's a bad day today so just stay away and it will be fine." They stay out of my way and I wander round the garden and get over it.

'It's a load of crap to say that comedians want to play Hamlet. A good comedian has more Hamlet in him than any straight actor. Harry Secombe is no exception. At home he collapses in a chair and goes down like a balloon. The thing with Harry is that he feels he's got to be funny all the time.'

Sykes was born in 1923 in the North—'where all good comedians come from'—in Oldham, Lancashire. 'You had to have a sense of humour to survive,' he says. 'That's why there's so much more to northern humour than Cockney humour. Ours has a definite character.'

His father was an overlooker in a cotton mill and before young Sykes followed him into the mill he was a woodworker, a painter and a greengrocer's assistant. But he was writing all the time.

'I was trying to write the act that didn't have one word in it, the complete mime act, and I'm still trying. My favourite comedian was Sherkot, the French mime who did a goalkeeping act. Never said a word on stage, died of cancer of the throat—strange. I wrote piece after piece but I was stumped—I always had to put some words in.'

Sykes joined the R.A.F. as a wireless operator but was seconded to the army, in which he acquired sergeant's stripes. He also served aboard naval vessels. There was so much confusion about his precise place in the forces that it took a parliamentary question to gain his release.

While still with, but not in, the army, Sykes became a comedian with an army concert party using, as a basis for his act, a gag book he had bought for 15/-6 through an advertisement in *The Stage*. Frankie Howerd was operating in the same area in Germany with another concert party.

'Afterwards,' says Sykes, 'while I was with Oldham Rep, Frankie wrote to me asking if he could have the act I did in the army show. I let him have it and he asked if I had any other stuff, so I started to write for him. It took me about five minutes to write Frankie's whole act. It was nothing to me to write it. I could write on the top of a bus or sitting in my dressing-room waiting to go on. I didn't really want to do it. I didn't want to be a writer and I didn't want to be in rep. I wanted to be up there as a principal comedian myself. Eventually, I badgered Frank so much that he recorded an act with me. I had written it, and after we listened to the recording Frank said, "Now do you believe me?" And I said, "Yes." "Right," said Frank, "forget the stage; just be a writer."

'Frank's voice was so full of life—there were so many nuances in it. Mine was dull and flat. Every time he stopped speaking and I started it sounded as if there was something wrong with the record. It was terrible and I curled up. I only came back as a performer because I used to put myself into sketches as a flunkey in order to be able to direct the others properly.

'Later I did a series for ITV and was promised all sorts of guest artists like Frank Sinatra and Bing Crosby for fortnightly spectaculars. They didn't materialise so I found myself having to play the leading roles.'

Sykes never made it as the stand-up comic of his ambitions, but showed what a good situation comedy performer he was with a number of television series with Hattie Jacques, a lady of ample proportions and excellent timing who had earlier been such an admirable foil—though no rapier, she—to Tony Hancock. She and Sykes varied the usual domestic comedy situation by playing brother and sister, and the humour was warm and full of invention. The series were, of course, written by Sykes.

He had joined Frankie Howerd as a full-time writer in 1949 at £10 a week, but other people rapidly became interested in him. He wrote *Educating Archie* for radio, a series for Hancock and, because he worked alone, was at one time the highest paid comedy writer in the country. He also wrote three *Goon Shows* with Spike Milligan. 'But we fought about everything, and I couldn't stand it any longer. We did alternate weeks for about another four programmes and then I gave it up.'

Sykes believes that the only way the country will get another crop of writers like Milligan, Muir, Norden, Speight and himself is by reintroducing conscription.

'Take away the necessity of earning a living,' he says, 'provide food and bed so that you can just sit on your backside for two years and you will find that the violinist will practise his violin, the language student will learn a language and the comedian will create comedy. It's no use expecting it to come from people who are in boring, undemanding jobs, for they have already half-settled for what they've got. Conscription is an obvious staging-post. A war is even better if you can keep alive.'

A writer, Sykes believes, writes from his past. 'It is all derived from a period in your life when you were absorbent like a sponge. You keep writing and rewriting that period and ring the changes but you don't change fundamentally. My period was bowler hats and watch chains and highly polished boots—the Sunday best of the 'thirties. In the week there'd be clogs going past from quarter to seven till five to seven when the mill opened, millions of clogs. They would all stop and then you'd get the odd one running like mad. At half past five the whistle would go and all the clogs would clatter back again. It was a funny period. Look at the way they posed for portraits or the way they dressed for motor cars or aeroplanes. They felt that they should be wearing different clothes for doing such interesting things, so they turned their caps back to front.' He shakes his head in wonder at the thought.

'I love that period,' he reflects. 'It's full of warmth and humour and it's very funny. I think we've lost a lot of humour because we've lost a lot of humanity. People talk in terms of humanity now and forget what it's all about.'

4 | *The Six-Letter Word*

About midnight on the night of August 22nd, first day of the 1960 Edinburgh Festival, the man sitting in front of me in the Lyceum Theatre noisily vacated his seat and stumped out. That unknown citizen, puffing in indignation at irreverent references to the Queen, the Prime Minister, the Right Honourable Harold Macmillan, and other respectable institutions, was the first victim of what became known as the Permissive Age—a term used, as someone once pointed out, in contrast to the repressive ages which had preceded it.

After that night came mini-skirts, long hair, nudity in the theatre, 'bum', 'bleeding', and worse on television, the right to commit sodomy in private, student protest, pictures of John Lennon and Yoko Ono naked on a record sleeve and sundry other manifestations of a changing world. It is a wonder that the City Fathers of Edinburgh, ever-watchful that a Festival event should commit no moral outrage, do not lie awake at night thinking of the havoc caused by the show they played host to for one week a decade ago.

Of course, times are not changed by one show, however influential. But *Beyond the Fringe* ushered in the changes, may have hastened them, and certainly indicated the disrespectful directions in which they should go. It was, after all, only designed as a late-night distraction for theatregoers judged to be sated by *The Seagull* (which, in fact, had held the Lyceum stage earlier that evening) or concertgoers heavy with Hindemith. Local and transient, even its title was meaningless outside the context of the many unofficial and mostly university productions that had accrued over the years as a fringe to the main cultural curtain that descends on Edinburgh every autumn. Later, in America and even in London, the title was taken as a declaration that the contents of the show were designed to go beyond the fringe of decency (political rather than sexual) or accepted standards. This was an idea that never occurred to its creators, or, it seems, to the examiners of plays in the Lord Chamberlain's office who let pass material for this revue, concocted and to be performed by four young men from Oxbridge

—in such a place at such an event at such an hour—which would never have been tolerated for a West End theatre and a normal commercial run. In doing so, they helped to create the climate necessary for their own happy abolition.

Jonathan Miller was a doctor of medicine and an intellectual. True, he had appeared in Cambridge footlight revues and had been compared very favourably with a camel, but his work as a doctor clearly came first, as he had stated on many occasions.

Alan Bennett was a lecturer in medieval history at Oxford, was something of an expert on the years 1388-99 and had said that he felt he was best suited for an academic career. He had been to Edinburgh the year before with an Oxford group in a real fringe revue.*

Dudley Moore was a serious musician, a Bachelor of Arts and Music who had won an organ scholarship to Oxford.

And Peter Cook, though professionally in show-business, having written most of the hit revue *Pieces of Eight*, had also been to Cambridge.

Surely there was nothing insidious or seditious about these young men, and if they wanted to poke mild fun at Mr Macmillan, the Queen, or God, it was just the high spirits that young gentlemen often indulged in before settling down to steady and sober careers.

The rules, never clearly defined, were bent, and references were permitted to persons and offices kept free from discussion in the so-called serious theatre for two centuries.

The Lord Chamberlain's men should have noted the sharpness with which the four principals defined their own places in the social system in one of the sketches submitted.

COOK : I think at about this juncture it would be wise to point out to those of you who haven't noticed—and God knows it's apparent enough—that Jonathan and myself come from good families and have had the benefits of a public school education, whereas the other two members of the cast have worked their way up from working-class backgrounds. Yet Jonathan and I are working together with them and treating them as equals, and I must say, it's proving to be a most worth-while, enjoyable and stimulating experience for both of us. Wouldn't you agree, Jonathan?

MILLER : Oh yes, extremely so. Very stimulating.

---

* I cannot resist a critical 'I told you so', for in 1959 I wrote a piece about him in which I said he should pack in the amateur clowning and turn professional.

BENNETT : Well, I suppose we are working class. But I wonder how many of these people realise that Jonathan Miller is a Jew.
MOORE : Yes, well, he is a Jew but one of the better sort.
BENNETT : I would rather be working class than a Jew.
MOORE : Good Lord, yes—there's no comparison, is there? But think of the awful situation if you were working class *and* a Jew.
BENNETT : There is always someone worse off than yourself.

(They exit and Miller is left alone with the audience.)

MILLER : In fact, I'm not really a Jew. Just Jewish.

Of the four, Miller is the most articulate. Words and ideas flow from him in an unending but unboring stream. Bennett, who now lives opposite Miller in trendy Victorian N.W.1 on the borderline between rough, working-class Camden Town and genteel, middle-class Regent's Park—the perfect area for someone with a social conscience and a good income—was, at one time, he says, 'deeply envious of Jonathan's verbal gifts. He was the perfect person to talk to the press. It was ready-made copy and Dudley and I used to sit there, not really having much to say and feeling quite neglected. Jonathan has this ability to talk in rounded sentences'.

Rounded paragraphs—or even rounded chapters—might be a more appropriate description.

'*Beyond the Fringe*,' says Miller, 'was original, though its subject matter may seem on superficial glance to be the same as all previous revue material—parodies of Shakespeare, parodies of dons, parodies of civil servants. Nor was satire its principal appeal. What was unique about *Beyond the Fringe* was that it succeeded in telling the truth about certain clear-cut idiosyncrasies and follies of the English character. And made some good jokes.

'The original things were, for example, the re-creation of the Second World War as a sort of folk memory turned upside-down. Now that had been done before. People had done parodies of certain war films. What they had not done was to parody the tone of voice within which patriotic nostalgia had existed in the post-war years. That was new. The fact that we pasted together in a collage so many disparate elements—folk memories, film memories, radio memories and so forth—that was original. The overall manner within which the thing was conceived was original.

'The first *Footlights Revue* I appeared in, in 1954, was the old-fashioned type of classical intimate revue full of blackout sketches and all based on, "We thought it would be funny if . . . Noël Coward had rewritten *Hopalong Cassidy*" or something. It all depended, as it were, on these unlikely fictions. It had a lot to do with style and parody.

'Parody, of course, is a preoccupation with style. It reproduces a manner, an idiom, and shows, in fact, that the idiom is independent of the context in which it arises. It is this incongruity that makes it funny. In that sense, *Beyond the Fringe* continued some of these traditions. We parodied Shakespeare, but we didn't parody him by saying how funny it would be if, say, his style was applied to nuclear war. What we did really went to the centre of what was funny in Shakespearean productions and was also funny about Shakespeare's own diction and verse.

'Our basic idea with *Beyond the Fringe* was not "Wouldn't it be funny if . . ." but "Isn't it funny that . . .".

'We had no conscious motive at all. We simply sat around a table for six weeks and tried to think of the things which amused us the most. Retrospectively, one could look back over it and say, "Look, this seems to be something with a rather satirical trend to it, a certain mood of youthful scepticism, an overthrowing of old standards and so forth." That was inherent in the fact that we were young men from the university, but it was a university which no longer represented simply privilege. Two of our members were, in fact, straightforward working-class scholarship boys. The old style of university revue had been eroded in the same way that the university itself had been eroded. The old standards were no longer accepted. Privilege was no longer regarded as binding. It wasn't that we wanted to kill sacred cows, and we certainly did not cruise round the countryside looking for them. It was just that the whole field of human foibles seemed open to us. There were no embargoes.'

In one sketch Miller, as a television vicar, talks to some television youths :

You see, I think we have got to get right away from this stuffy old idea of thinking of God as something holy or divine and once we do that we'll get you youngsters flooding back into the churches—I know that for sure. Now—Alan—is there anything in the Bible that actually puts you off religion? . . . it's my aim to get the violence off the streets and into the churches where it belongs. . . . We've now got ourselves a young, vigorous church where youngsters like yourselves can come in off the streets, pick up a chick, jive in the aisles and really have yourselves a ball. The result is we are playing to packed houses every night—except, of course, for Sunday, when we are forced to close our doors because of the Lord's Day Observance Society.

'We simply said,' Miller continues, ' "The following things seem to us to be very funny." And then along comes the critic who has, as it were, to artificially harden the outlines of a thing of this sort and create a movement out of it, and because it makes a good journalistic point, turn it into satire. There is an innate tendency in all intelligent human beings to classify novelty. Novelty, as it were, cannot be seen unless it is put into a class of some sort. People were diffusely aware of the fact that this was new in some way, but in order to make it identifiable and therefore talkaboutable, it had to belong to a category, had to be labelled. Labelling also tends to artificially sharpen certain elements at the expense of others and means, in the end, that the thing acquires in memory a purity which it never had at the outset. I don't think we had satirical intentions but we acquired them. We were influenced by the reaction. Having been told that we were satirical, we then looked back at ourselves and said, "Yes, it is rather satirical isn't it? Oh, and look at ourselves—we are part of the tradition that goes back to the German cabarets and George Grosz and the early Brecht and so on." And, as we were at the time young and relatively innocent of public life, we were quite willing to accept these various labels because they seemed to us to be honourable and, indeed, rather courageous. I think we began to see ourselves as matadors drawing blood from ageing bulls. But it was only after people had told us that that was what we were.

'I think probably Alan Bennett had a little more anger in him than the rest of us, was much more bitter. Strangely enough, he of all of us has become perhaps the most conservative, although he retains a certain sense of bitter cynicism. His sense of the absurd, his sense of the unjust, has not become blander but less political, less clearly associated with the Left. He is now capable of simply standing in a rather isolated conservative stance from which he sees injustice and absurdity perpetrated by both the Right and the Left.

'Peter provided an absolutely unique form of verbal surrealism, a sort of insane linguistic facility which is in a tradition that includes people like N. F. Simpson, Ionesco and Pinter. It extracts peculiar surrealistic effects from the endless repetition of middle-class and lower-middle-class clichés. What Peter reproduces is mechanical thinking.'

Yes, I could have been a judge but I never had the Latin, never had the Latin for the judging. I just never had sufficient of it to get through the rigorous judging exams. They're noted for their rigour. People come staggering out saying, 'My God, what a rigorous exam'—and so I became a miner instead. A coal-miner. I managed to get through the mining exams—they're not very rigorous. They only ask one question. They say, 'Who are you?' and I got 75 per cent on that.

Of course, it's quite interesting work, getting hold of lumps of coal all day, it's quite interesting. Because the coal was made in a very unusual way. You see, God blew all the trees down. He didn't just say let's have some coal. No, he got this great wind going, you see, and blew down all the trees, then over a period of three million years—he changed it into coal, gradually over a period of three million years, so it wasn't noticeable to the average passer-by . . . it was all part of the scheme, but people at the time did not see it that way. People under the trees did not say, 'Hurrah, coal in three million years.' No, they said; 'Oh dear, oh dear, trees falling on us—that's the last thing we want', and of course their wish was granted.

I am very interested in the Universe—I am specialising in the Universe and all that surrounds it. I am studying Nesbitt's book, *The Universe and All That Surrounds It, an Introduction.* He tackles the subject boldly, goes from the beginning of time right through to the present day which, according to Nesbitt, is October 31st, 1940. And he says the earth is spinning into the sun and we will all be burnt to death. But he ends the book on a note of hope. He says, 'I hope this will not happen.' But there's not a lot of interest in this down the mine.

The trouble with it is the people. I am not saying you get a load of riff-raff down the mine, I am not saying that. I am just saying we had a load of riff-raff down my mine. Very boring conversationalists, extremely boring. All they talk about is what goes on in the mine. Extremely boring. If you were searching for a word to describe the conversations that go on down the mine, boring would spring to your lips—Oh, God! They're very boring. If ever you want to hear things like : 'Hallo, I've found a bit of coal.' 'Have you really?' 'Yes, no doubt about it, this black substance is coal all right.' 'Jolly good, the very thing we're looking for.' It is not enough to keep the mind alive is it? Whoops.

Did you notice I suddenly went Whoops? It's an impediment I got from being down the mine. 'Cause one day I was walking along in the dark when I came across the body of a dead pit pony. Whoops, I went in surprise, and ever since then I've been going Whoops and that's another reason I couldn't be a judge because I might have been up there all regal, sentencing away 'I sentence you to Whoops' and you see the trouble is under

English law that would have to stand. So all in all I'd rather have been a judge than a miner.

And what is more, being a miner, as soon as you are too old and tired and sick and stupid to do the job properly you have to go. Well, the very opposite applies with the judges. So all in all I would rather have been a judge than a miner. Because I've always been after the trappings of great luxury, you see, I really have. But all I've got hold of are the trappings of great poverty. I've got hold of the wrong load of trappings, and a rotten load of trappings they are too, ones I could've well done without.

'Peter's miner,' remarks Miller, 'makes what philosophers call mistakes of category. He makes the mistakes of thinking that the idea of capability is optional. He says, "I could have been a judge if only I'd had the Latin." He has the idea that these things are sorted out in some cosmic game of Russian roulette and that he could have had it if it had only worked out in a particular way. He talks about the trappings of luxury or poverty as if, in fact, they were lying around in a wardrobe and he happened to lay his hands on the wrong lot. What is funny about that is that it involves what again the philosophers call a misdescription. It is, in fact, automatic thinking and the humour about it is automatic thought, automatic cliché, a seizing of the superficial and then investing it with an artificial authority and importance. It is hysterically funny because it involves this fundamental mistake about the essential feature of the situation. This goes back to Bergson's theory of laughter when Bergson* said that what makes us laugh is confronting someone who has lost his humanity, by which he means his flexibility, his versatility and his initiative, and is becoming a machine. The reason why we laugh at a man falling on a banana-skin is because he ceases to be a person in full charge of his will and becomes a thing in the control of gravity. That's why we laugh at so many of Peter's creatures—these are mechanical men, clockwork creatures. It's the same with the comedian's catchphrase, because by using it he becomes a sort of jack-in-the-box, a mechanical toy.

'Peter's contribution was original, but it is important to see him in the line that goes right back to Dickens and even some of those peculiar cliché'd characters in Shakespeare like Costard in *Love's*

---

* Bergson, who was Miller's great uncle, said: 'The attitudes, gestures and movement of the human body are laughable in exact proportion as that body reminds us of a mere machine. But it must be subtle; the humanity must show beneath the rigidity.'

Labour's Lost who endlessly goes over the word "remuneration" It's very similar to what Peter does: "Boring is the word I would choose to describe this. If you were looking for the right word to describe this, boring would be the one that would leap to mind. Boring is the word." He hits the word again and again. Repetition is a fundamental element of all humour because repetition implies the mechanical.

'Alan brought two things: (1) a sense of austere intellectual severity and (2) the belief that fatuity is abroad. He recognises this fatuity in social manners rather than in styles of thought. He recognises it in people who are otherwise very highly respected— Foreign Office officials, clergymen and people who generally enjoy the privileges of office.

'Certainly, clergymen have always been the butt of comedians, but never with quite the same accuracy as Alan has got. He has pinned down the clergyman's idioms, his sanctimony, his emptiness. Alan is a literary man whose great heroes are people like Sydney Smith, himself a clergyman. Alan has very strong religious feelings. I think he probably dislikes these forms because he so highly respects the Church and also in a sense he rather likes these forms because they remind him of the Church. To imitate accurately is to love what you imitate. Peter is indifferent to the people he imitates. He would dismiss them as twits.

'Alan is not so much fond of his people as of the security of the various institutions they represent. Alan likes the Church. He is outraged and despairing about the loss of choral evensong on the radio. Alan sets great store by traditional forms and gets great comfort from the simplicity of the language of the Anglican Church. He likes churches and, like Philip Larkin, recognises that they are serious places, fit to grow wise in. While at the same time he also recognises that they are places which have bred fools.'

(Alan Bennett, straw-thatched, lips ready to purse into a tight, solemn and prim line, enters and moves down to a balcony which he uses as a pulpit. He wears a clerical collar.)

The 29th verse of the 14th Chapter of the book of Genesis— 'But my brother Esau is an hairy man, but I am a smooth man'— My brother Esau is an hairy man, but I am a smooth man. Perhaps I can paraphrase this, say the same thing in a different way, by quoting you some words from that grand old prophet Nehemiah, Nehemiah 7-16: 'And he said unto me, what seest thou and I said unto him, lo I see the children of Bebai numbering six hundred and seventy-three and I see the children of

Asgad numbering one thousand four hundred and seventy-four.'

(*He repeats the last four lines.*) There come times in the lives of each and every one of us when we turn aside from our fellows and seek the solitude and tranquillity of our own firesides. When we put up our feet and put on our slippers and sit and stare into the fire and I wonder at such times whether your thoughts turn, as mine do, to those words I've just read you now.

They are very unique and very special words, words that express as so very few words do, that sense of lack that lies at the very heart of modern existence. That 'I don't quite know what it is but I'm not getting everything out of life that I should be getting' sort of feeling. But they are more than this, these words, much, much more—they are in a very real sense a challenge to each and every one of us here tonight. What is that challenge?

As I was on my way here tonight I arrived at the station and, by an oversight, I happened to come out by the way one is supposed to go in and as I was coming out an employee of the railway company hailed me. 'Hey mate,' he shouted, 'where do you think you are going?' That, at any rate, was the gist of what he said. You know, I was grateful to him, because, you see, he put me in mind of the kind of question I felt I ought to be asking you here tonight : Where do you think you're going?

Very many years ago when I was about as old as some of you are now, I went mountain climbing in Scotland with a very dear friend of mine. And there was this mountain, you see, and we decided to climb it. And so, very early one morning, we arose and began to climb. All day we climbed. Up and up and up. Higher and higher. Till the valley lay very small below us and the mists of the evening began to come down, and the sun to set. And when we reached the summit we sat down to watch this most magnificent sight of the sun going down behind the mountain. And, as we watched, my friend very suddenly and violently vomited. Some of us think life's a bit like that, don't we? But it isn't, you know. Life, life, is rather like opening a tin of sardines. We are all of us looking for the key. Some of us— some of us think we've found the key, don't we? We roll back the lid of the sardine tin of life, we reveal the sardines, the riches of life therein and we get them out, we enjoy them. But you know, there's always a little piece in the corner you can't get out. I wonder—I wonder, is there a little piece in the corner of your life? I know there is in mine.

So now I draw to a close. I want you, when you go out into the world, in times of trouble, sorrow and helplessness and despair, amid the hurly-burly of modern life, if ever you're tempted to say, 'Oh shove this for a lark', I want you to remember for comfort the voice of my first text to you tonight: 'But my brother Esau is an hairy man, but I am a smooth man.'

Dudley Moore's solos in the show were all musical. He sat at the piano, fixed the audience with a winning, confident leer and launched himself into some catastrophic German *lieder* or British folk song, making huge moans in a falsetto voice full of flourishes.

'Dudley,' says Jonathan Miller, 'brought a peculiar, almost pagan frivolity, a strange, cloven-hoofed, Panlike sense of the comic which is libidinous, childlike, goatlike. Very primitive in the very best sense. I often think of him as the embodiment of some peculiar mythical satyr. There is a very important stream of humour which is this antic, mythic, shaggy-thighed anarchic joy—primal.'

And obsessional, as in the sketch where he had been to see a show 497 times in the hope of seeing the Royal Family.

I read in the newspapers that the Royal Family were planning a visit to this theatre, so naturally I came along. You see, up there, that's what they call the Royal Box. But I don't know if you've noticed, there's no Royalty in it. No Royal People there at all. No Royal Personage actually gracing the Royal Box . . . unless, of course, they're crouching. But, I mean, that wouldn't be Royalty, would it?

He hopes against hope that 'one night the Royal Family will turn up and make my having to sit through this rotten, awful show each night worth while'.

'Do you really mean to say?' asks Cook, 'that you spend fifteen shillings every night just on the off-chance you may catch a glimpse of the Royal Family?'

'Well,' says Moore, 'they're not worth the pound.'

Miller describes himself. 'I'm partly a fantasist. I don't know what it was that I brought to it at all. Primarily, I'm a director. People think of me—thought of me—as a sort of capering ostrich or camel. I've been fighting off this awful thing of the clown wanting to play Hamlet—"Dr Miller's brow has been getting higher and higher. . . ." The fact is that if people want to use the word highbrow, I've been highbrow all my life because I've been brought up in an absolutely academic household.

'I can make people laugh a great deal when I'm talking. I find myself performing. When I tell stories a fantasy overtakes me.'

Alan Bennett, born in 1934 in Leeds, son of a butcher, went to Oxford via a grammar-school scholarship. 'We were not poor, not well off,' says Bennett. 'I once told Jonathan we were working class and he came home expecting us to be crouched over the kitchen hob with a pot of stew.

'I don't think I was funny at school, really. I was quite acid and sharp and probably sour and unpleasant. I'm very close to my mother and father. My mother is unconsciously funny and my father is more aware of being funny and together we tend to be rather critical. They very often abuse people on the television and say things about people they see outside. That was a big influence on me, I think.

'I remember seeing George Formby in a film in Leeds and wanting to stop laughing because it was so painful. I liked *Take It From Here* a lot because of those outrageous far-fetched puns. I remember a take-off of *The Crowthers of Bankdam* and Jimmy Edwards sitting down and eating some soda scones. Then he said, "I shouldn't have eaten them soda scones so late; they make me so disconsolate." You can imagine Muir and Norden's glee when they thought that one up.'

Bennett's addiction to the pun was thoroughly indulged in his play, *Forty Years On*, which ran at the Apollo Theatre throughout 1969. From the rich rag-bag of British tradition, Bennett plucked literary, political and social memories of times, places and states of mind which he himself could never have experienced, and set them working in a public school, end-of-an-era atmosphere at a time of changing headmasters. Bennett himself blandly threaded his way through numerous roles ranging from Victorian dowager to Bloomsbury literary man.

The first deliberately funny thing he remembers doing was a small contribution to a cabaret evening while he was in the army. He spent an unusually rarefied conscription period on the Joint Services Russian Course at Cambridge. No one knows what effect this course had on our intelligence agencies' evaluation of Russia, but it certainly produced a crop of writers, among them Dennis Potter, Michael Frayn and Bennett himself, who look upon England with a distinctly critical eye.

'Then I went to Oxford,' says Bennett, 'and read history. I opted out of the social scene. I wasn't in any of the dramatic clubs. It took me a long time to find my feet and I tended to imagine that the standard was enormously high. It was only in my third year when I was about, as I thought then, to finish, that I felt confident enough to do anything. I did the sermon, the one I did later in *Beyond the Fringe*, at a smoker we held in Exeter College. I wrote it in an afternoon, not thinking very much about it.

'I was very religious between the ages of about fifteen and eighteen and I'm still not anti-religious. I go to church in the village where my parents live now, but not in London because I regard it as part of the fabric of life there but not here. I suppose it was things unconsciously absorbed in those years that came out in the sermon and later in *Forty Years On*. Sort of Church of England things. Anyway, I did the sermon for the first time in 1957 and then I got my degree and stayed on to do research. My period was 1388-99. That's not as ludicrous as it sounds. I wasn't very good at research, very slapdash. But I taught as well. I never got a Fellowship and I don't think I ever would have done. I didn't do anything particularly dramatic until 1959 when I went to Edinburgh with the Oxford Theatre Group revue. It was written by Stanley Daniels, but I asked if I could do some of my own material. By that time I had started writing odd bits of things. They didn't really fit in with his scheme so I wasn't allowed to do them. Except that on the last night I persuaded the technicians to alter the thing so that I could do the sermon without telling him. It was an unforgivable thing to do and there was a tremendous row about it but it was a great success. I just wanted to see whether it was a sort of viable proposition. John Bassett, then assistant to Robert Ponsonby (Director of the Festival), saw the revue. He had also seen Jon and thought that perhaps we could get together for the 1960 Festival. We started having meetings about Easter in a restaurant in Charlotte Street. My knowledge of London was so hazy that whenever we went about I never quite knew where we were. I remember being appalled by how prolific Peter was. He was still at Cambridge. Dudley had left Oxford and Jonathan was at the Middlesex Hospital. Peter was the youngest and the only real undergraduate. He threw off jokes all the time. I realised I couldn't actually provide material at the meetings, that I'd have to think of things beforehand and come along with them. But even so I think Peter had the largest percentage of material. Some of it, like the Macmillan piece, was satirical.'

It was called TV PM and Cook stood beside a table on which was a globe. From time to time he pointed to the globe to illustrate his talk. Rarely did gesture coincide with words.

Good evening. I have recently been travelling round the world on your behalf and at your expense, visiting some of the chaps with whom I hope to be shaping your future. I went first to

Germany and there I spoke with the German Foreign Minister, Herr . . . Herr . . . and there. And we exchanged many frank words in our respective languages. From thence I flew by Boeing to the Bahamas where I was having talks with the American President, Mr Kennedy, and I must say I was very struck by his youth and vigour. The talks we had were of a very friendly nature and at one time we even exchanged photographs of our respective families, and I was very touched, very touched indeed, to discover that here was yet another great world leader who regarded the business of government as being a family affair.

Our talks ranged over a wide variety of subjects including that of the Skybolt Missile programme. And after a great deal of good-natured give-and-take I decided on behalf of Great Britain to accept the Polaris in the place of the Skybolt. This is a good solution because, as far as I can see, the Polaris starts where the Skybolt left off. In the sea. I was privileged to see some actual photographs of this weapon. The President was kind enough to show me actual photographs of this missile, beautiful photographs taken by Karsh of Ottawa. A very handsome weapon we shall be very proud to have. The photographs, that is. We don't get the missiles till round about 1970—in the meantime we shall just have to keep our fingers crossed, sit very quietly and try not to alienate anyone.

This is not to say that we do not have our own Nuclear Striking Force—we do; we have the Blue Steel, a very effective missile as it has a range of 150 miles which means we can just about get Paris—and by God, we will.

While I was abroad I was very moved to receive letters from people in acute distress all over the country. And one in particular from an old-age pensioner in Fyfe is indelibly printed on my memory. (*He fumbles for it in his pockets and eventually finds the letter.*) Let me read it to you. It reads : 'Dear Prime Minister, I am an Old-Age Pensioner in Fyfe living on a fixed income of some £2.7s a week. This is not enough. What do you of the Conservative Party propose to do about it?' (*He tears up the letter.*)

Well, let me say right away Mrs Macfarlane, as one Scottish Old-Age Pensioner to another—be of good cheer. There are many people in this country today who are far worse off than yourself. And it is the policy of the Conservative Party to see that this position is maintained. And now I see the sands of time are, alas, drawing all too rapidly to a close, so I leave you all with that grand old Celtic saying that is so popular up there, Goodnight and may God be wi' ye.

'I think,' continues Bennett, 'that Dudley also felt a bit lost and didn't quite know what to do. I think that until a fortnight before we actually did *Beyond the Fringe* he was very diffident about putting forward his own things. I remember the lovely Benjamin Britten parody he did. He said he was just trying it out, he couldn't possibly do this, could he?

'I don't think we were at all easy with one another. We had enormous rows. One was about a joke about anti-Semitism which I wanted to put in. We didn't have a director really, so there was no impartial figure to give a decision. If something had to be taken out it was three of us ganging up on the fourth. I remember being very upset about this joke that went out. I'm quite sure now it was right that it should go. I've forgotten what it was, it was so unfunny.

'The same kind of thing happened later on when we opened in Cambridge before coming to London. We had to cut half an hour out of the show and I had to keep going to Oxford because I was still teaching. Of course, it's fatal to go away in a situation like that. We weren't very cosy with one another until America, and even then Jonathan and I used to have enormous rows. The relationship is much better now that we are not working together.'

Beyond the Fringe opened at the Fortune Theatre in London in May 1961 and finished, with a different cast, in 1966. It ran for two years in New York with the original cast.

'We are very disparate personalities. Jonathan is very exuberant and I'm sort of inward-looking. Dudley's sort of cuddlesome and Peter's a sort of mad lunatic. The things we did tended to be in line with the way we are. Jonathan's humour is very verbal and very physical. He runs about and does things on the spur of the moment, tending not to do the same thing twice. When he gets into a rut he starts to stutter. One of the best things was the sketch about the war at the end of the first act. Peter originally didn't want it in. I think Jon and I had to sell the idea quite hard. But once it had been accepted Peter was the mainstay of it and did some very funny things. He improvised the man who met every crisis with another cup of tea during the time we were writing.'

That was the night they got Pithy Street. I always remember it. I was out in the garden at the time planting out some deadly nightshade for the Boche. My wife came out to me in the garden and told me the abominable news. 'Thousands have died in Pithy Street.' 'Never you mind the thousands of dead,' I says to her. 'You put on the kettle, we'll have a nice cup of tea.'

Bennett did a piece about a Battle of Britain pilot which he brought ready-written to the meeting.

> I had a pretty quiet war really. I was one of the Few. We were stationed down at Biggin Hill. One Sunday we got word Jerry was coming in over Broadstairs, I think it was. We got up there as quickly as we could and, you know, everything was very calm and peaceful. England lay like a green carpet below us and the war seemed worlds away. I could see Tunbridge Wells and the sun glinting on the river and I remembered that last week-end I spent there with Celia that summer of '39.
>
> Suddenly Jerry was coming at me out of a bank of cloud. I let him have it, and I think I must have got him in the wing because he spiralled past me out of control. As he did so, I will always remember this, I got a glimpse of his face and, you know, he smiled. Funny thing—war.

'One could always make fun of the stiff upper lip,' Bennett comments, 'but in the particular context of the war sketch it was quite shocking and did annoy some people. And yet it made people realise that it *was* slightly ridiculous and it also made people who had already realised this that they were not alone.

'When we got used to working together, that is when it was running in London, things tended to expand and change and to be improvised upon the stage. There was a sketch that Peter wrote called "Royal Box". Originally it was just Peter and Dudley doing it. Then we came on to corpse one another really, not because we could make any contribution. There were three chairs there and I just went and sat in the third chair. The first time I did it they just became helpless and couldn't get on with the sketch. Then, gradually, they got used to this situation, though I didn't do it every night. Peter began to improvise some dialogue and the sketch began to alter. Sometimes Jonathan would come in as well.

'Jon's sense of humour is verbal in the sense that it comes out of very exact and very odd descriptions, whereas Peter is more schizophrenic in his use of words. I think this is what schizophrenics do—associate words that sound alike. Peter's old man sitting on a bench rambling on will leap from subject to subject through similarities in word form. The other aspect is insult. It's very much an upper-class thing—somebody who is so secure in his position that he can be insulting to everyone else. In a sense the imitation of Macmillan was rather like this. It was someone who was very much looking down on the people who were listening to him. It's very cruel humour really.

'Dudley did a Kurt Weill parody in New York which was a lovely thing. He's a great mugger, he really does make the most appalling faces. But he'd be rather hurt about that. It's funny, but we're all very sensitive about what the others say about us.

'I'm extremely competitive and edgy. I remember fighting very hard against a lot of Peter's vaudeville exuberance, though whether it was because I genuinely believed it would submerge any purpose the show might have or whether it was because I thought I should be swept away because I produced so little, I don't know. It was probably a bit of both. Peter at that time had written *Pieces of Eight*, he was a wonderboy really. I feel quite easy talking about Jonathan because I know him so much better now. But in New York in particular we really used to get on each other's nerves and it was a great relief when he left. As soon as he did, it was all right. It's just that he's difficult to work with. Simply because I know him so well I tend not to trust his judgment at all. He makes me laugh enormously—socially.

'It is very peculiar when you've worked with three other people and know them better than anybody else. In New York we lived together for a time, but that was a disaster. Yet, at the same time, looking back on it as a whole I do value it enormously and one shares something with the others that nobody else can comprehend.

'I don't think we ever thought we could change things, but each of us, to some extent, concentrated on the things that irritated us. Some of these were small irritations, others had larger implications. I used to do a sketch which Peter called "your boring old man sketch". Originally it was about South Africa but, as circumstances changed, other things like capital punishment became the subject. And it was rather boring. There were great stretches of boredom in it. There were few laughs and I'd never dare do it today, but I was sustained because I did feel that it was sort of hard-core material. In fact, it was noticed as being a sort of departure. But if there had been more of that sort of stuff the whole thing would have failed miserably. It was prestige really.

'I did a series on television with sketches about this area, N.W.1, of which I am a part, and so in a sense it was making fun of myself. But it pinpointed something and since then N.W.1 has been used as a catchphrase to indicate Sunday supplement trendiness which people now find rather suspect. But it is a very small gain and it doesn't mean anything to anyone in Leeds or Bradford.

'The older I get and the more I do the less confident I am that one can achieve anything by comedy. I did a spoof documentary about a northern writer on television, which is the only thing in the series that I can say was exactly what I wanted to do and I thought it would be quite hard to make documentaries like that afterwards. In fact, I've seen several since.

'There was only one television series because I'm so slow. I ate up so much stuff that I can't afford to do it again, not in terms of money but material. I realised there that I enjoyed making jokes for the sake of the joke rather than anything else. The funniest thing I ever wrote, I think, was for *Not So Much a Programme*. . . . It was a sketch in which I played a clergyman who was being visited by a parishioner who is having it off with a girl in the office and he's worried about it and wants to talk to the vicar. The opening shot was of a cross and the vicar takes out his pipe and it is seen that the cross is also a pipe-rack. It raised a great sort of hoo-hah, but once I'd thought of it I couldn't resist doing it.' Bennett giggled.

'People read all sorts of things into that kind of joke, but it's simply like witty remarks you make about some people—you just can't resist making them.'

Miller blossomed as a director with a talent for upsetting traditional concepts with Highly Original Thoughts. He directed *Alice in Wonderland* for television in a way which brought out all its schizophrenic qualities and set a National Theatre production of *The Merchant of Venice* with Olivier as Shylock in a late-Victorian, money-dominated society.

'One of the reasons I don't do comedy any more,' says Miller, 'is that I'm much more interested in the theory than the practice of it.

'Class plays a very complicated part in English humour. First of all there is working-class humour, and then there is humour about the working classes. Working-class humour has two or three main strains to it. First of all there is the natural strain of people laughing at their own misfortunes, a parallel with Jewish humour. Then there is the humour that arises from self-recognition. If you name a familiar place which has special significance for the group they laugh and by laughing together they confirm their group solidarity. The third thing, which is what George Orwell found out in his essay on Donald McGill's seaside postcards, is that the working classes are the unwilling and unconscious victims of various systems of repression, mainly sexual repression. There are particular ideas about decency, marriage and in-laws, and there are simple elementary rules to determine family conduct. The language of the working classes is, by and large, very context-bound. It's fixed in the situations themselves. It is about what those people are doing at the moment, about the immediate circumstances. It does not make reference to general principles and therefore there is very little room to manoeuvre and criticise the standards in accordance with which they act. The result is that the intelligent ones among them are aware of the fact that they are constrained in their behaviour but are not eloquent enough to be able to describe the reasons why these constraints are felt to be binding.

'So the only way in which they can deal with this situation is by humour which, as it were, criticises the standards without seriously calling them into question. So what you have is a parallel world of postbox-coloured ladies with bulging breasts and bottoms, a world in which little wizened men are endowed with superhuman sexual capacities. A little bowler-hatted, moustached figure is seen alongside a lady of enormous proportions wheeling a pramful of children, while a neighbour questions his capacity to produce them. "He's a nightworker," says the mother. "I'll bet he is," says the neighbour. It's a half-arsed criticism of the real world; it's a place in which the unofficial self is recognised.

'The working classes have a very vague, cloudy sense of unfairness about certain constraints and the sense of unfairness expresses itself, not with reference to any dialogue, but to the safe confines of a music-hall or a picture postcard. Say it with a smile and it's safe. The smile means that you don't mean it really. And yet you do mean it. Humour is used as a primitive technique of moral criticism.

'What happens in the intellectual classes is that there is no need to resort to these pantomime, masquerade techniques. Criticism can become explicit and made with reference to abstract principles. The laughter of the literate classes is very much more reflexive. It is laughter about the use of language, not necessarily about situations, though they are common to all humour. It's laughter about strange uses of linguistic bathos—above all, irony. Irony is the distinctive feature of educated laughter and it is something which, in fact, the working classes are pretty awkward in the presence of. Irony becomes a distinctly threatening thing because it represents to them a linguistic facility which they don't have.

'Laughter as a means of survival is used to diminish threat. To call a bomb a doodlebug diminishes its size, turns it into a toy. It's like children in hospital playing doctors and nurses with dolls. By being masters of the doll situation they act out the possibility of their being masters of their own destiny. We make linguistic dolls of our oppressors in jokes and seem therefore to be in control.

'Bergson said laughter was injected into the human species at a very early stage. Whenever a person became mechanical, unversatile, his survival was threatened. To be unversatile is to be mechanical and to be mechanical is to be unable to adapt to circumstances, and to be unadaptable means that survival as a biological creature is threatened. Laughter is the reminder of the group to the individual that he is slipping into a dangerous style of behaviour.

'Up to the late 'fifties, university humour was characterised—as indeed most educated humour was—by making figures of fun out of the working classes. There were comic shopgirls, comic servants, comic workmen, gnarled, inflexible figures whose language habits were extremely limited. We laughed at their clichés. But almost all upper-class humour about the working classes was itself a cliché. We cannot any longer laugh at the working classes in the same way that we cannot any longer exploit them.'

Cook and Moore continued in comedy with a number of films but, more notably, with their television series, *Not Only . . . But Also.*

Dudley Moore is small, slight, dark and vulnerable, an arouser, it appears, of strong maternal and other passions in women. He was born in Dagenham in 1934, son of a railway electrician. Peter Cook is tall and very nearly as willowy as Frank Muir. He was born in Torquay in 1937, son of a colonial administrator. As they said in their *Beyond the Fringe* sketch, Moore is working class, Cook upper class. Cook effervesces, Moore tends to brood. Moore, at first, was overshadowed by the other three in *Beyond the Fringe* and while they juggled with words he displayed his dexterity through music, a form which does not lend itself to illustrative quotations in critics' reviews or interviews. It was not until later, in an unlikely partnership with Cook, that his personal comedy developed. The BBC acted as marriage-broker. But it is more a liaison than a marriage. Cook and Moore are not padlocked together in the mind's eye like Morecambe and Wise. Each can work alone, unaffected by the other's absence.

Moore has a club foot and it was the most important single factor in the fashioning of his life.

'I spent a lot of time in hospital when I was young,' he says. 'There were a lot of operations. I think it gave me a masochistic nature which still exists to this day.'

He says this jokily but . . .

'The club foot is something that dominates my whole life—or has done. I think it still does to a certain extent. I think everyone

The Goons light up: Spike Milligan, Peter Sellers and Harry Secombe

The original cast of *Beyond the Fringe*: Jonathan Miller, Alan Bennett, Dudley Moore and Peter Cook

Tony Hancock

Michael Bentine

has something on to which they project everything, but it was a force that has given me drive in many ways and also a great deal of repression. It is not an unusual combination.'

He had an unhappy time at Oxford.

'I found it very difficult to fit in. I came from a working-class background and everybody seemed to be very suave and smooth and assured. I was very angry, I suppose, for a long time for no reason at all. I despised any sort of friendliness. In fact, I despised friendliness from a very early age, when I come to think of it. You used to get wheeled into the operating theatre and told things like, "Now you are going to see a Mickey Mouse film". And I used to say whatever was the equivalent of "Oh, for fuck's sake, I'm going to have an operation". It was as if they were looking down on me, but again, it was one of those situations where things can't be perfect. I had a number of operations, but a club foot is still a thin leg and a deformed foot. I was always in what were called manipulative plasters and due to them the leg never really grew.

'I don't want to play with words, but, funnily enough, it gives one the feeling of being manipulated. I spent a long time in hospitals. I used laughter as a safety valve, both for myself and as a defence against others. I remember the exact moment when it happened. I was about twelve and in an English lesson and I thought, "I can't stand this any longer", and I summoned up my courage and made some silly little remark that made the children look around and laugh. I could see them thinking, "Did that come from him?" I was a very solemn sort of pompous boy and I was treated rather warily or gently by the masters which, of course, didn't exactly endear me to the boys. The sight of people actually smiling at me was a new thing and I wanted to keep them doing that, to get their approval. So I kept on fooling about. Consequently my work went down, which was a great sorrow to me because I was a very hard worker and unless I was top of the class I felt humiliated. When I discovered this way of making people laugh I felt a bit more comfortable, but my work dropped. So I pleased the children and the teachers were slightly confused by the fact that I wasn't working so hard. I didn't really feel too great about it, but it was a safety measure.

'I really wanted to be a maths or language teacher, but I dropped the subjects that involved extra work and fell back on those I could do instinctively and easily. Music was one of them. I didn't have to work very hard at it and didn't really think of it as a career at first. I retreated to it, as it were.'

Moore's family was musical. He wanted to play the violin but his mother thought he should learn the piano first. While still at

D

the local grammar school he won a junior exhibition to the Guild-hall School of Music, where he presented himself for four hours each Saturday morning to learn basic musicianship. He also sang in the local choir, and, at sixteen, learned to play the organ. He then won an organ scholarship to Oxford. 'It was,' he thinks, 'a convenient way of getting to university. In a way, it was the same at Oxford as it had been at school. I wanted attention and I started doing revues just at the wrong time—in my third and final year for my B.A. Then I stayed on an extra year, ostensibly to do a Bachelor of Music in composition. In revue I did some rather hideous mime. When I think of it now my stomach turns over. I did a Western scene which involved coming through swing doors and being hit in the back by them. There were other tiny snippets of fairly useless stuff. When I left Oxford I didn't really know what I wanted to do except that it would probably be in revue or cabaret. I did all sorts of rubbish at first—commercial jingles, incidental music for the Royal Court Theatre, bits of cabaret.'

Moore had started playing jazz when he was still at school. After Oxford he went to America with the Vic Lewis Orchestra and stayed in New York when the other musicians returned to England. He auditioned for the Jack Paar and Ed Sullivan television shows without success and for a time played in a Greenwich Village bar. He returned to England and joined the Johnny Dankworth Orchestra. Then came *Beyond the Fringe*.

'I don't think,' he says, 'I was responsible for anything of the feeling of *Beyond the Fringe* except in terms of performance. I felt very out of place with the other three—totally out of place. I mean, I didn't contribute anything textually. Jonathan has a mercurial quality. He's fascinated by words, though not in quite the same way as Peter is. Peter bends words and twists them and follows them through. Jonathan juggles with them. He throws them up in the air and you get a great firework display. I was quite shocked at their lack of inhibition. I kept saying things like, "But you can't do that . . ." Now I'm just as unthinkingly outrageous, sometimes.

'We were all very competitive when we met. We had had some success in our respective fields, but I couldn't compete on the literary, philosophical or political level at all. I had no knowledge there. I was probably lucky to be the only musician in the group. Peter and Jonathan sparked each other off a lot; Alan worked very slowly and used to put his bit in. I didn't say anything at all. I was all right in my solo pieces, but until we got to New York I felt totally constricted and overpowered. There was still a niggling thing in the back of my mind about not being able to contribute as a writer. In America I started to feel that I could perform with Peter very well, that we had some sort of *rapport*. In the course of the run I think Jonathan gradually got more ill-at-ease with himself and the show, got tired of doing it. Now and again, tensions built up between Jonathan and Alan, between myself and Alan. I remember doing a sketch with Alan and he was very angry about the way I did it and that kind of froze us up for a long, long time. It was a display of disapproval that I was unable to cope with and I think he couldn't either.'

Moore's real involvement with comedy did not come until some years later when Dudley, the swinging jazzman, came up with Dud, the meek little male virgin in the shabby raincoat, while the elegant Peter Cook donned a dirty white scarf and torn cloth-cap and turned into Pete the ignoramus know-all of dominating character. For Cook, Pete was a performance. For Moore, Dud was a disclosure. Their partnership will be considered later.

Peter Cook started performing at his public school, Radley. 'I developed it as a protection against being bullied,' says Cook. 'Not that I was particularly weedy or small but it just seemed an added bulwark. If you were pretty funny then, on the whole, people didn't hit you. We did revues at school and I wrote things which mainly took the piss out of the masters. I wrote a terrible musical play for marionettes called *Black and White Blues*. It was about a jazz band which went to Africa in order to convert the natives to Christianity. It had a very obscure plot, was written in doggerel and was very smutty. It was a great success. It was neither pro nor anti religion, it just made a farce of the whole thing.

'I had a marvellous time at school during my last three years. A group of people, all of whom were friends of mine, became prefects by default. We'd always thought that a lot of the rules were ridiculous so, when we came to power, so to speak, there was a silent revolution. We didn't say anything; we just did not enforce any of the really stupid rules like the ones about buttons. In your first year all your buttons had to be done up, in the second year you could have one button undone, in third year two, and when you became a prefect you could undo all your buttons and walk over certain bits of grass. We also abolished beating altogether and a great deal of laughing went on. I couldn't imagine beating anybody, though I'd been beaten by no less a figure than Ted Dexter (the England cricketer) for drinking cider at Henley Regatta. I've followed his career with interest but I haven't thought of a good way of getting my own back.

'In my last year I passed all my exams and won a scholarship to Cambridge. While I was waiting I had nothing to do so I taught a little and was waited on hand and foot because, as a prefect, you had two fags. I once mistakenly described this period on television in America, where fag means homosexual. It caused some confusion.

'I didn't join the army because I'm allergic to feathers. It was on my medical record that I used to have an allergy and asthma, but puberty had rather got rid of it. They asked me if I would sneeze if I were in a barrack-room full of feather pillows and I said, "I'm terribly sorry, but I would." So I was turned down. I said, "You will call me up in case of an emergency?" and they said they would. A bloke behind me in the queue during the examination said, "You seem to have got them concerned about somethink." I told him about this allergy to feathers. When he was asked if he had any medical history he said, "Yeh, I got this allergy to feathers and dust." They asked him how it affected him and he said, "I get this terrible pain in the back." I think he was passed A1 and was probably killed somewhere, poor sod.

'I had a year to fill in before I went to Cambridge so I went to France to Tours University, allegedly to learn French. I think my parents tried to make sure that my first hesitant sexual manoeuvres took place outside the country. It was a very good plan, but unfortunately I didn't meet with much success. Interesting remarks such as "*Je suis un étudiant anglais*" didn't seem to get the girls going in quite the way I had hoped.

'At Cambridge I studied French and German and got my degree by pinching Eleanor Bron's notes. I toyed with the idea of going into the Foreign Office, but I don't think the Foreign Office toyed with the idea of my joining them. I was writing and performing at Cambridge, wrote stuff for *Pieces of Eight* and then came *Beyond the Fringe*.

'We all hated the title but couldn't think of anything else. Alan was completely different then. I think he was genuinely shocked by the degree of filthy badinage. He was quite puritanical then; now he's the smuttiest of the lot of us. Alan's contribution was the most severe and the hardest, I suppose. He took a tougher line than the rest of us.'

Cook adopts the voice of a particularly grisly compère : 'Now,' he says, 'it is boring old man time which will severely restrain the audience from laughter and lash them with guilt. . . .

'There were all sorts of things I would have liked to change in society but I didn't think they would be achieved by *Beyond the Fringe*. I thought it was important that the sketches had some real content and weight but primarily they were there to make people laugh. Dudley and I weren't actually racked by guilt at the fact that we were doing a stage show.

'Jonathan had masses of material from the past when he had been called the Danny Kaye of Cambridge. He was fed up with most of it, but nevertheless it was very funny. It was with great difficulty that he was persuaded to be in the show at all. He had this doctor-comedian conflict and Alan had this academic-comedian conflict. I had no conflict whatsoever, nor had Dudley. It was rather boring. We kept trying to think of something—"By day he is a Trappist monk, by night he is on the boards". That sort of thing.

'Dudley was much quieter in those days. Jonathan talks a great deal and very lucidly about any subject under the sun. On first meeting, his loquacity is rather inhibiting. Alan would be quietly brooding in a corner while Jonathan would be theorising and Dudley was quite subdued. I was sort of the ghastly show-business element in the sense that I had actually done something. I also had an agent and got paid £10 a week more than they did, but as I had to pay commission I ended up with £5 less. That was a great source of amusement.

'The coal-miner who wanted to be a judge was in my mind—not based on observation of anyone. Somewhere within me must be lurking a schizophrenic with a mackintosh. I hope he never surfaces and takes over. During four years of doing "If I Had the Latin" I must have done about fifty hours of different material. I wish I could remember some of it.

'We used to try and throw the others off during sketches. In Boston, when Jonathan and Alan were doing the philosophy sketch and Jonathan's wife, Rachel, was standing in the wings with their two-week-old baby, I became a butler and brought it on and said, "Excuse me sir, but your wife's just had this sir, and I wondered what I should do with it." Jonathan said, "Oh, bung it in the fridge." He was very cross, actually, he was certain that I'd drop the baby. Dudley was always trying to corpse Alan during the Shakespeare scene and Alan reacted rather unfavourably to this. There were frosty periods which used to last a week or so, but it was a very amicable show really, compared to other shows I've been involved in.'

Oddly enough, it was the uncommitted Cook, more concerned with comedy than comment, who played the major part in spreading satire to the wider audience of television. He was also one of the founders of the magazine *Private Eye*.

While *Beyond the Fringe* was running in London Cook started the Establishment Club in Soho, where a number of outrageous performances took place. 'I'm still amazed,' says Cook, 'at some of the things we did there. We had sketches in the most appalling taste. Many were extremely libellous and there were a lot of crucifixion things. One about class ended up with two working-class robbers looking at a very upper-class Jesus and saying things like, "How come he is three feet higher than us and getting all the attention?"

The BBC approached the Establishment with a view to doing a television show of a similar nature. It did not get off the ground because there was opposition to promoting a commercial enterprise. Another factor was that John Bird, who was the lynch-pin of the Establishment productions, did not want to compère a television series, preferring to go to America instead. The BBC decided to mount its own show with David Frost as the front man and Ned Sherrin as producer.

That Was the Week That Was started on November 24th, 1962, a month after the original *Beyond the Fringe* company opened in New York. For the first few weeks there was an average of three million viewers. By the end of February 1963 there were twelve million. This was extraordinary for a late-night show. A great deal of the interest had less to do with comedy than hard-hitting political journalism, usually disguised as biography, and partial to an extent never known on television before. There was, for instance, an item by David Frost and Christopher Booker which dealt with Henry (now Lord) Brooke, the then Home Secretary. It made large use of quotations from newspaper cuttings and adopted the form of *This Is Your Life*, the popular and deliberately inoffensive television show which can be depended upon to ignore a subject's four broken marriages, three cases of drunken driving and a charge of rape, while giving an exhaustive account of a youthful orchard raid.

The way TW3 did it was quite different.

And so, Henry, to this week-end and the case of Chief Enaharo, the Nigerian Opposition Leader who has asked for asylum but whom you are sending back into danger. He got in without you noticing him—like Rockwell and Bidault. You've changed your mind—as you did with Carmen Bryan. And you've ignored the spirit of British tradition to please another government—like Soblen. Your policy, Mr Brooke, has been one of trial and error. Their trials. Your errors. On behalf of us all—particularly of

Dr Soblen and Chief Enaharo—THIS IS YOUR LIFE, HENRY
BROOKE—and was theirs.*
HENRY : Just shows, if you're Home Secretary, you can get
away with murder.

There were cries of 'unfair' from supporters of those who were
attacked, but these were mild compared with the outbreak of
shock, horror, disgust alarm and letter-writing occasioned by such
items as a 'Consumer Guide to Religions' by Robert Gillespie and
Charles Lewsen, and a sketch by the late Steven Vinaver about
a man being told by his girl friend in a café that his fly-buttons
were undone.

Seven years later, Benny Hill was to perform a sketch on
television in which a sporting vicar hurries to a television interview
with his fly-buttons manifestly seen to be undone without, as far
as is known, one murmur of protest.

This radical change in the careful BBC posture of avoiding
controversy at all costs, was engineered, not from the shiny, modern
Television Centre, but from a small Victorian house adjoining the
old studios in Lime Grove. Here, in an upper room once reserved
for the private fantasies of drapers or clerks, Ned Sherrin, then
thirty-one and David Frost, then twenty-three, spurred on an ever-
increasing number of writers to ever-greater productivity, Frost
with cries of 'super' and Sherrin with a bland urbanity that inspired
both confidence and audacity.

On Saturday nights Frost blossomed aggressively on to the screen
itself, occasionally hitting large portraits of victims with his fist
and transmitting a general hostility which, now that he shines
with a softer light on commercial television, has been firmly
discarded.

There were, of course, lapses of judgment—rarely of taste—
and the stormier the resultant row, the more reassuring Sherrin
became. He was a masterly memo-writer and manipulated the BBC
machinery of delegated responsibility with total authority. He
sustained his writers with much praise and small money. He was
secure in the knowledge of the formidable support he was getting
from the policy-makers at the top. On the wall of his office was a
memo from Kenneth Adam, the Director of BBC Television. It
was received after the first week's show and read : 'D.G. (Director
General, then Sir Hugh Greene) says that he wants there to be no

* Rockwell, the American Nazi leader, Georges Bidault, Soblen and Carmen
Bryan were all the subject of controversial decisions by Brooke during his
term of office.

delay in his offering warmest congratulations to all those concerned with the production of *This Was the Week That Was* last Saturday night.'

There is little doubt that not all subsequent memoranda were so whole-heartedly in support, but it was good to know that the general principles upon which the show was conducted were approved by the top brass, even if they could not get its title quite right.

Freedom to unfetter fly-buttons was the smallest of the breakthroughs achieved by Sherrin and Frost. Areas of comedy were opened up which could never again be declared out of bounds. They are not, perhaps never can be, precisely charted. To a large extent, what is permitted and what is proscribed depends upon the men in charge of each department of the BBC.

It is more difficult to gauge what political effect, if any, the Saturday night sniping had. But as Jonathan Miller cautiously puts it : 'After several years of this sort of activity, I think you can say that a generalised scepticism in the face of political behaviour became characteristic of the British public.'

5 | *Not in Front of the TV Audience*

If it is mainly words, it is the responsibility of Michael Mills, Head of Comedy; if it is words and music, it comes under Billy Cótton, Junior, Head of Variety and, since Tom Sloan's death in spring 1970, in charge of the Light Entertainment Group of the BBC which controls both sections. The Variety Department, therefore, looks after programmes that feature such artists as Morecambe and Wise, Rolf Harris, Cilla Black, Cliff Richard, Roy Castle and Val Doonican. The Comedy Department is in charge of situation comedies like *Till Death Us Do Part, Steptoe and Son, Up Pompeii!* and, by some extraordinary quirk of administration, *Dixon of Dock Green.*

The demarcation line, however, is fluid. The Peter Cook-Dudley Moore show, *Not Only . . . But Also,* was technically a variety responsibility, but the producer was a Comedy Department man and the scripts had a tendency towards the controversial—a problem rarely encountered in variety circles—so decisions were made by Michael Mills, a brisk, bearded man, buffeted between stormy writers who want to use 'bloody', 'bum', 'arse' and 'tit', and gales of protest from puritans who get the vapours at the drop of a damn.

Mills, born in Prestwich, Lancashire, in 1919, educated at Westminster and in Germany, France and Switzerland, joined the BBC in 1938 as a junior producer's assistant after working as stage manager at the St Pancras People's Theatre. He spent the war in the Royal Navy, returned to the BBC, resigned to work in the theatre and as a free-lance writer and television producer, rejoined the BBC as a producer, won awards for *The World of Wooster* and *Misleading Cases* and was made Head of Comedy in 1967.

Some fifty people work under him. No other television service in the world has a comedy department. In America, independent organisations like Desilu produce about 150 shows a year for the networks, while the BBC Comedy Department turns out between 225 and 250.

'It is,' says Michael Mills, 'a very serious business. The fond idea that we all sit here laughing our bloody heads off is not true. We don't have many failures. There are many shows that are failures as far as individuals are concerned but not from the public's point of view. *As Good Cooks Go* (an undistinguished series which misused the distinguished Tessie O'Shea) didn't make me laugh, but it is the old belly-laugh pratfall thing which is appreciated by bus-drivers in Stoke-on-Trent who don't want to know about Marty Feldman or Monty Python. It was simple and old-fashioned, the kind of thing which, as a matter of fact, we in this department don't do very well. We're a bit too cerebral. We don't do the broad knockabout comedy very well and I'm constantly trying to find something like that.

'We'd like to do comedy right across the board. Ideally, in every week there would be a Spike Milligan, two middle-of-the-road shows like *Not in Front of the Children, Dad's Army* or *Oh Brother!* and somewhere out on the wing a real corny banger like *The Rag Trade*, the kind of show that ITV do very well. It seldom happens this way but you hope it averages out over a period.'

Mills's two main functions are to find or originate new comedy and, at the same time, to define the limits to which it can go. There are no longer any rule-books.

'You buy people,' admits Mills. 'You buy their brains and intelligence. It was, for instance, Barry Took who was responsible for the *Monty Python* show reaching the screen.'

Took, a one-time stand-up comedian himself, later a writer who, in partnership with Marty Feldman, wrote *Round the Horne* for radio, *Marty* and a number of other shows for television, was a 'comedy script adviser' at the BBC, a new name for what used to be called script editor.

'Script editor,' says Mills, 'became a dirty word to a lot of writers. Script editors were baseless creatures rendering everything down to the lowest common denominator. We don't do it. We have script advisers who are writers as well and it makes a big difference. Took came in one day and said that the boys who were doing *At Last the 1948 Show* were tired of the other side because they didn't get enough rehearsal time and had to work in a tiny studio. He thought that if we got that team together on a long-term basis we would get something. Barry gave them a long session and told them what they could do in the writing. Then I had them down and told them what budget they had. I said, "Don't get too clever. If you try and do too much you won't get away with it and you'll bugger your show up. Now start quietly." And it worked. Mind you, it will never be a walloping great twelve million audience show. I know the British public won't go for it that much. I think it will wind itself up to six million eventually, but you reach a point at which you've got to be fairly bright to get that stuff. It comes at you pretty sharpish. They don't stop for anything and they don't explain anything.'

Took himself later moved to the 'other side' as Head of Light Entertainment for London Weekend Television, resigning in February 1971 after newspaper owner Rupert Murdoch gained control of the company.

Every successful show brings its imitators.

'For about two years after *Till Death Us Do Part,*' says Mills, 'we got scripts about rude families shouting at one another. They were not very good.'

Technical advances put new ideas into the minds of the inventive. *Monty Python* experimented with cartoon, and a process called colour overlay was seized on by Marty Feldman for a sketch in which he opened a number of classic novels out of which all the characters fell, squabbling.

But basically, comedy comes from the mind of the creator and the art of the performer. The camera can turn a scene upside-down, transmit it in negative, dissolve it, split it up, black it out, miniaturise it. But it never does anything funny.

The minds of some of the best creators of comedy are apt to be sharp and firmly linked to reality. They find their comedy in human passions and patterns of speech and behaviour. They wish to call a spade a spade even if it upsets the Race Relations Board and tend to get tetchy and touchy over any kind of censorship. Censorship is indefensible when imposed from outside, but a case can be made out for giving the man who takes the responsibility the power to exercise his judgment on what is and is not permissible. Mills takes advice, but the final decision is his. He confesses that it is a dictatorial power and subject to personal and frequently illogical consideration. Today you can say 'Winter draw(er)s on' and 'strewth'. More fundamental rights are in question.

Hugh Leonard, an Irish writer who is a great craftsman with the television play, is the creator of the comedy series called *Me Mammy*, which has as its two central figures a middle-aged male virgin (Milo O'Shea) totally dominated by his mother (Anna Manahan), a lady of fervent religious feelings and almost total ignorance. Leonard gets a good deal of comedy mileage out of the fringe manifestations of Irish Catholicism—its attitude to sex and its abundance of saintly statues.

'The idea,' says Leonard, 'was to ally satire with farce, and in one script a priest takes an overdose of a very powerful purgative. I was told that Michael Mills did not accept anal jokes. That was the only major piece of censorship. The others were on words or attitudes which might—which, indeed, were intended to—give offence. The mother can get away with anything because, whatever she says, she is an absolute innocent. She is a monster, but genuine. She uses all sorts of language without even knowing the meaning. Her son, Bunjy, comes home the day the Pope has thrown some twenty saints out of the calendar and finds the hallway littered with statues. But he is bringing his mother another one and she says, "Here I've spent all day putting the buggers out and you've brought me in another one."

'Out went the word "buggers".

'When she finds that the saint he has brought her is, in fact, the greatest of the refugees from the Roman calendar, she says, "Well, you festering gobshite." That went out. He says, "Happy birthday, Mother," and she says, "Birthday, me arse. I'm destroyed." Arse went out. Sometimes if I wasn't there, the cast invented an alternative. I wasn't so much concerned with its aptness as with the rhythm of the line which is something you need with idiomatic Irish. It became "Birthday, me backside" and "festering gobhawk".

'I found my way round it in a later series by inventing words. Mother sees a girl in a bikini and says, "Look at her, showing off her hoojas." They keep asking her what "hoojas" are and she boxes their ears and says, "Never you mind." When the doorbell rings while Cousin Ender, who is very queer, is saying his prayers, he gets annoyed and says, "Oh balloons and ballcocks." I'd much rather have had bollocks, but there you are!

'There were two attempts to slice up a tape after it had been done. One was where the mother was praying and she said, "Protect us from all women except holy nuns, women over sixty and children under ten." Someone said this seemed to imply that it was all right to rape children over ten. Eventually, though, it was left in. There was another case where Bunjy snarls at a coloured girl, "Go back and eat your water-melon." They may have had a point there, though it wasn't intended as a racialistic line. In one script, there was a girl called Miss Paisley—"that name beloved of Satan and his Orange angels"—and trouble started in the North while we were taping. Jimmy Gilbert, the producer, took the tapes to Belfast and played them there for the BBC and several city councillors and asked them if there would be any objections and they just fell around laughing.

'In one episode, Sidney Tafler played Bunjy's boss and is referred to by the mother as a "hook-nosed old Jew man". Then he is very nice to her and she says, "Oh, that man's a real Christian." Sidney came in to play it and discovered that all references to "Jew man" had been cut out. He said he wouldn't have agreed to do the script if he had thought it was anti-Semitic and wasn't going to do it unless they restored the lines and made him a "Jew man" again. So they put them back. It was the only time the censorship was reversed—and it took an actor to do it.

'There was one example of sexual censorship. Yootha Joyce plays the girl Bunjy is secretly engaged to, and she is no innocent. She's looking for it and wants to get it. In one of the episodes where they were due to go to Paris he says to her, "I'll show you the Eiffel Tower." She looks at him as only Yootha can look and says, "Something like that." Her next line was, "And I'll show you the Arch of Triumph." But they changed it to Arc de Triomphe, so it went for nothing.

'I go over the top about censorship because I grew up in the middle of it in Ireland. I won't even go and see a cut film.'

Australian comedian Barry Humphries also had his troubles in his BBC 2 series, *The Barry Humphries Scandals*. He says, 'The BBC has split standards. Anything can be said in BBC drama or documentaries, but light entertainment is the most circumscribed of all the departments. Why a show that goes out at ten past nine should be subject to any kind of censorship I don't know particularly, when one isn't a deliberate smut-pedlar. I wanted to do an Edna Everage cookery piece (Edna Everage is his archetypal Australian matron) with a real recipe for "Spiced Indonesian Balls" which I got from an Australian cookbook. I followed the recipe precisely and wanted to cook it on the set. But they said the whole thing had to be cut because I mentioned the word "balls" more than once. Once would have been all right.

'There was also a patriotic song I wrote called "British Spunk", a song about British courage through the ages with a chorus that went :

> We're so full of British spunk
> We're never in a panic, never in a funk.
> But in a time of crisis
> There is nothing quite so nice as
> Seeing spunk, spunk, spunk, spunk, spunk.

'The song went through the Black Death, the Dissolution of the Monasteries, the Black Hole of Calcutta, the Wreck of the *Titanic* and the Second World War. There was a final chorus with the George Mitchell Singers, the dancers and the orchestra as landgirls, WRNS, ATS—it was the greatest ending. But there is an infantile, schoolboy meaning to the word. There's no doubt that I was not unaware of this but the BBC were very embarrassed and the song was banned in its entirety. I did it in the studio and it was a great hit with the audience. I've sung it to Lord David Cecil, Professor of English Literature at Oxford, and Edward Heath at a *Spectator* party when I was a bit drunk and they all loved it.

'It's a word that worries people. They feel guilty about it. It's associated with adolescent guilt, schoolboy fears and the fact that it is of all naughty words *the* most ambiguous. But it's in the *Oxford English Dictionary* with only one definition* and the context of the song was totally patriotic. There's no question that I wasn't trying to get away with something, but I think it was very legitimate.†

'The thing they objected to more than anything else was a quickie sketch. I was to appear completely bald and go into the bathroom in pyjama trousers and singlet. There are a lot of bottles with all sorts of hair restorer. I sprinkle some on my bald scalp, rub it in, look in the mirror, shake my head. I sprinkle some more in and there is still nothing. Suddenly I look surprised at the camera, raise my right arm and a cloud of hair uncoils from my armpit to the floor. The technicians screamed and the studio audience loved it, but the BBC said, "Armpits! No!" And when I protested they told me: "Not every BBC viewer has been to an Australian university." That was a bit of a put-down.'

All the same, the BBC allowed Humphries to perform his 'Gladdy' song, probably the most phallic bit of fun since Blackpool built its tower. He had earlier used it to close his stage show at the Fortune Theatre. Dressed as Edna Everage, he threw great armfuls of gladioli—which he insists are the Australian national flower—to the audience, commanded them to wave their gladdies and said things like: 'You've got a poor specimen, haven't you sir? Never mind, it's not the size that counts, is it ladies? Not much. . . . Now up with your glads. Up. Up. Good heavens, there's a gentleman down here who took me a bit too literally. Are you all right, dears? Can you get it up? Gladdies up, Up with your glads. Up. Up. All together.'

He leads them in a line or two from his gladdies song—

> We've got a lovely bunch of gladdies
> Watch us hold them high above our heads . . .

* 'Spunk, n. (colloq.). Courage, mettle, spirit; anger.'—*Concise Oxford Dictionary.*
† In February 1971 the BBC bought and transmitted an American series featuring Mary Tyler Moore, the virginal comedienne. In the first episode the word 'spunk' was used twice.

Then comes more patter.

> Return your gladdies to the erect position. Now we're going
> to join in a chorus, all of you—Up. Up. Up. And when I give the
> word I want you to hit the nearest Catholic. There's a moment
> in the chorus when I want you to tremble your gladdies.
> Let's just practise that. Stand and tremble! You *have* had a
> busy day, haven't you sir? Stand and tremble! Not too hard,
> you might go blind. Heavens, he's a professional gladdie
> trembler. . . .

Superficially, it would seem that the ways of censorship are
indeed strange, but it is also possible to follow Mills's view that a
great deal of funniness excuses a little filth and agree that the
gladdie routine is far funnier than the spunk song.

Of all the writers, Johnny Speight aroused the greatest outcry
from viewers, who were horrified, shocked, disgusted and alarmed
by his outrageous bigot Alf Garnett in *Till Death Us Do Part*. Yet
millions laughed at, and some agreed with, his sentiments. Unlike
Mrs Malaprop, Speight remained unperturbed by outside attacks
on his language and aspersions on his parts of speech, while
protesting volubly at any attempts to curb it from within the BBC.

'Worried?' Speight comments. 'Christ, no. The thing that amused
me was when the BBC said I was allowed twenty "bloodies" a
script and no more. It's ridiculous. If bloody's a bad word, the
more you say it, the more inoffensive it becomes. A Garnett would
never say ruddy. That, to me, is bad language. Bloody is good
language because that's what he would normally say. I can't stand
words like frigging. It means fucking. Frigging is bad language.
Bloody was the worst word we ever used, though he said "cobblers"
a couple of times and "that's a lot of crap". But I don't think they
were really attacking us for the bad language. They used that as a
stick to beat us with. What they didn't like was the subject-matter
we discussed—religion, sex, politics and royalty—all subjects you
must not discuss in polite society. They are the only ones worth
discussing. The BBC censored the last show like mad.'

'Over the years,' says Mills, 'the taboos and inhibitions have
disappeared. How far the process will go I haven't the faintest idea.
I don't know what's going to happen next week. In the end it
comes to my judgment. I go to other people like the Head of
Religious Broadcasting for advice, but *I* decide whether something
is in or out. In the long run, I'm afraid, it comes down to a dic-
tatorship. *Up Pompeii!* is outrageous, of course, and the innuendo

is awful—it falls round your ears like autumn leaves. You wouldn't be able to do it except for three things—one, it's funny, which excuses almost anything, and two, it's Frankie Howerd. If it were Benny Hill or Terry Scott doing the same script it would be horrid, but because it's Frankie with that pursed-up, outraged school-mistress look, it's marvellous. Thirdly, it's done very well, with great style, lovely sets, good costumes and good artists like Max Adrian and Elizabeth Larner. So it doesn't look like a tatty music-hall sketch that's been put on to get a dirty laugh.

'But I'm quite certain that somebody will come in with a completely different comedy and when I say "No" to something in it, he will say, "But Frankie said worse." Then something else comes in and it looks funny and I let it through.

'I make mistakes, of course, but this question of what we can or cannot laugh at—I really don't know, honestly. I just sit tight sometimes after I've let something go by and wait to see if the roof's going to fall on me. All you can possibly hope to do is to try and be somewhere between the full avant-garde people who would say anything and do anything, and the sticky ones who would let nothing through. If you let them have their way, you would end up with television like the French and the Americans have.

'The most difficult part of this job is finding people who can write, but the next one is balancing on this tightrope of how far you can go. It is a problem which hardly arose until about five years ago (1965). Everybody knew the conventions then; the taboos were set and nobody bothered to try and break them. Now you have to play it by ear week by week and hope that you don't make a cock of it.

'Barry Humphries did a sketch about cooking a dish called "Spiced Indonesian Balls". Once would have been all right. Mrs Everage says it and the comedy of it is that she doesn't know what she has said, doesn't know that Spiced Indonesian Balls has got a dirty connotation. Once! Do it a second time and you kill the whole thing. I said he could have it once and if he did it any more it would be offensive.

'One of the most difficult scripts was a *Till Death Us Do Part* about the meaning of God. Johnny specialises in bringing scripts in at the last minute and he hopes they will get by in the rush. However, Dennis Main Wilson (the producer) came in and plonked it down. I'm not a theologian and I don't know what is or what is not offensive, theologically speaking, to Christians who take these things seriously. So I asked for two more scripts and sent one to Tom Sloan and the other to the Head of Religious Broadcasting. The following morning they both arrived on my desk with marks

on. I'd already marked my own script with what I thought ought
to be cut. The three sets of marks were almost identical. So Johnny
came in and we had a little barney and argued the toss. I yielded
on a couple of things and insisted on a couple of others and eventually Johnny accepted it and everyone was happy. Then he goes
round the corner and screams blue murder about being savagely
censored. One of the television critics said, "Having seen the show
and what was said, in God's name what did they cut out?" What
we cut out, in fact, was two and a half pages of rip-roaring
blasphemy which would have offended more people than it would
have pleased.

'Of course Johnny Speight's ration of twenty "bloodies" a script
is absurd, but what we were doing at the time was rescuing him
from himself because the word "bloody" just went on and on and
became rather boring.

'Pete and Dud did a script for *Not Only* on exactly this subject.
It's a marvellous sketch. Pete plays me and Dud plays Johnny
Speight and, so help me God, they weren't in the room but the
dialogue is exactly as it happened.'

COOK : May I say straight away, Johnny, that this script, this
comedy script, is one of the funniest I've ever read in all my
years at the BBC. It's witty, it's visual, it's earthy—it's terrific,
and, by golly, we're going to do it.

MOORE (*with a slight, Speightlike stammer*) : The point is, it's
got something to say. It's a social comment on the b-bloody world
we live in. I mean, you've gotter 'ave a go in life 'aven't yer?

COOK : Exactly, exactly. We love it, we are going to do it and,
as I said, it's terrific. This script is really terrific.

MOORE : But.

COOK : But what?

MOORE : You were about to say but . . .

COOK : No I wasn't about to say but. I was saying the script
is really terrific, but—er . . .

MOORE : There you go.

COOK : I think you'll agree with me that the BBC has been a
pioneer in the field of controversial comedy. Look at the record,
TW3, *Steptoe, Till Death* . . .

MOORE : What are you t-t-trying to say?

COOK : What I'm trying to say, Johnny, is that you've got
twenty-seven bloodies in your script. We've led the way, I don't
care how many bloodies you have, that's fine by me . . .

MOORE : It reflects life, dunnit? I mean, I use bloody the
whole b-b-bloody time.

Cook : That's true. You're welcome to use it in life and in the script. The only thing that worries me about this script is the number of bums you have.

Moore : So what's wrong with that? So I've got thirty bums in the script.

Cook : Thirty-one.

Moore : Thirty-one, give or take a bum. The bums are all there for a dramatic cumulative effect. You're not going to tell me that bums don't exist.

Cook : No.

Moore : I've got a bum, you've got a bum.

Cook : We've all got a bum, Johnny. I would not pretend that bums don't exist. But what I do ask you, Johnny, and I ask you this very seriously, does an ordinary English family sitting at home early in the evening want to have a barrage of thirty-one bums thrown in their faces in the privacy of their own living-room? I think not, I think not. I don't think we're ready yet to break through the bum-barrier.

Moore : Don't give me that. Only two years ago Kenneth Tynan said f-f-f . . .

Cook : I don't care what Kenneth Tynan said. That was a live, unscripted programme over which we had no control and I must tell you, Johnny, that it is very seldom indeed that we allow a bum to slip out before 11 o'clock in the evening.

Moore : What miracle happens at 11 o'clock in the evening that takes the sting out of a bum?

Cook : Now then, I know it's illogical, you know it's illogical. It *is* illogical. But believe me, trust me. I believe in your bums. I'm going to fight tooth and nail to preserve your bums. I'll leave as many bums as I possibly can. Trust me, trust me. But there's one other word that worries me even more than bum. And that is your colloquial use of a word for a lady's er—chest.

Moore : You mean my comedic use of the word t-t-t- . . .

Cook : Your comedic use of that word. Now this is a word that used on a nature programme to describe the bird of the same name would cause no objection whatever. Or you could use it in the phrase tit-for-tat. No trouble at all. But not in the way that you have used it Johnny. I'm sorry, we just can't wear that, it's impossible.

Moore : Look, I'm not dropping them, I'm not dropping them. They are a vital part of the idiom of the script. I would not be true to myself as a writer if I dropped them. The whole flavour of the script would be impaired if I snipped out the Bristols.

Cook : Now Johnny, you have put your finger on it. Bristols! Bristols, Johnny, are the answer. You'd get away with Bristols, I think.

Moore : But Bristols don't have the impact of t-t- . . .

Cook : I think Bristols are terrifically strong. I think Bristols are tremendous. You could use other rhyming slang. Let's see, you could use sans or fainting.

Moore : Sans or fainting? What are you talkin' about?

Cook : Rhyming slang—San Moritz, fainting fits.

Moore : That'd be great! This bird in the tight sweater goes past and the bloke says, 'Cor, I'd like to get my elastics round them faintings.' Elastics—elastic bands—hands.

Cook : I prefer it to the original. I think it's better.

Moore : This script is more than just a comedy, it's a social document.

Cook : I realise that . . .

Moore : A social document, in respect of the whole cosmic spectrum of . . .

Cook : I know this Johnny. I realise how important these bums are to you.

Moore : Not to mention the t-t-t . . .

Cook : Not to mention them if you possibly can. Now, Johnny, because I respect you as a writer of integrity and fire and passion I'm willing to allow you all your twenty-seven bloodies. No questions asked.

Moore : Right.

Cook : Furthermore, I'll let you have, let me see—this is more than I've done before—you can have seven bums. And because it's you and only because it's you, Johnny, I'll allow you one—er—one thingummy.

Moore : Not even a pair?

Cook : I'm sorry, Johnny, I wish that I could.

Moore : Look, I'll tell you what I'll do—I'll lose some bloodies if you give me an extra bum and another t-t-t- . . .

Cook : Well, let's see, if you lost some bloodies it might be feasible. Why don't we make it seventeen bloodies, eight bums and a pair of—er—um—doodahs.

Moore : So how many bloodies is that to a bum?

Cook : Ten bloodies to a bum, I'd say.

Moore : Right, now I could lose ten bloodies in the pub sequence, that gives me an extra bum to play about with. I really think the scene in the launderette really cries out for another t-t-t- . . .

Cook : Look Johnny, if you feel you need another one of those in the launderette I'll raise that, so that will give you, let's see, seven bloodies, nine bums and three of the—er—the other word which you have.

MOORE : I'll raise you one bum.

COOK : You're really driving me into a corner here, Johnny. Tricky. Look, I know you, you know me, why should we let one bum stand between us? It's a deal.

MOORE : I'm glad we could discuss this in an adult fashion.

COOK : Thank you for being so co-operative. And I'll whip this script off to Sooty just as soon as I can.

MOORE : Well, bottoms up.

COOK : Cheers.

(They drink to each other.)

The key men under Mills, the ones who bear the responsibility for getting a show together and putting it out in some kind of shape are the producers and directors. Sometimes the two functions are separated, but the two men considered here prefer to combine them—that is, to take total charge of the casting, the content and the need for the cameras to be pointing at the right place and at the right performance.

Duncan Wood is a big, broad-shouldered man of whom Spike Milligan once said, 'He would have made the perfect Tank Corps sergeant.'

Dennis Main Wilson, immediately dubbed 'Spanish Main' Wilson by the Goons whom he directed in his radio days, is small and sharp with the quick, eager movements of a particularly curious and gutsy squirrel.

Duncan Wood was born in Bristol in 1925. His father was a bank manager and his mother a professional musician. Wood himself played piano and trumpet in semi-professional bands. When, in 1941, the BBC Variety Department was evacuated to the West Country they advertised for sound-balance engineers. The requirements were a musical background and a basic knowledge of electronics. Wood bought a book on electronics and got the job. He was seventeen. After three years of balancing dance bands, Wood went into the army and played in unit bands, writing bits of comedy and compèring. After the war, he rejoined the BBC in his old job, became a studio manager and eventually was appointed variety producer for the West Region.

In 1955, Wood transferred to London, to work in television. He worked on *Come Dancing* and panel games like *Down You Go* and *Find the Link*. His first situation comedy was *Great Scott!*—

It's Maynard. Then came a series with Terry-Thomas followed by
fifty out of the fifty-one *Hancock's Half Hour* series. He has also
produced most of Frankie Howerd's work for the BBC, *Steptoe and
Son, The World of Beachcomber* and *Oh Brother!*

It was while working with Hancock that Wood experimented
with techniques of cutting and editing and found ways of presenting
a show without the flaws inevitable in continuous recording,
achieving a speed impossible when changes of scene or clothing had
to be masked by laborious and devious devices. Muir and Norden,
for instance, recall that whenever such changes were needed in
their *Whacko!* series, the viewers were given a shot of the school
clock. Many performers used to have to wear two pairs of trousers
at a time.

'The role of the producer,' says Wood, 'is to accept responsibility for the show and its background organisation, for the
handling of money, for casting. The job of a director is to get the
performances out of the artists and the script and to transfer those
performances to the screen. I've always believed in the handmade
product, so I like doing both. I find it very difficult to divide it
down the middle.'

Galton, Simpson and Wood were regarded as a team after their
experiences with Hancock, so they were kept together for the ten
Comedy Playhouse productions from which *Steptoe* sprang.

'I look for playing ability in a script,' says Wood. 'I don't like
scripts which are merely a succession of gags, because then you are
depending purely on the strength of the jokes. Sometimes they
work and sometimes they don't. A joke is a matter of personal
opinion anyway. Attitude is just as important as dialogue. All the
old silent comedies were based on attitude. If you are writing for
comedians like Hancock, Morecambe and Wise or Benny Hill,
you have before you start a series of predetermined facets and it's
the writers' job to exploit them. Working with a name comic you
start with a set of limitations—no, that's not fair—a set of assets,
which arc limited. Everything has to be geared to presenting the
comedian. In a comedy playlet like *Steptoe* you present the script
as interpreted by actors and you have to put comedy actors in far
more of a directorial strait-jacket than comedians. There are only
two things that count in television—immediacy and perfection.
If you are using a comedian and capitalising on the immediacy
angle you can allow a certain amount of ad-libbing as long as he
is funny. But if you are working in terms of perfection, then any
deviation from the set-up would throw out all the things you have
worked for all week. Take a two-handed scene in *Steptoe and Son.*
As a rule, we use six cameras to shoot two people. This allows you

to concentrate on facial expressions, and television lives and breathes in faces. It amounts to using film technique while still keeping the stimulus of performing in front of an audience. Ten years ago, *Steptoe and Son* would have averaged 150 shots to the half-hour. Now it is 270.

'There is nothing worse than for performers to say a funny line and then stop dead while the laughter is heard. This is false and it means coming totally out of character in order to accept the laugh. So I like to rehearse at exactly the pace that is needed for transmission, say 29¼ minutes in each case. This means allowing for the laughter in rehearsal. Any fool, given certain technical qualifications, can shoot dialogue; it takes far more to shoot reaction to dialogue. So you get a man who says a funny line and you stay on him for part of the laugh and then switch to the man at the receiving end of the line and accept the rest of the laugh while showing his reaction. Then you go back. It makes it look as if neither of them has stopped. It makes it flow. You can be thrown both ways—by some inconsequential line getting a laugh and by a stone-bonk certainty getting nothing.

'A producer has to be something of an architect so that you can tell your designer the kind of room you want because you are already in your own mind visualising how the actors are going to work in that room, where they're going to move and what they're going to do. He has to be a bit of a musician because he has to explain to the musical director before rehearsal what he is going to get out of a scene so that the music can be written. All this means that he is committing himself to a certain mood before he's even spoken to the actors. He has to know something about writing. Cutting a script is a very difficult thing and it's no use working on the principle of leaving out the bits that aren't funny, because you end up with a script full of gags and no situation. It often pays to cut, with a bleeding heart, very funny things and keep to other things which maintain the story-line. He need not act, but he has to have a feel for acting so that if an actor tells him he cannot say a line, the producer has to be able to say it himself, suggest another way of doing it or agree. The producer not only has to have a technical ability with his cameras, the tools of the trade, but sooner or later must ask his performers to accept some of the technicalese because without a basic knowledge of how the camera works they will never do the producer or themselves justice.

'You put your head on the block every time you televise comedy, for everybody in the audience is an expert in a way that they never are with drama.'

Main Wilson says his father was 'a very sober, very conservative gentleman who worked his way up from tea boy to boss of the factory', and his grandfather 'a drunk who died of alcoholic poisoning at the age of eighty-eight. I gather that he was a sculptor and that some of the better class of work in the Mansion House is his. He inherited a whisky distillery in Paisley and, by and large, except that I don't sculpt, he was roughly what I'd like to become. According to society he was a very undisciplined man. Genetically, it would appear that I was born to be some kind of anti-social bum. Eric Maschwitz dubbed me as "Doctor", which was short for "Doctor Weird". Actually, I am utterly, utterly normal. No, it's not everyone else who is weird; they are dull. They've got no courage and they've got no guts.

'Of all the arts, comedy is the most difficult, the most heart-burning, the most soul-destroying. You put your entire emotional self on a plate before the public and you are extremely vulnerable. This applies to directors as well as the fellows in front of the camera. A lot of rubbish is talked about comedy. You can't define it and anybody who tries to pontificate is either a liar or the head of a television department. Or a critic. Comedy is a thing that God, if God there be, gives you. You are born with it. Comparisons are not only odious, they are libellous as well. But there are half a dozen star names who play the Palladium, get television shows, work in the clubs and earn £2,000 a week who are not comedians. They tell jokes.

'I don't think I know one single great comedian who is secure or happy or who thinks that he's got where he wants to get.

'A comedy show is an organic thing. How does it get on the air? It happens in a boozer or a club or at a party. You cannot sit in an office and say, "I say, I've got a smashing idea." Johnny Speight will hate this, but it's true. Johnny was bored out of his mind after the Arthur Haynes shows and I was bored out of my mind after whatever I'd been doing and we used to meet about town and over a couple of years we talked about doing a show which he would write and I would direct. You have to start somewhere and the somewhere was the fact that we both loathed *Coronation Street*, *Peyton Place*, *Crossroads* and all the other space-fillers. If they are the best television can do there should be two-hour blanks on the screen. After a couple of months' drinking on and off we got to the stage where we decided to write about a street and a family which would show *Coronation Street* what writing for streets and families was about. We started with one idea—to knock *Coronation Street* out of the ratings. What resulted came out of Johnny Speight's gift, out of his genius. Nobody sat in an office.

'What bugs me about the university fellows is that they stand there in front of the cameras and entertain themselves, and if the public don't get it, it proves how clever they are. Comedy is communication. If you dare step on the stage or in front of the cameras as a comedian it means that you have accepted the holy writ of entertaining the public. But not if you sit there entertaining yourself and believe that the less they laugh, the more stupid they are, the more clever you are.

'I don't mean *Monty Python*, though I do say the sketches go on too long. They do the joke on page 3 and go on until page 94. It's their bad luck that they have never had to go out and work to an audience, say Monday night at Glasgow Empire. If you were five seconds too long you had cabbages and rotten tomatoes thrown at you, and if you were rebooked a year later, nobody would turn up. What happens now is that you learn your craft live on television from the London Palladium and bore the entire nation while you're doing it.

'The music-hall was killed through greedy agents who would send out a major star who could do twenty-eight minutes and they'd put in rubbish for the other two hours and take 60 per cent of the gross. For the last twenty years or more, the BBC, ITV and the film industry have lived off the proceeds of the war—Harry Secombe, Spike Milligan, Eric Sykes and all the others who came out of the war. We have exhausted that source and we're getting very thin on the ground. We have been saved by the new ones from the universities, by *That Was the Week* and by Pete and Dud. But there is an enormous gulf between the university educated—the university *superficially* educated, that is—and the working-class fellow.

'Most so-called comedy writers only write jokes. They can get stuffed. There are half a dozen great writers of comedy in this country—and that's an overstatement. There are even fewer comedy directors who can take a line of dialogue or a piece of action and make it happen. What goes wrong in both the BBC and commercial television is that "they" book a star, or "they" book a star writer or writers. They are then given a director to service them. His job is interpretative rather than creative. This is utterly wrong and is one of the reasons why we have such bad television. If you have the nerve to call yourself a director then you presumably should have some creative gift. The trouble is the pension at the end. All directors should be compulsorily made to free-lance and be paid ten times the money they get now and be fired ten times more often. You would then notice an immediate improvement in television.

'Tony Hancock spent fourteen years learning his craft and had the good fortune to work with a director like Duncan Wood. He could equally have had the misfortune of getting a director who was a year and a half out of university.

'The art of the director is to be (a) creative in the best abstract terms—in other words, to have a gift from God or nature. Whether he is a good administrator or not doesn't matter. All you need for that is a tidy mind. (b) He should be, to a certain extent, a writer himself. He should know show-business backwards and cast intuitively. He's got to know his craft so well that when he says to the star actor or the comedian of the year, "You are playing it wrong mate", he is right. You cannot impose an authority; you've got to convince him that you, creatively, are right and that he, creatively, is wrong.

'I have on two occasions in my twenty years with the BBC actually bashed an actor round a rehearsal room. This was towards the end of a series when we were all very tired. A very big star. With megalomania. He had to be sorted out. It can go emotionally that far. I see nothing wrong with it. At the end it was all love and great friendship. But mine is a system which, if applied generally to a large outfit like the BBC, might not work.'

Main Wilson, in his mid-forties and with radio shows like *The Goons* and *Hancock's Half Hour* behind him, with television credits that include *The Rag Trade, Till Death Us Do Part* and *Marty,* dismisses the craft of camerawork as within the capacity of anyone with, again, a 'tidy mind'.

'The director's job on television in general, but in television comedy in particular, is solely to make sure that what is happening in front of the cameras is an entertainment. Stick Frankie Howerd in front of a camera for twelve minutes and he will stop the show four times without a camera-cut anywhere. If direction is noticeable it is bad direction. The camera is an ancillary thing. Is the show funny or not is the only thing that matters. And if it is funny, it is funny without cameras.'

6 | *Three Writers*

Comedy today is keyed to the television set, liberated by its resources, confined by its limitations, stretched and stimulated by its demands and, in parts, worn thin by its rapacity. It is astonishing, not that so much is mediocre, but that so much is good. The supremacy of the BBC over 'independent' television is unchallenged, and though the commercial companies now and again come up with a highly polished series such as *Please Sir!* or *Doctor in the House* they are not noted for their pioneering spirit and seem to cater exclusively for Michael Mills's *idea* of a Stoke-on-Trent bus-driver, though how far that matches up to reality is hard to say.

The BBC have created conditions in which comedy can flourish and develop by providing room for the single half-hour show which, if successful, forms the jumping-off point for a series. In this way, *Till Death Us Do Part, Steptoe and Son, Up Pompeii!* and a number of others were born. *Not Only . . . But Also* grew out of a single show built round Dudley Moore, on which Peter Cook made a 'guest' appearance. The BBC ability to recognise potential stems from the long experience garnered during radio and the early, monopolistic years of television. But a crucial factor is the better resources. Offer a performer a few days more rehearsal time, a larger studio and a high calibre director like Wood or Main Wilson and he will follow you anywhere. Providing the money is also right.

For writers, the BBC, despite, or because of, its institutional nature, offers a certain amount of liberation from the need to chase after instant mass-appeal and gives them producers who are secure enough to feel that they can fail occasionally. At least, these are the qualities which conditioned its superiority. The fact that it is now partly in question is not due to any directive from the Chairman, Lord Hill, but to the knowledge—or belief—among the staff of his conservative and conformist nature. His presence acts more as an obstruction than a dam.

The star comedian can, and indeed does, perform on both commercial and BBC channels with only peripheral differences. It is writers like Johnny Speight and Galton and Simpson who appear to find fulfilment, despite little local difficulties over one or two words, through the BBC's more relaxed attitude to so-called situation comedy—which is essentially character comedy. Whatever the situations in which Alf Garnett or the Steptoes are involved, they stem from their own hard-shelled obstinacies. Their situations were established at the beginning and are unchangeable in the present format. It is this which has reached its limits and is due for a change. Denis Norden once said that Galton and Simpson's achievements were those of a major novelist. But the fundamental property of a good novel is that by the last page some change in circumstances or character has been effected. In so-called situation comedy this is impossible. This has nothing to do with the quality of the comedy itself. The worst and the best circle in a rut created by the convention of the form. Writers, actors and directors strive for the utmost reality of character, but the one reality they constantly ignore is the viewer's awareness that all alarms are false; that all must end as it began so that next week's adventure or the next series can take place as though the past had never happened. If twenty-five minutes are spent in setting up Harold Steptoe for marriage or Albert Steptoe as a possible victim of tuberculosis, nevertheless the viewer knows for certain that some way out must be found in the final few minutes to re-establish them as they were before and leave them untouched by their experiences.

Hancock tried desperately to get out of this predicament by insisting on moving from East Cheam to Earls Court. But he was, to use Duncan Wood's phrase, limited by his assets and, like all great comics, found—but never learned—that his own funniness enclosed him like a cage.

For the writer there are no such limitations. The comedy series must change to the comedy serial, not a never-ending *Peyton Place* or *Coronation Street* but a finite progression allowing room for development, surprise, climax and resolution. Once completed, however long it may need, it then makes way for another. The Drama Department does *The Forsyte Saga* or a David Mercer trilogy and moves on. Certainly, they do not expect to come back to the same characters year after year.

Something of this may have already been sensed for, at the time of writing, Galton and Simpson were working on a television adaptation of the comic novel *Clochemerle*. They could equally well produce something original.

Johnny Speight also seems to be seeking a way out of the restrictive half-hour form as now established by bringing Alf Garnett back without his family, possibly in a pub setting or in argument with a neighbour just as stupid and bigoted in a Marxist way as Garnett is in his true-blue stance. One of the reasons for this, however, is that by the end of the last series of *Till Death,* so many strains and conflicts had developed among the cast that it seems unlikely that they will ever be able to get together again.

Speight is a stocky Cockney whose words, overlaid by stammer and accent, rush and bubble out of his mouth with such force it is as if he fears he will suddenly be struck inarticulate. He was born in Canning Town, one of three children. His father was a dock labourer. Being the eldest child, Speight had the privilege of wearing the boots first.

'Those awful boots,' he remembers. 'My feet are still bad from them. The mother would buy them two sizes too big and hope that you would grow into them. It took two years to grow into them and another two years to grow out of them. They put blakeys (studs) on the soles so that the sparks flew when you walked. I got the new pairs, but actually the other two were better off because I'd worn them in like.'

Speight was one future humorist who did not use comedy as a defence at school. He preferred, he explains, to run away. 'There was no time for comedy in my school,' he says. 'All the same, it makes a lot of sense. If you were born a handsome, good-looking feller who scored for the school team every Saturday you don't need comedy. But one day you look in a mirror and see your face and you say "Why? Why? Why me?" And if you're not going to cry you start laughing at it.

'All they turned out at the school was factory fodder and after I left at fourteen I worked in factories all down the Silvertown Way. It's about four miles long and I think I worked in every factory. I lasted about a week or a fortnight in each place.

'Fortunately for me, the war broke out and I was called up into the army. I was nineteen. The war was a knockout for me. If it hadn't happened I may still have been in Canning Town. But I was dragged into the army and there were all kinds of people and I suddenly realised the world was a bigger place than I thought it was. I took a big decision when I was called up. I realised it was going to be a choice between being a coward and a hero so I decided that I was definitely a coward. I used all the ingenuity I had to get out of anywhere where there was a chance of a gun being fired. I managed it for most of the time. I stayed in England until I went to France on D-Day plus thirty-six. Then I shipped back to England, supposedly to be posted to the Far East, but the Atom Bomb was dropped. As a left-wing intellectual I should think it was awful, but it saved me from going out there and at the time I thought it was bloody marvellous.

'I wrote a revue in the army and I played drums in the unit band, but I was never with the *Stars in Battledress* lark. When I got demobbed it looked like back to the factory, which by that time I couldn't stand, so I thought I'd try to be a drummer. I got a kind of living out of it. I suppose if you average it out I made thirty bob a month. I was heavily subsidised by the National Assistance Board.

'Bernard Shaw was alive in those days and almost every day he was quoted in the papers. I thought he was a comic like Tommy Trinder and I thought I must catch his act one day. I was in Canning Town Public Library when I saw a big shelf of his books. "Christ!" I thought, "he writes as well." The first one I read was *Immaturity* and the preface knocked me out right away. "Christ!" I thought, "I'm not wrong after all. They're all wrong. What I think is right." I devoured Shaw after that. I used to go on sessions with some of the jazz boys with Shaw in the drum-cases. Shaw was a big name-dropper in his prefaces—Ibsen, Chekhov and so on—so I started to read them as well. I thought, "Christ, I'm going to be a writer," and sold my drums. I don't know why I thought I could be a writer, but Shaw gave me the feeling that I could do it. He gave me the feeling that if you want to be something you have a go. To me he was marvellous. I never met him, but I've been round the house at Ayot St Lawrence many times. It's a lovely, simple house.

'I started to write serious working-class plays and a lot of crap they must have been. I joined Unity Theatre and wrote these terrible, dreary, working-class dramas in which I tried to show how awful it was living in Canning Town. They were dreary bloody plays. They weren't put on. They didn't deserve to be put on. I think you must write all the rubbish out of yourself for about five years before you realise what writing is about.

'I met a friend of mine from the army who was a masseur and he had met Frankie Howerd and Tony Hancock. So he arranged a meeting with Frank and through Frank I met Eric Sykes and Spike Milligan and they saw some of the stuff I was writing and they said there were a few good lines in it. I was trying to write some comedy by then and there was one line that Spike and Eric liked. It was, "They pulled down my old house and built a slum." They said that anyone who could write that line must be a good writer. I think Hancock used it on a *Hancock's Half Hour* on radio and a few others have used it since. It wasn't a bad line actually. They asked me to join the office and the first show I did anything

for was Mr Ros and Mr Ray—Edmundo Ros and Ray Ellington—
Sunday lunchtime half-hour, two bands. I did about five gags
each show for thirteen weeks and I got about £15 a week. I had
become a professional writer; I had actually earned money from
writing. I couldn't get over the kick of seeing my name in the
Radio Times and hearing it broadcast. The next thing was Frankie
Howerd's radio show written by me and Terry Nation, Dick
Barrington and John Antrobus. Then I wrote for Morecambe and
Wise and Peter Sellers. The big breakthrough came with Arthur
Haynes. He was the first comic to come on television without an
already established character. So I wrote things which he actually
performed.'

One of his inventions for Haynes was the belligerent tramp with
a chestful of medals.

'Arthur had a marvellous, immobile face in which only the eyes
moved—malicious eyes. You knew that tramp was going to con you
the moment you saw him. I loved and enjoyed writing for Frankie
Howerd, but the point was that Frank's character was already
established.'

Speight wrote for Haynes for nearly nine years and during that
time produced a pair of television plays, *The Compartment* and
The Playmates, which were originally performed by Michael Caine
and repeated later with Marty Feldman as the weird, obsessive
central figure. He also wrote *The Knacker's Yard*, which was staged
at the Arts Theatre.

'I got fed up with the Arthur Haynes format. I tried hard to get
ATV to do a half-hour series on the two tramps—Arthur and
Dermot Kelly. We almost got to it, but every time Lew Grade
would say, "Why change a successful format?" In the meantime,
the BBC asked me to write a *Comedy Playhouse*. Arthur was working in the summer season at Blackpool and I would have gone back
to him when he returned, but this *Comedy Playhouse* thing took
off.'

It was *Till Death Us Do Part*.

A newspaper poll once established that seven out of ten people
thought Alf Garnett was real. In a sense he was. The combination
of Speight's writing and Warren Mitchell's performance was a
powerful mixture and a monstrous figure, totally credible in his
fixations, ignorance and bigotries was created.

'It's completely untrue that I based Alf Garnett on my father,'
affirms Speight. 'There was one little bit in the original *Comedy
Playhouse* piece that was my father. One Christmas he was going
down to the local with my cousin and my cousin said, "They're
not open yet." My father looked at his watch and said, "They're

open now." My cousin said, "Your watch is wrong. Mine's right, I set it by Big Ben." "You can't go by that," said my father. He had this thing about his watch. It was always right and you had to live by his time. He isn't like Garnett at all. He is a nice, gentle man. He told me some lovely stories that I put into Garnett's mouth. I don't think my father saw Alf Garnett much. He watches ITV most of the time. Once he said, "I hear you've got a good show on the other side."

'The more I wrote, the more the characters became alive. People didn't realise how good Dandy Nicholls was as the mum until the repeats. On the first showing it was all Garnett because he had the words. But on the repeats they could see how great Dandy was, just sitting there looking at him with marvellous eyes.

'Comedy, to have any point at all, has got to say something. I don't believe in a gag for the sake of a joke. I can't stand empty comedy. All great comedy has got some thought behind it. All the great comedians and comedy writers are having a go at society, trying to show what it is like. It was always in my writing, even with Arthur. I realised you can do more with comedy than with dreary plays but the thought is still there. You want to say something if you can. But first and foremost it's got to be funny.

'Someone once said that a lot of my work was derivative and I thought, "Oh, Christ, everyone's derivative, you must derive from something." The Glums in *Take It From Here* were a great influence on me. I always saw Jimmy Edwards as wearing a big belt and braces and being crude and vulgar and lovely. The Arthur Haynes character, Oscar Pennyfeather, who called his wife an old ratbag, was derived from Mr Glum and Garnett came down from him. But I didn't create Garnett, society created him. All I did was report him.

'I'm like him myself. There are times when my wife hates me when I'm grouching round the house. Warren once told his wife to wake him up early with a pot of coffee and breakfast as he had to be at rehearsal. So she oversleeps and as she's going round the house getting breakfast he keeps going on at her—"Look, I tole yer, didn't I, I tole yer I had to be there at 10 o'clock." Finally, she flung his breakfast at him and said, "You're getting more and more like Alf Garnett. The trouble is, you're not funny with it." He stormed out of the house and half-way to rehearsal he started laughing.

'Warren's made the character his in a lot of ways. We once discussed who else could have played it and thought Lionel Jeffries or Peter Sellers, but with the edge on Jeffries. He would have been different but could have done it just as well. We had the idea of doing another film. At the end of the last film, Garnett's moved into a block of flats in a new town—poor old sod—and we thought of starting the film in these flats where his next-door neighbour is Jeffries who is a bright red communist, laying it down by the book— "Look, according to Marx, your actual Marx now . . . as Karl Marx said. . . ." "Don't you talk to me about bloody Marx."

'There are all those lovely communist clichés from Unity Theatre days—"Now look comrades . . ." and "Now, that's reactionary. . . ." 'He'd be a left-wing Garnett. They'd hate each other and love each other because they'd be the same people and the only people who would talk to each other.

'I wouldn't like to see Alf go, but I don't think they'll come back to television as a family. The series got a bit uptight; there was strife.

'My mother told my sister I was spoiling myself when I did Garnett. She liked the Arthur Haynes shows but hated Garnett because of his language. She's a devout Roman Catholic and she's President of the Women's Guild in her area. She went to a big diocesan meeting and the County President said something to her about "your brilliant son who writes that show". She couldn't believe it. She was about to apologise. Now she's confused. I don't go to church, I'm an atheist. I've told her now and she can't understand why an atheist is doing so well and all the other kids who go to church regular and take Holy Communion are not doing well at all. She thinks that God has let her down.

'I don't know whether you can change people through comedy. Over a long period they will change themselves. Bernard Shaw thought he never changed anyone, but he did. He changed a lot of people. He changed me like mad. Art changes people. Good art.'

Living, you might say, up the road a bit from Garnett are Harold and Albert Steptoe, the rag-and-bone men bound together by indissoluble ties of working-class kinship. Harold aspires to the high life, to birds and fast cars and intellectual status, blaming his father for all the frustrations caused by his own frailties, and yet compelled by the laws of the poor to look after his father while breath is drawn in the meagre but wiry old body. Sometimes the situation proves so flexible and allows so much latitude that it almost seems as if Harold and Albert Steptoe are performing a script written for Hancock and Sid James.

One *Steptoe and Son* episode in the winter of 1970 opened with Harold soliloquising bitterly about the dreariness of a Sunday

Tommy Cooper

Frankie Howerd as Lurcio
in *Up Pompeii!*

Frank Muir and Dennis Norden

afternoon. While his father slumps and snores in an easy chair, Harold fantasises about life as Henry VIII at Hampton Court. Later, in an attempt to improve Harold's social life, the total absence of which is at the root of the trouble, old Albert gives him lessons in ballroom dancing.

It is strange that in this, so far the most Hancockian episode of *Steptoe and Son*, Galton and Simpson used a phrase that Hancock himself employed in his stage act—to which Galton and Simpson contributed—in 1954. He would pause in the middle of his patter, look at his feet and confide, "Cor, I don't know how they do an hour and a half at the Palladium—I've got toes like globe artichokes."

Sixteen years later, Albert Steptoe breaks off dancing with his son and complains, "I'll have toes like globe artichokes in the morning."

This was one of the rare episodes in which the father supported the son's aspirations. More usually, his function, like Sid James's with the high-flown Hancockian ambitions, is to cut them down to size, to bring the dreamer back to cruel reality. Harold, for example, hopes to be adopted as Labour candidate in the local elections. Albert, of course, is a Tory. Harold will turn their two-up, one-down junkyard cottage into a fashionable salon: ". . . a place where fine minds gather to exchange ideas. There'll be choice wines, superb food, elegant conversation. Theories will be propounded, decisions will be made. Here in this very room. It'll become such a power-house of intellectual thought and political thinking that people like C. P. Snow and Bertrand Russell will be busting a gut to get in. I see my gatherings more like the pre-war Cliveden set . . . Lady Astor's place. The week-end house parties . . ."

ALBERT: Oh yeah—there'll be plenty for them to do here. Table tennis, rat hunting. I can see you all now going for long tramps across the yard deep in intellectual conversation and horse manure.

But the old man walks a shaky path between belligerence and fear. His paternal authority is a relic of his younger and stronger days. He knows he is utterly dependent on Harold and that Harold could, if he ever took it into his head, push him into an old home or just walk out and leave him helpless. He takes refuge in a cunning pathos.

ALBERT: Die, that's what you were going to say wasn't it . . . why don't you die?

E

HAROLD : No I wasn't.

ALBERT : Yes you were . . . you can't wait to hear the first shovelful of dirt hit the coffin, can you? I wouldn't be mourned, I know that . . . you'd be dancing on my grave . . . well, I'll tell you, it'll be a relief to go, get away from this hell-hole.

HAROLD : You die . . . don't make me laugh. You'll get your telegram from the Queen, don't worry.

The series could just as well have been called *Till Death Us Do Part*.

So, for that matter, could the partnership between Galton and Simpson. Nothing is certain, but it seems inconceivable that they could ever part. Many collaborators find a professional empathy, an interlocking of thought and word which results in a better class of work than either could achieve independently. Galton and Simpson go further and deeper. Their relationship works on a personal level as well, each supplying what the other lacks in areas which have nothing to do with their work. It could come through both having faced up to the possibility of death at an early age through tuberculosis; they met, in fact, in a sanatorium.

Galton says : 'When we got out of it we used to go to parties where we would look on people of the same age enjoying themselves in a way that we could never . . . we couldn't join in. We'd look across the room at each other and there was a knowing smile. We didn't have to say anything. We knew that we were both regarding the goings on with the same degree of amazement.'

It does not follow that they share the same interests and mirror each other's attitudes, though there is a painting of both of them in their office which shows them sunk in seriousness and a slight, mutual melancholy.

'Unfortunately,' says Galton, 'I haven't any all-consuming passion like Alan and his football. I really mean unfortunately. I really miss it. I'm conscious that there's a lack in my life. I'm too serious, for my liking. I keep saying to myself, "My God, you've got to try and enjoy yourself sometimes." Especially when I hear of people dying at the age of forty or so. I say to myself, "Oh God, what am I doing? Time is slipping by, why don't you buy that boat or go on more holidays." I've always been too serious, much too serious. It was more marked when I was younger. The teenage bit escaped me. The things I'm really interested in are the things you can't really pursue, like reading, architecture, town planning, politics. These are the things that really get me going. I get worried about things. I'm terribly worried about overpopulation. I don't mean in the world as a whole, I mean in this country. These are the sort of things that really get me going, what I worry about all the time.'

Simpson says: 'I don't laugh easily but I'm not miserable. I'm very easily amused. No, not amused—contented—very easily contented. When I look around at the things I really enjoy, the great majority of them are things that cost very little.'

They live close to each other, Galton in Hampton, Simpson in Sunbury. They travel to work separately but usually arrive at their office in Mayfair within a few minutes of each other. They have never written anything independently. They started together twenty-one years ago and have earned money from writing for nineteen years.

Galton was born in Paddington in 1930. His father was in the Royal Navy and, between the wars, worked as a bus conductor. He was called up in 1938 and Galton 'hardly saw him after that'. He left school in 1944 with no idea what he wanted to do except that he did not fancy working in an office. For a year he repaired bomb damage with the vague intention of becoming a plasterer. He followed this with a year as an office boy in the Transport and General Workers' Union office; then he became ill. He was sixteen years old and he was given a few weeks to live.

'It was the sanatorium that gave me some kind of education. I met a lot of interesting people, mainly servicemen. I was the youngest there and I suppose I was spoiled a bit. But it was there that I found the desire to read and learn things.'

Simpson was born in Brixton in 1929, son of a milkman. He left Mitcham Grammar School when he was sixteen. 'I had the choice of staying on, but I hated it so much I couldn't wait to get away,' he says. 'I was always keen on football and wanted to be a professional footballer. At one time I wanted to be a sports journalist, mainly because I thought it was the only way of getting into football matches without paying anything. My mother wanted me to be a civil servant because the biggest success in our family was one. He was the only one who had a car or a pension. I decided I wanted to go in the navy and be a ship's writer. I fancied the uniform. In the end I got into shipping. I thought it was romantic. I was a postal clerk at thirty bob a week. I had about three jobs in two years, then I was taken ill.'

They were in different places at first. Galton had already been in his sanatorium for two years when Simpson was sent there.

'In those days,' says Galton, 'people were in sanatoriums for years, so you were allowed a lot of freedom. The fellow I was in with was mad on engineering and electronics and the whole room was covered with radio equipment. There were vices rigged up at the end of the iron beds and he had an electric drill screwed down in his locker. He and another fellow installed a radio network throughout the sanatorium and we used to have record programmes and quizzes. Alan and myself were keen on comedy. We used to listen to everything and discuss everything. We decided to write a short series of comedy programmes for our radio. We intended to do six but we dried up after four. We performed them ourselves. Basically, they were about hospital life.'

Simpson says : 'We listened to all the professional comedy programmes—*Take It From Here, Much Binding in the Marsh*, Braden, Tommy Handley. We thought that if we could do something like that we could make our radio a little BBC. We wrote to Frank Muir and Denis Norden saying how much we admired their show and asked them how you became a scriptwriter. They wrote back saying that the best thing to do was to submit something to Gale Pedrick at the BBC.'

Shortly afterwards, they were allowed to go home. They found some facts about Captain Henry Morgan from an encyclopedia and spent eight weeks of evenings writing a *Take It From Here* style pirate sketch full of puns. They sent it to Gale Pedrick.

'I remember,' continues Simpson, 'getting on the bus and rushing over to Ray and shouting and waving the letter from Gale Pedrick. He wrote that the sketch was highly amusing and asked us to go to see him. We were knocked out. Even to get a letter from the BBC was fantastic. If it had said nothing else we would have been showing this letter to everybody saying, "Of course, we know something about writing—did you see this . . . er . . . letter from the BBC. They say the stuff we sent them was quite amusing." We would have lived on that for the next forty years.

'Derek Roy got hold of the sketch and the first joke we ever got paid for was in it : "They're down in the hold playing Jane Russell pontoon." "What's Jane Russell pontoon?" "The same as ordinary pontoon except that you need thirty-eight to bust." Change the name to Raquel Welch and we could do the same joke now in the right show. If we put it into *Steptoe* it would require the old man saying it with a "Ha, ha, ha, ha—that was a good 'un wasn't it?" and making it a deliberate bad joke.'

The producer of the Derek Roy show was Dennis Main Wilson, and Tony Hancock had a regular spot in it as a scoutmaster in charge of a troop called the 'Eager Beavers'. Main Wilson had been called in to take over the final four shows of the series and did not not like the scripts he inherited, so he threw them out.

In an earlier book* I quoted Main Wilson's account of how he

* Freddie Hancock and David Nathan, *Hancock* (William Kimber, 1969).

was instrumental in bringing Galton, Simpson and Hancock together : 'I consulted Gale Pedrick,' he said, 'and asked him if he had any young writers he wanted to get experience for. He showed me a script that was a knockout. It came from two boys who had started together when they met in a sanatorium. I liked the script so much that I said they should do the remaining shows.'

It was during the rehearsal for the second of these, held in the Paris Cinema, a BBC studio in Lower Regent Street, in October 1951, that Alan Simpson and Ray Galton met Hancock for the first time. Hancock was slumped in a seat when Galton and Simpson walked past him. 'You write that sketch?' he inquired. Simpson said, 'Yes.' 'Very good,' said Hancock. They walked on.

Later Hancock asked them to write him some material for a *Workers' Playtime* broadcast and, when they discussed payment, Hancock said they could have half his £50 fee. This was a big increase on the eight guineas they were accustomed to splitting between them.

Ten years later, after they had written 101 radio scripts and fifty-one television shows, one film and a lot of stage material, Hancock virtually dismissed them. They had, however, grown into artists by then.

'When we started,' says Simpson, 'we worked within the terms of reference of the time. This was that all comics were stand-up comics and did five or six minutes of patter. Comedy sketches were five minutes of puns and parodies and funny voices. This was how it was in the first two or three years until *Hancock's Half Hour* on radio—we just wrote according to the demands of the time. The big man was Bob Hope and smart, witty, American-style patter was very much in demand.'

'The intention with Hancock,' says Galton, 'was to try to get away from funny voices and jokes. We didn't quite succeed as far as the funny voices were concerned, but we did get some sort of credible story line. Mind you, if you look at them today, they're not credible at all. Everybody talked in those days about domestic comedies and they were about families. The idea of doing thirty minutes non-stop with one basic situation without a singer coming along to split it up was unthinkable, even in America where they had been doing situation comedy for years. The BBC always maintained that *Hancock's Half Hour* was the first non-domestic situation comedy anywhere in the world that went on for thirty minutes without being interrupted by music.'

'The difficult thing,' says Simpson, 'is to find an idea that will run for thirty minutes. Once you've got that, the ending will come.'

'Sometimes,' says Galton, 'we find an ending for a show that makes it appear as if we were writing towards it, and it's perfect.'

'Many times,' says Simpson, 'particularly in the early Hancock series, we used to be known as the talk-out enders with everybody saying things like, "Well, I've never heard anything so ridiculous in my life" and "How dare you!" and then the music would come over. It used to be called the hit-everybody-on-the-head-with-the-script-ending because that's what Hancock and the others would start doing.

'You write from instinct, but over the years you acquire a certain craftsmanship.'

The break with Hancock and the manner of it left them hurt and angry. Hancock called them to his flat in London one day and told them that he did not wish to work with them any more. He was under the illusion that his creative talents were as individual as his interpretative genius and had reached a stage at which he could no longer share acclaim with anyone else. Tom Sloan at the BBC tried to salvage what he could from the wreckage and offered Galton and Simpson ten comedy half-hours, all different, each to be cast as required. *Steptoe and Son* was the fourth.

'From a technical point of view,' says Simpson, 'we were used to thinking in terms of two characters—Hancock and Sid James. The first one was about two undertakers, the second about two something else. We were thinking about two something just to get us started. It seemed better than four something or ten something. It at least gives you a dialogue. Once you start involving more then two people in a situation it becomes like *Coronation Street*. You have to create histories and manipulate.'

'We had seen a couple of rag-and-bone men in a pie and eel shop in Tooting,' recalls Galton. 'We listened to their conversation but we had no idea what they were talking about. I wouldn't have thought that was the inspiration because that was some years before.'

Simpson : 'We've also seen two chimney sweeps and two of everything else.'

Galton : 'I said to Alan, "What about doing a show about two rag-and-bone men?" It evoked some sort of response. He said, "Yeah, all right."'

'At the time,' says Simpson, 'it was just another piece of writing. When we got down to the show itself and saw it in rehearsal it became obvious that this one had a lot of good things. We told each other that they were going to ask us to do a series.'

Galton says : 'When Tom Sloan said, "Of course, you realise what you have written don't you?" we played dumb and said,

"No, what?" He said, "It's marvellous, it's a series." We said, "Oh no, no." For about six months we resisted him.

'It was because of the eight years of Hancock,' explains Simpson. 'We had had eight years of working for one man, or one show—and we were fed up with it. When the BBC gave us the chance of writing comedy half-hours and casting them as required, we thought it was real freedom.'

'In the end,' says Galton, 'we were persuaded because Harry and Willy (Corbett and Brambell) were keen as well. We had suggested them, but if either had not been available someone else would have done it and the show may not have been a success. It is one of those imponderables. As they were actors we didn't think they would want to do a series. When we ran out of arguments we agreed. We thought it would be one series but it developed into five.'

After the fourth series, Galton and Simpson announced that they would do no more *Steptoes*.

'After enough time went by,' says Galton, 'we thought it wasn't such a bad situation and they were still attractive characters to write for. There is enough in the situation to go on writing them for as long as we can think up stories.'

Simpson says : 'We saw the first one recently with one we did three years later and there is no doubt that the performances were certainly far superior in the later one. The idea was good in the first and there were some lovely moments in it, but it was a little bit raw and crude really.'

'Slickness,' says Galton, 'could be the thing that makes you think they're better and they're not really. I don't think they're particularly better or worse. You've got to take them as they come. Some weeks they are better than others. I think that's the way it will always go. A lot of people think there's no development in the characters, but we have deliberately not tried to make them "progress" because I don't think people do change. They talk about different things but in the same way. They would talk about Biafra in the same way as they would talk about the bloody Munich crisis. I don't see the point in having Harry married off. That's not progress. The sort of thing reporters ask is, "Are they going to be trendy?" or "Are they going to reflect 1970?" How can they reflect 1970 other than in a few comments they make? They can't *be* 1970. Logically, they wouldn't have changed their ideas with the calendar.'

'We didn't,' says Simpson, 'sit down and decide to write a show that said something that needed to be said. But if you are writing about real people in real situations, this inevitably comes into it and people say, "Ah, social significance!" But it's not deliberately socially significant. The first thing is that it's got to be funny. That's not a cop-out, it's a starting-point.'

'Breakthrough' is a word frequently misused to describe developments in television comedy which are ludicrously unimportant in every other medium.

'The only time we said to each other, "This has never been done before in comedy", says Simpson, 'was when, after about three or four Hancock series, we deliberately tried to pick boring situations. We did it three or four times. One was about a Sunday afternoon. There were great long pauses full of ho-humming and sighs and a lot of inconsequential stuff like picking out Hitler's face in the wallpaper pattern. Hancock and the others were knocked out by the idea of doing half an hour of nothing happening. It's the only time I can think of when we were conscious of the fact that we were exploring new ground.'

Galton says: 'People are doing it today in smaller doses. What we were trying to do, what all writers are trying to do all the time, is looking for areas that haven't been exploited to saturation-point. Once you can find virgin territory you can write quickly.'

They have written five screenplays, *The Rebel*, for Hancock, *The Bargee* with Harry H. Corbett, *The Wrong Arm of the Law*, *The Spy with the Cold Nose* and *Loot*, an adaptation of Joe Orton's black comedy. They were asked to write a *Steptoe and Son* screenplay but turned down the idea because it appeared to them at the time that it would not stand much chance of success, that people would refuse to pay to see something they could see for nothing at home. Then came the film version of *Till Death Us Do Part* which made handsome profits.

'The dilemma,' says Galton, 'if we made a film of *Steptoe*, would be to decide whether to make a picture that had no reference at all to the television series, a film that could be shown throughout the world, or a domestic film made in the awareness that everyone had already seen them on television. In that case it would have no market outside Britain.'

'*The Rebel*,' says Simpson, 'was virtually written as a television piece. We approached it in exactly the same way and, as it happens, it was very successful. It wasn't the Hancock from East Cheam; it was a man working in an office who wanted to be an artist. But, essentially, it was the same Hancock.'

Of the two classic comedy series they have created, *Steptoe* and *Hancock*, it is the former which gives them the greater satisfaction.

'We got a tremendous kick out of writing *Hancock*,' says Simpson, 'particularly when we had a good one. We used to look forward to going down to the read-through because they laughed and fell about so much. It was great. But *Steptoe* is ours. We've got two good actors but it is our thing, whereas with *Hancock* we were just Tony's scriptwriters. Sometimes we got mentioned, sometimes we didn't. And the *Steptoe* situations are much more realistic, deeper, less fantastic.'

'They are more satisfying to write,' says Galton.

'*Steptoe*,' says Simpson, 'is in many ways an extension of *Hancock* but much deeper, less superficial than he was. The sort of situations we get them involved in are things that Tony and Sid couldn't have done.'

The search for a new subject for a series occupies a great deal of their thinking time. 'I only hope,' says Galton, 'that I recognise it when it hits me. They are rare. I mean not just rare for me but rare for the whole medium. The number of shows that have really captured the imagination of the public are very few—*Garnett, Steptoe, Hancock* . . . after that you've just got good shows.'

'During my early twenties I used to think that given the time and an easing of the economic pressures I could write serious plays. But as you get older you realise that you know fuck all, that all the things you really felt strongly about are no longer black and white. This is the tragedy of getting old, I suppose—that you cannot see things as clearly as you could when you were younger. You say, "Christ, let's leave it to a younger man to say things that are pertinent and real and let us have the full blast of his cynicism." '

Galton's tone is regretful. The point is that young, cynical men who see things in black and white are rarely funny. Nor do they have a monopoly of truth.

7 | Men's Doubles

Dud and Peter were left in Michael Mills's office illustrating the intricacies, the wheelings and dealings of BBC-type censorship. There was, it may be recalled, the memorable exchange:

> 'You could use other rhyming slang, let's see, you could use sans or fainting.'
> 'Sans or fainting? What are you talking about?'
> 'Rhyming slang. San Moritz, fainting fits.'

The original line was 'You could use Gare or fainting'.

> 'Gare or fainting? What are you talking about?'
> 'Rhyming slang. Gare Austerlitz, fainting fits.'
> 'Gare Austerlitz? What's that?'
> 'A large railway station in Paris.'

'I would have preferred,' says Cook, 'to have had Gare Austerlitz rather than San Moritz. I liked the deliberate obscurity of Gare Austerlitz. It's such a ridiculous thing to have rhyming slang for, because nobody has ever heard of it. That's the kind of thing Dudley and I will argue about. The occasional obscurity doesn't worry me provided there are enough things that are clear.

'We have a strange, haphazard way of working. Dudley's very keen on actual motivations and reasons for things. I can get carried away thinking up a series of funny things and Dudley will ask why we are going in that direction, apart from the fact that I've thought up a series of funny things.

'A lot of the time is spent arguing over whether something is legitimate or not. We usually both agree on what's funny. But I do fight to maintain rather obscure lines. We're both very anti-tag, that thing bunged on to the end of a sketch to round it off. We tend to prefer rather slow fades. Sometimes a sketch will have a natural tag, but I hate it when something is bunged on.

'There are lots of changes after the script is written. In one Dud and Pete, Dudley was going to say, "I can get back to dreaming about Jane Russell" and we changed it to Debra Paget. Debra Paget is funny and Jane Russell isn't. I don't know why.'

Occasionally, things are 'bunged in' as the show is being recorded for transmission and they tend to send tremors over the face of whoever is at the receiving end of the bunging. In one sketch, Dud blacked up and explained that, wearing an African costume, he had been refused entry at the Savoy Hotel on the grounds that he was improperly dressed. He recounts how he had told them that it was the equivalent of full evening attire up the Zambesi, to which the retort was that he should get back up the Zambesi and tuck into some best end of missionary. Pete hopes that Dud treated this with the contempt it deserved. Indeed, he had. Moreover, he had rung up the Race Relations Board about it. They had promised to take it up eventually, but at the time they were busy investigating an allegation that a Welshman had been refused Irish coffee in an Indian Restaurant.

It was at this point that Cook added, 'Oh yes, I read about that in the *Jewish Chronicle*.'

Cook and Moore deal in fantasy but like to see at least one sketch in each show firmly based on a recognisably human situation or emotion. Once having got it, they then push it as far as it can go.

'If I'm really desperate for material,' says Cook, 'I usually ask friends if anything really ghastly has happened to them recently, horrible domestic situations and so on. Practically everyone I know is involved in some superficially hideous disaster of one kind or another and I don't hesitate to use them. I use things which happen to me the whole time—like domestic rows. One of the ways of getting out of anything which you find you are taking over-seriously at the time is to escalate it into comedy. A lot of the Molière situations deal with the most awful emotional situations but are immensely funny. That's why *Steptoe* is funny, because of its reality. It's basically a hideous situation.

'I saw an actor I knew vaguely in the BBC Club one day and I asked him if he was working. "Not for a long time," he said. So I asked him what he was doing at the club. He said, "I'm hoping to meet my accountant." I asked him why he had arranged to meet his accountant there and he said he hadn't arranged anything. His accountant, it turned out, would not talk to him on the telephone because he was not important enough but frequently came to the BBC Club hoping to pick up future clients. "It's really my only chance to get together with him," the actor said.

'It struck me as being very sad and ludicrous, drifting along every day to the BBC Club hoping to see your accountant. To make it less obscure you might change it to an agent and when he eventually does come along get him to say, "You don't know me, but I think I could do things for you." It's a tag-end but its fair.

'Dud,' says Dudley Moore, 'came from me. I didn't want to do literary or political or philosophical things, but stuff which came from my own experience.'

The area which Moore owns lies in the shadow of the Dagenham Dye Works and not all the waters of the Hampstead Ponds, near which he now lives, are sufficient to wash away the stains it left on his character.

'My own experiences,' Moore says, 'were possibly more mundane than Peter's, but they were mine. Dud came from a rather sorry-looking bloke I used to see in my father's church at home. He would walk up the aisle so deferential and meek. I never heard him speak. The innocence of the Dud character is, I suppose, the sort of ideal innocence that I wanted to have. Pete is the know-ledgeable bloke, and Dud is easy for me because it really is my side of the story in a sense—ill-digested knowledge or lack of it and repressions and inhibitions all bubbling beneath the meek surface.'

Pete feels very depressed and asks Dud the meaning of life.

> DUD : Life is a precious gift. We're on this earth but for a brief sojourn; the more we put into life, the more we get out of it and if, on the way, I can spread a little sunshine, then my living shall not be in vain.
>
> PETE : Thank you, Patience Strong. Have you ever thought about death? Do you realise that each and every one of us needs must die?
>
> DUD : Yeah, of course, but it's only half past four of a Wednesday afternoon.
>
> PETE : No man knoweth when God in His Almighty wisdom will vouchsafe His precious gift of death.
>
> DUD : Granted, but he's unlikely to make a swoop at this time of day.
>
> PETE : As far as I'm concerned he can get a bloody move on.
>
> DUD : Aw, that's morbid. Think of the good things in life.
>
> PETE : Like what?
>
> DUD : Well, all you gotter do, Pete, is look out of the window. (*Dud looks out of the window and changes his mind*) P'raps not.

PETE : I think it was rightly said : see Dagenham Dye Works and die.

But Dud is not easily discouraged. He urges Pete to think of all the happy times they have had, their memories of such joyous adventures as going up the GPO Tower and visiting the London Planetarium and the National Gallery.

PETE : You spent four hours with your nose glued up against one of Rubens' more voluptuous nudes.

DUD : I was interested in the Dutch master's handling of light and shade.

PETE : With special reference to her enormous knockers . . .

'Really,' says Moore, 'the television series was a bit of a release for me because I could actually delve into my own existence. It was something I couldn't do in *Beyond the Fringe*, which seemed to be very clever. I don't think for that reason it was cold—it was not a cold show by any means—but I wanted to do something I could actually lay my hands on in terms of experience.

'We ad-lib very little, though we leave certain phrases very loose. Other things have to be said exactly right in order to set up a joke. I prefer to know exactly what I'm going to say. Peter doesn't because he tries to find something different every time. He never seems to be at a loss and always comes out with something different, phrasing in a way that's surprising. He makes me laugh a lot. I make him laugh, too, especially when I'm drunk. Whenever we go out to dinner he tries to pour wine down me because he knows that I get very loud and obstreperous and start making speeches. I get up on the table and start declaiming.

'I enjoy his company tremendously and I hope he enjoys mine, otherwise it would be intolerable. We have had some gloomy days, but I think we've got to the stage where we can be very heavily sarcastic with each other and say the most wounding, personal things. It's such a relief to say them and go hammer-and-tongs and know that it's non-damaging. That particular frankness has probably only come recently.'

There is a temporary, improvised air about the partnership. 'We both do our separate things and come together when we feel we want to,' says Moore.

Morecambe and Wise are more permanent, two of a kind who are so professionally inseparable that when Morecambe was pole-axed by a heart attack for some months Wise wore the bravely puzzled air of a man trying to scratch a newly amputated leg.

They live miles from each other, Morecambe in Harpenden, Wise in Peterborough, stay in different hotels when on tour but look at each other when performing with a deep unfakeable affection. Now in their early forties, they have been working together since they were twelve years old. They have the ability, after days of rehearsal, to listen to each other with the total attention of someone who is hearing something interesting being said for the very first time and very often, especially when Morecambe is speaking, this is the case. Their basic routine is the pure cross-talk comedy of the old music-hall and variety stages, the invariable ping-pong chat of comic and feed. But in this case the comic is a master and, over the years, the feed has developed a comic personality of his own, a compound of vanity and puritanism that gives him a kind of equality. Morecambe without Wise is almost as unthinkable as Wise without Morecambe. Together they have brought to television the sheer fun and warmth of an older way of comedy. They create, not only laughter but that much rarer commodity, happiness. They give a lift to the spirit.

Morecambe can talk about the basic properties of their act without throwing much light on it. 'It is based,' he once said, 'on the theory that he (Ernie Wise) is a fool, but I'm a bigger fool. He comes on in all the gear and says he is going to dance like Fred Astaire. But he's not a bit like Astaire, so he's a fool. I watch him and I think he is Astaire, so I'm a bigger fool.'

This may have been true in the early days. Today they have developed to a point where the comedian, the bigger fool, can win some of the time. 'Now,' says Morecambe, 'I'd turn to the audience and say, "Look at him—he believes it all you know", which is something I wouldn't have done before.'

When Wise tells something to Morecambe, Morecambe watches him warily, desperately determined not to be a mug this time, not to be conned. Morecambe comes on holding a pair of bongo drums, a real swinger. Only he holds them with one hand and strikes them with the other. 'Use both hands,' instructs Wise. Morecambe looks at him as if he is quite mad. 'Put them between your knees,' says Wise. Morecambe's face mirrors total disbelief, followed by a dawning realisation that there may be more in this than meets the eye, that in fact something a bit dirty might have been said. It is the way he looks at Wise that is the joke, that wins him the exchange.

Another time he will resort to a sudden belligerence.

'The success of this act is due to me,' claims Wise smugly.

'It isn't, is it?' asks Morecambe in what seems to be a spirit of genuine inquiry.

'Yes it is.'

'I'll smash your face in.'

Superficially, Wise is the suave one who bullies the simple Morecambe. Wise is the one who gets the girl, or at least the good-looking one, while Morecambe is left with the boot-faced best friend. But one confiding glance at the audience or a point-blank refusal to take seriously Wise's pretensions as actor or playwright establishes the superiority of the fool over the know-all and ensures total audience identification.

Eric Morecambe was born Eric Bartholomew in Morecambe, Lancashire, son of a corporation workman. Ernie Wise was born Ernest Wiseman, in Leeds, Yorkshire, son of a railwayman. Wise's father did a semi-pro act in the working men's clubs and, though it was against the law, young Eric joined him at the age of seven and they became 'Carson and Kid'.

'We sang songs like "Winter Wonderland" and "It Happened on the Beach at Bali-Bali",' says Wise. 'There was one where I sat on my dad's knee and he sang "Little Pal, if Daddy Goes Away" and they all cried into their beer.'

Morecambe also worked the clubs as a youngster. They know about incidents in each other's lives which happened before they even met and prompt each other's memories like reminiscing brothers. They talk like a script.

WISE : Eric did the gormless kind of comedy.

MORECAMBE : A proper northern comic. I used to sing a comedy song called 'I'm Not All There'. I think it belonged to Ella Shields.

WISE : He used to wear a beret . . .

MORECAMBE : Kiss-curl, big glasses.

WISE : And carried a big lollipop.

MORECAMBE : I was about eleven.

WISE : There was one basic thing common to the two of us— we both wore cut-down evening dress suits with the jacket pinned together by a big safety pin.

MORECAMBE : Our comedy was what our parents thought was funny and what they'd seen the major comics do.

WISE : I was influenced by Charlie Chaplin. I have pictures of me with a bowler hat on and a little tash.

MORECAMBE : And I was influenced by Shirley Temple and I still am. When I first went to dancing class with my cousin Peggy I learned to tap-dance and I used to do a double act with a girl called Molly Bunting. I was Fred Astaire and she was Ginger Rogers. Then I'd black up and do G. H. Elliott.

WISE: We weren't influenced by music-hall. I never saw any as a kid. We were influenced by the cinema.

MORECAMBE: I never saw G. H. Elliott. My mother and father had. And Flanagan and Allen. I used to do 'Underneath the Arches' by myself with an invisible partner.

WISE: And radio—*Monday Night at Eight.*

MORECAMBE: I remember as a kid listening to Ernie before I'd ever met him. He was on *Monday Night at Eight*. I was working the clubs now and then and my mother used to say, 'There's that Ernie Wise on again.'

WISE: Bryan Michie discovered me. I gave an audition to him in Leeds and Jack Hylton was my mentor. He changed my name to Wise. I was a clog-dancer and I wasn't introduced to sophisticated tap-shoes until much later on. Hylton changed my style, otherwise I would have been an out-and-out comic. He put me into a straw hat with a white jacket and evening-dress trousers and I used to do numbers like 'Run, Rabbit, Run'.

MORECAMBE: His father was really upset when Ernie went professional.

WISE: He was bringing up a family of five on £2 a week he got from the railway and we used to get 30/-, sometimes £2.10 in the clubs. But he wasn't upset about the money. I was a very big thing in his life. He enjoyed those week-ends and he glowed in the small glory there was to them. He was offered a job by Jack Hylton with me and he turned it down because he needed the regular railway money.

MORECAMBE: I used to play tennis with lollipops or swing one like the pendulum of a clock. I hated every second of it, but I got laughs. I've got thousands of relations in Morecambe.

WISE: All his laughs were based on his gormless face with that little kiss-curl at the front.

MORECAMBE: At thirteen, fourteen, fifteen you start to feel your feet a bit, girlwise.

WISE: Vanity.

MORECAMBE: All those fellers like Ernie who used to wear the smart suits got more chances with the girls than this gormless idiot comic did. I used to get terribly embarrassed about it. I insisted that my mother bought me a long dressing-gown down to the ground and I wouldn't take it off until half a second before I went on. But of course I still had the lollipop in my hand, the kiss-curl and the big, horn-rimmed glasses. So if I did have any luck with any of the girls it was genuine.

WISE : He also objected to wearing a hat with the brim turned up at the front.

MORECAMBE : I won the Lancashire and Cheshire contest at Hoylake, near Liverpool. The first prize was an audition for Jack Hylton which I did in Manchester.

WISE : And I saw him do it.

MORECAMBE : Hylton put me into *Bryan Michie's Discoveries*. I was thirteen.

WISE : He did 'I'm Not All There' and 'Underneath the Arches'.

MORECAMBE : And 'Lily of Laguna'.

By this time Wise had actually left *Bryan Michie's Discoveries* and was touring with the Hylton band. He rejoined the *Discoveries* when Hylton broke up his band show at the beginning of the war. He and Morecambe met in Swansea. Morecambe's mother looked after him on tour but Wise was left to fend for himself, as his mother had another four to care for at home in Leeds. At Oxford he couldn't find any digs and finished up on an airbed in More-cambe's lodgings. After that, Mrs Bartholomew looked after the two of them.

MORECAMBE : The first job we ever did together, Ernie came on and sang, 'How's About a Little Ramble in the Moonlight' and I walked on with a chair and a cane fishing-rod which had a piece of string and an apple tied to it.

MORECAMBE : 'I'm fishing.'

WISE : 'But you can't catch fish with an apple; you catch fish with a worm.'

MORECAMBE : 'That's all right, the worm's inside the apple.' That was the first gag we ever did together.

WISE : We got that kind of gag from people who told us what to do—things like 'What are you doing down there?'

MORECAMDE : 'Getting up.'

WISE : We never thought of anything ourselves. We got all these gags from old pros and Abbott and Costello films. We used to steal like hell. Eric would come running across the stage with a bicycle pump. 'Where are you going?'

MORECAMBE : 'I'm going to put the wind up Hitler.'

WISE : We did that in a recent television show. But purposely. 'Where are you going with that coat-hanger?'

MORECAMBE : 'For an aeroplane.'

WISE : 'What for?'

MORECAMBE : 'I've got the hangar.'

WISE : Rubbish. It was all rubbish.

MORECAMBE : You've got to start somewhere.

WISE : If someone else did a gag and it got a big laugh we would do it.

MORECAMBE : If they weren't with us the next week, that is.

WISE : We even pinched from Moon and Bentley—Georgie Moon and Dick Bentley. They were the first double act we ever saw really. At one time we used American accents. We pinched one from Morris and Cowley which we didn't understand. 'Why are you walking like that?'

MORECAMBE : 'Because I'm a businessman.'

WISE : 'A businessman doesn't walk like that.'

MORECAMBE : 'Ah, but you don't know my business.'

WISE : We didn't know its implications. All we knew was that it got a big laugh. But when we went into ENSA we got complaints from the padres.

MORECAMBE : We never really said anything personal to each other, never spoke to one another. It was all cross-over gags. We only had five minutes. Ernie would start singing, 'How's About a Little . . .' and then I'd come on and he'd say . . .

WISE : 'Just a moment.' And I hoped he wouldn't take too bloody long because I didn't know how the song went on.

MORECAMBE : Then we got good numbers in like 'The Waiter and the Porter and the Upstairs Maid'. We used to do that with a girl called Jean Bamforth who is now a dresser with the BBC.

WISE : We built up to *Strike a New Note* with Sid Field at the Prince of Wales but we went on as separate acts. People wouldn't accept the double act.

MORECAMBE : Let's be honest, it was bad. It wasn't a good double act. It was two sixteen-year-old kids. I expect today young fellers are copying us like we copied Abbott and Costello. But they can't do it like us and we couldn't do it like Abbott and Costello.

WISE : At the time, though, we didn't think we were bad. We went to matinées at the Palladium and thought we were equally as good as the acts we saw.

MORECAMBE : We used to watch Jewell and Warris and they would do twenty-five minutes and we used to think it was bloody awful. In fact, they weren't, it was just our envy and jealousy.

The war separated them for some three years. Wise went into the Merchant Navy and Morecambe went down the mines, from which he was released with a tired heart. For a while he worked as a feed to Gus Morris, lesser-known brother of comedian Dave Morris. 'I was straight man to Gus,' says Morecambe, 'and he was a very good comic. But very northern, very Middlesbrough. Taught me a hell of a lot about timing.'

In 1947, Morecambe and Wise teamed up again and joined a travelling circus.

WISE : I think the first original gag we thought of was the door gag.

MORECAMBE : I thought of that on top of a bus in Dewsbury. I used to come on carrying a little sliding door in a frame just a little bit bigger than my head. Ernie would be singing and I would go up to him and hand him the frame. He would turn to look at me but wouldn't be able to see me for the door. I'd knock on the door. He would open it and I'd say, 'Can a feller get a drink in here?'

WISE : 'Yes, come in.'

MORECAMBE : I'd walk past him, take the door, turn round, give it back to him, knock on the door and he'd open it again and I'd say, 'Wha's the marrer? The bar's closed.'

WISE : We saw a routine that Abbott and Costello did in a picture with a beard and a cigar.

MORECAMBE : The cigar was attached to the beard. Ernie used to send me off with . . .

WISE : 'I never want to see your face again. You understand? Gerroff!' Then I'd turn to the audience and say, 'I'm very sorry about that interruption, ladies and gentlemen. Now I'd like to sing my favourite . . .'

MORECAMBE : And I'd come back on with this beard but with my back to Ernie. He would recognise me from the back and say . . .

WISE : 'How dare you come on like this! I've told you . . .'

MORECAMBE : But I'd turn round with the beard on and he'd say . . .

WISE : 'Oh, I'm terribly sorry, sir.'

MORECAMBE : Then he'd look at the audience and I would take the cigar out of my mouth—because I couldn't talk with it in—and the beard would come off with it and I'd say 'That's all right' and put it back on.

WISE : 'I'm terribly sorry, sir. I mistook you for someone else.'

MORECAMBE : 'What's he look like, this feller? Did he look like this?' And I took the cigar and beard off for a fraction.

WISE : 'Yes, he looked exactly like you, but of course you've got a beard and a cigar.'

MORECAMBE : 'Of course.' And to say it I would take off the beard and cigar and replace it upside-down.

WISE : The act was forming.

MORECAMBE : Today we need ten routines like that. We found it very difficult to get in down south. We never considered ourselves northern comics but everybody else used to.

WISE : We had to make a determined effort. We decided we must get on the radio—*Workers' Playtime, Variety Fanfare* and things like that, to get known to the public. We wrote special scripts. We got gag books and would get together a string of gags on one subject like suits, with an occasional original joke here and there.

MORECAMBE : Anybody who starts from scratch as Ernie and I were doing must start by copying, but what happens is that eventually, if you have it, this originality for want of a better word . . .

WISE : Starts coming through.

MORECAMBE : Now the thing to do is to build up on that originality and it becomes part of you. The ones who can't do that and just carry on doing copies never really get anywhere.

WISE : That's why some comedians reel off jokes as if they've just come out of a book. There's no future in that, or at least it's limited. You bring yourself into the public eye but where do you go from there?

MORECAMBE : We do very few jokes nowadays. There are usually about three in the show but they are done purposely as 'jokes' in quotation marks.

WISE : Like, 'I haven't got time to do a commercial; my schedules are very tight.'

MORECAMBE : 'I must say you've gone a funny colour.' It's only one step away from 'I want to take down your particulars' but if you only do them occasionally and in the right place they're very funny. But it's more personality now. It's 'You're working well, Ern' and 'You can't see the join'. It's all personality.

WISE : If we had stayed in variety we would never have advanced. We did the radio shows but we couldn't get into London. We became, more or less, northern stars.

MORECAMBE : We started to move forward in 1961.

WISE : We had been to Australia and when we came back we decided we weren't getting anywhere.

MORECAMBE : That was the only time the idea of separating could ever have cropped up. But it didn't.

WISE : We went to Billy Marsh, the agent, and asked him to get us some television. He said he could do it if we supplied the material. We sat down and wrote the judo sketch and a lot of other spots were adapted from radio. The judo sketch is the one where Eric knows all about judo and wants to demonstrate it to me but he's the only one who keeps getting hurt and he can't understand it. We did a *Sunday Night at the London Palladium* and some *Saturday Night Spectaculars*. We used to get £100 for them. They began to take notice. Lew Grade asked us if we'd like to do a series and we agreed if we could have Hills and Green to write it and Colin Clewes to produce it. They were then writing for Jimmy and Ben (Jewell and Warris).

MORECAMBE : There was trouble about that, but we said if they couldn't get them we couldn't do the series, so in the end they agreed.

It is no wonder they were cautious. They had, in fact, done some earlier television, as far back as 1954, and about the best word they got for the series was 'feeble'.

MORECAMBE : The first show of the series with Hills and Green was exactly the same as all the other televisions we had been doing. The following week Equity went on strike. We were in the V.A.F. (Variety Artistes Federation, now combined with Equity) so we were allowed to work. But we were not allowed to work with anybody—only Sid (Green) and Dick (Hills). So we sat in an office and asked ourselves what we could do and Sid and Dick said they would appear with us. We called it the lonely show. Sid and Dick had written some very good stuff for Dave King and we had seen their potential.

Eric and Ernie and Sid and Dick stayed together and grew together until Morecambe's heart attack in 1968. Then Green and Hills, who, during all this time had also written for other comedians and other shows, left them. Recently, they announced that they were emigrating to Hollywood because of the greater opportunities and more money.

MORECAMBE : They were good writers, excellent writers.
WISE : Sid and Dick are good sketch plus music-hall writers.
MORECAMBE : I'd never decry Sid and Dick. For their writing anyway.
WISE : We have every respect for them.
MORECAMBE : For their writing.

WISE : We're a little sad about it all, but . . .
MORECAMBE : This is a gift from heaven, isn't it?

The 'gift from heaven' is Eddie Braben who, actually, comes from Liverpool. He is dour and down-to-earth and used to write for Ken Dodd. With him, Morecambe and Wise have overcome the tremendous practical and psychological obstacle of changing writers at what seemed to be the peak of their success. It was a danger that Hancock failed to negotiate, though he had brought the situation on himself by his own folly. With Morecambe and Wise it was unsought. The difficulty was increased by the need for Morecambe to take things easier after his heart attack, to cut out the club work, the summer shows, the winter pantomimes, the films, the frequent American appearances. All depended on their new long-term contract with the BBC and they faced it with a new writer.

WISE : It was a very critical time.
MORECAMBE : Through Eddie's influence there have been changes that you don't even notice at the time. We're doing what we always wanted to do—that is, grow up with the comedy. It's no good, say, in another five years when we're forty-eight, for Ernie and I to act like two college boys with all the little dollies floating around.
WISE : I think we've brought a lot of the public with us. They watch us so closely now and know us so well that we can actually talk about Sunderland or Leeds Empire and all the old variety days and they know what we're talking about. I think we're part of the history of the theatre and a lot of our comedy comes from that.
MORECAMBE : At the moment, because of the heart attack, theatres are out. We've been offered the Palladium, the Prince of Wales—and you name it, we've been offered it. But we don't want them. We've done thirty years of it anyway. It's a long time.
WISE : We could get very bored doing theatre, doing the same thing every night. We've got to the stage where we want to *create* comedy more than we have ever done before.
MORECAMBE : At the beginning of the last series I happened to say that we were going to jump even further, higher. People said, 'But you can't, you're as high as you can be.' But we weren't because we have jumped higher. Who would have thought it? We don't know why. We can't put our finger on it and say, 'Ah—Eddie Braben.' But he's part of it, and us, and Johnnie Ammonds (their producer). But would we have jumped

higher if we had done the televisions and played Batley and done pantomimes and summer season? It's what we put into it.

WISE : We now spend three weeks on shows that used to take one week.

MORECAMBE : And still don't know half of it when we get there.

WISE : Remembering continuity is the hardest part, not remembering the lines.

MORECAMBE : The trouble is that you know the script but you want to get even more out of it, so you start to put a little bit extra in and it might throw you for a second. It's like the classic one I did. Instead of saying 'Corridors of Power' I said, 'There's Charles Hill, running around the powers of corridor.'

WISE : I said, 'Corridors of Power.'

MORECAMBE : And I said, 'Ah, yeah, but he's doing it backwards.' It was a good ad-lib but I forgot what came next so I missed a little piece out.

WISE : On one show I had to put on a red nose and the elastic broke.

MORECAMBE : With all our years of experience we carried on. What we should have done was to stop and get a new one fitted. We could have gone back but we didn't because of the variety training. You get on and do it. It doesn't matter if the prop breaks—do it all the same.

But they were right to carry on. It showed them as being vulnerable, human and liable to accident. The spontaneous performance when something trivial is seen to go wrong sets a challenge the audience likes to see met—and overcome. To fail is embarrassing. The comedian must cope and win. There was one occasion when they did not win.

WISE : The scar's still vivid. We were working pantomime twice daily and we were exhausted. They talked us into doing a television from the London Palladium. We should have refused. It was 1964 and we had just won an award. It was one show six years ago and it still hurts. Eric didn't feel well and as we walked on somebody shouted out. It was live and it was the London Palladium and somebody shouted out and it threw the whole thing. We came on and Eric said, 'What shall we do?' and somebody shouted, 'Why don't you stand on your head?' Eric said . . .

MORECAMBE : 'We're not in Australia are we?'

WISE : It got a good laugh but it threw the routine. Then things went wrong mechanically. We didn't go to pieces but the act went to pieces in our grasp. We couldn't pick it up, we couldn't get out of it. All the timing went. We were racing and touching hysteria.

MORECAMBE : And trying to look casual at the same time.

WISE : Mixed emotions—like your mother-in-law driving your new car over a cliff. Mixed emotions. Don't forget that the great relaxation that appears is acquired.

MORECAMBE : It always makes me laugh 'cos Ernie gets the shakes and I get the dry lip.

WISE : Oh, I shake all right. It doesn't happen if it's a routine we know backwards, but when it's all new. . . . You go out there and it's not the last show that counts, no matter how good it was, it's this one, the one you're doing now. We're as insecure as our last sketch, believe me. . . . As we went off, Eric said . . .

MORECAMBE : 'This must be the worst television we've ever done.'

WISE : Over the whole network! It rang out over the whole country! Clifford Davis (*Daily Mirror* television correspondent) telephoned us and asked what happened. 'What happened?' I said. 'It was no bloody good.' What else can you say?

MORECAMBE : We'd done about fifty good shows before that.

WISE : Of course, the level we try to attain these days is very high. We feel the strain more than we did before. When Eddie started writing for us he knew who he was writing for. He knew what the relationship was and he didn't have to create something from scratch. But he has brought more out than ever before for the simple reason that he can see more in us than we can see in ourselves.

MORECAMBE : We're quite happy to go out there and do a half-hour of stand-up material as long as it's funny. We'd do that every week until we had driven everybody into the ground. But Eddie's not. We're getting a little more way out in certain respects. We come basic now and again—I think you've got to. I'm a great believer in basic comedy.

WISE : The people are not looking at caricatures. The comedy that comes out is actually Eric and I. When we walk on he doesn't adopt another personality. Neither do I.

MORECAMBE : We only know what makes us laugh and we feel that we've got the experience now to say when it won't make them laugh. But we're not 100 per cent sure. We know what not to do. We never ever leer, we're never oversexed. We had a lot of beautiful girls round us but we didn't want to look like dirty old men. That's why when Eddie joined us we cut down on the girls and got Ann Hamilton, who is a little older than sixteen or nineteen, and it's a better relationship than with those big-busted dollies and me ogling them all the time. We don't do blue stuff as such, but we do a lot of innuendo that we feel we can get away with because I have a blank look, an innocent face.

WISE : And, of course, my attitude all the time is 'Please . . . how dare you !' The prude.

MORECAMBE : It's never carried through. It's done very quickly and then left.

Once or twice they have shared a double bed in a sketch. When he shared a house with Sid James, Hancock once refused to wear a pinny and do the washing up because he feared it might make him look homosexual. Galton and Simpson had to rewrite the sketch.

WISE : There's no question of homosexuality. It goes back to old-style Laurel and Hardy humour, the early silents.

MORECAMBE : When I first read this script of Eddie's I never thought of anything in the homosexual line at all.

WISE : Neither of us did. But it was mentioned. The producer said, 'I'm a little worried about two fellers in a bed' and we said, 'What for?' and he said, 'Well, you might offend . . . ah, sod it, you won't.' But it could have done, I suppose, played in a different way.

MORECAMBE : Twenty years ago it was accepted that men slept together. Now you wouldn't think of it.

WISE : I must say, that was a step . . . this is Eddie, not us.

MORECAMBE : We did two like that, and kept them well apart.

WISE : It's a point you have to watch, but I don't think it crosses the public's mind.

Very occasionally, they differ about what is funny.

WISE : We are constantly proved wrong, both ways, time and time again.

MORECAMBE : It's an unwritten law in our association that eventually I would have the last say on comedy. If I had thought hard and long enough I would say to Ernie, 'Look, it is funny. I can make it really funny.'

WISE : And I would say, 'Well, you're the comic, so we'll do it.' He's the one who's got to get the laughs.

MORECAMBE : Ernie is only just becoming a comic. This is

good, it is another facet. It's taken him longer because he's never had the lines before. He's not a comic, but he's becoming a character, a personality.

WISE : For years we worked on the premise of straight man and comic. But with the amount of work we do on television it's not possible to continue like that because you can't ring the changes enough.

Does he resent the years he spent without getting the good lines?

WISE : No.

MORECAMBE : He might have resented it on a Monday, but when he got paid on a Friday . . .

WISE : No I didn't resent it. I've always really been a song-and-dance man. I call myself the thin line of sanity. You've got to have sanity somewhere.

MORECAMBE : I've got to have somebody to lean on and to react against.

WISE : Sometimes Eric wins now, sometimes he even gets the girl. We do try to outfox the public. If it's obvious what's going to happen next, we try and switch it on 'em. It's a constant game beween us and the public to try and outfox them.

They have made three films, *The Intelligence Man, The Riviera Touch* and *The Magnificent Two.*

WISE : They were successful at the box office.

MORECAMBE : But from our point of view they were not successful at all.

WISE : Nobody knew how to approach it.

MORECAMBE : Nobody knew how to handle us. We were willing to be led. You get a man who's putting up £300,000 and you think he must know something about it. And the director says, 'Leave it to me', so you do.

WISE : We did what we could, but we found that what came out was diluted Morecambe and Wise.

MORECAMBE : They were early Abbott and Costello. Any two reasonably funny fellers could have done them. I'd give my right arm to do a really good film because that's about all the ambition that is left. There was something wrong with our pictures and I'm not going to blame the producer, the director, the writers or the comics. But it was one of them. Otherwise we'd have been very good indeed. We wanted to do an extension of our television, but the film boys said this was impossible. If I had to do a thing seven times, it had to be on the same mark and done in the same way each time.

Morecambe finds it difficult to do something the same way twice —sometimes even once.

WISE : As long as I know what comes next I don't mind Eric's ad-libs.

MORECAMBE : There was one I did when a doctor tells Ernie to take his clothes off and I say, 'Yes, take 'em off and give us all a laugh.' I added, 'And while you're at it you can do that impression of a teapot.' Eddie never wrote that and it got a belter and a round of applause.

If either fluffs a line, the other rarely lets it go.

WISE : I had to say, 'I play the part of her overbearing tyrant of a father.' It was a very hard line, but I didn't realise until I came to do it on the show I couldn't say it. And the more I couldn't say it, the more Eric attracted attention to it.

MORECAMBE : This is good, it's back to the human element.

WISE : There is a different attitude; you pick me up, I laugh at you.

MORECAMBE : I know comics who work with straight men and they'd come off and have a fight over that.

WISE : If we started a ding-dong we wouldn't get anywhere.

MORECAMBE : All those things against Ernie were all ad-libs originally—the short, fat, hairy legs, you can't see the join, you're working well, that double-handed slap on the face. They're all based on fear. You think, 'Christ, what's next', and you've got to say *something*. It's all thinking time. Ernie always gets it in the neck and I get all the sympathy.

WISE : We're not brimming over with confidence; we are no more secure than we used to be.

MORECAMBE : We say, 'We've only got to do another three or four years', but in another three or four years we're going to say, 'All we want is another two years.' The clever thing is to make the money while you can and if you can get out . . .

WISE : With dignity . . .

MORECAMBE : With dignity, then get out. If it gets to the stage where we have to work in clubs to make ends meet it will be our fault.

WISE : This is good in theory but in practice you're so stage-struck that you'll perform anywhere. This applies to a lot of people. Whether it applies to us as well I don't know. But in many instances they don't carry on for the money, they carry on because they want to. I think in the long run we'll just get fed up.

MORECAMBE : If we're still on top in another five years I think we'll start thinking of giving it up.

WISE : They might give us up anyway and save us the decision.

MORECAMBE : I think we'll go more into situation. The writing's the important thing. Our life is in the writing.

So, for that matter, is Eddie Braben's. The fact that he is writing at all is a source of joy to him; that he is writing for Morecambe and Wise sometimes makes him blink with amazement. Not that there are many outward signs of a constant inner ecstasy. Braben goes about with the air of a man who doesn't believe in luck but is keeping his fingers crossed. In fact, he is not lucky; he is a highly gifted writer steeped in the great northern mixture of down-to-earth flat-cap comedy and rich flights of fantasy. He relishes his memories of comedians like Jimmy James and Dave Morris, and recounts their stories for the umpteenth time with undiminished zest. He tells how Jimmy James would explain to the audience that the tall, gangling Eli standing beside him would perform a great feat of daring. He would jump out of an aeroplane 20,000 feet above that very theatre, would crash through the roof and then, ten feet from the ground, would pull the cord that would open the parachute.

Eli stammers : 'W-w-w-what if it doesn't open?'

Jimmy James shuffles the bent cigarette from one side of his mouth to the other. 'Yer can jump ten feet can't yer?'

Or Dave Morris claiming to be the greatest defence counsel ever seen. 'Defended Crippen, you know. Yes, I defended Crippen. Got him off the murder charge. They hung him for having his chimney on fire. But I appealed. The appeal was dismissed. They hung him again.'

Or as the greatest lion-tamer on earth—was in a cage with fifteen forest-bred lions when the chair broke. So these thirty forest-bred lions clawed their way out of the cage and started chasing him through the streets. There he was, pursued by fifty forest-bred lions when he found that he had run into a cul-de-sac with a ten-foot wall with these 150 forest-bred lions behind him. Picture it, in this cul-de-sac with the 100-foot wall and those 350 forest-bred lions after him.

'And you think to yourself,' says Braben, 'how the hell is he going
to get out of this and he knows that you are thinking that and
someone asks, "What happened?"'

'What happened?' said Morris. 'I just turned me 'at back to
front, gave a false name and walked away.'

And Braben remembers and marvels at the skill and the timing
and the fantasy.

Braben was born in The Dingle, a poor part of Liverpool. His
father was a butcher. He was a shy boy at school and was still shy
when, as a young man, he ran a greengrocery stall in St John's
market. A shy market trader is something of a rarity. But all the
time he was writing hundreds of gags a week and sending them off
to comedians all over the country. The first one he sold—bought
by Charlie Chester—was 'Hopalong Cassidy's mother always knew
he'd be a cowboy—he wore a ten-gallon nappy.'

For ten years he was, as it were, Ken Dodd's staff writer.

*'At school I was teacher's pet—I used to sit in a cage at the back
of a classroom.'*

In those ten years, he reckons, he wrote some half a million gags
and puns like that. It is a prodigious, mind-boggling output. He
left Dodd because he wanted to do more television work than Dodd
was prepared to undertake and it was the BBC who brought him
together with Morecambe and Wise.

'It is probably a little easier to write for two than one,' says
Braben. 'They bounce off each other all the time.'

Braben still lives in Liverpool. 'There's no point in leaving it,'
he says. 'Anyway, it's only two and a half hours away from London
—if you walk quick.'

The first piece he wrote for Morecambe and Wise, the one that
clinched the deal, was an opening patter spot in which Morecambe
said he had changed his name by deed poll. He was now Robin
Catbush and he had been to Somerset House and would have
changed his sex as well, only the door was closed.

'All you need for a sketch,' says Braben, 'is a very faint thread
to run through it. You've got to have the funny lines inside. I get
boys now, starting off, who send me sketches and they are not
really sketches but stories that can be acted, but they have no
funny lines inside them. It happened that the way I do it was the
right way, but it was more by accident than design. It is a tremendous help writing for two people. Ernie is rather retiring, rather
Victorian. You can make him conceited, pompous, shy or boastful
and it's still Ernie Wise. You can play on a lot of traits.

'Eric is the disrespectful one. He shows complete and utter dis-
regard for all that Ernie stands for. That's where the humour

comes from. If Ernie's pleased with a new suit, Eric will tell him
it's the worst suit he's ever seen in his life. Providing neither of
them win all the time, it's all right. You deal with the same subjects
all the time—the girl friend, the car, income tax. The trick is how
you approach them. It's impossible to dream up new subjects. You
can't use something that nobody knows anything about. But,
oddly enough, the more familiar the audience are with the subject,
the funnier it is. A classic example was Eric going on about his
hands. We've all got hands but we very rarely stop to think about
them. He did in one show : "Think of all the places this hand's
been. Been to some funny places, that hand—Bournemouth, the
West Riding. . . ." It just happened when I sat down and looked
at my hands one day.

'Back home I have a blank wall and I have drawn a screen on
it, a television screen drawn with a pencil. And I sit and watch it
sometimes. I'll see a man walk on and I just don't think; I let my
mind make something happen. Anything can happen to that man.
It's not Eric or Ernie, just a man, a figure. Then a second figure
will come on carrying something outrageous, a beer barrel or a
broken bike. And they just carry on from there. It's as if they did
it before my eyes. It's not as easy as it sounds. But it's a trick that's
worked once or twice.

'Every morning at 8.30 I say to my missus, "I'm off to work,
where's me cap and shovel?" To me, it's like going out into the
road and saying, "Christ, I've got to dig a bloody great hole there."
So you get on with it. You get on with it because you've got to do
it. The biggest trick of all to learn—and the most difficult—is self-
discipline. Particularly if you write at home like I do. It's the easiest
thing in the world to say, "To hell with it, I'll go down and have
a cup of tea and watch the telly." That's why my office is very
frugal. All I need is a table, a chair, a typewriter and some paper.
I don't have an easy chair, just a stool. If there was a nice, comfortable chair in the corner, it would be too easy to sit in it and,
once you're in, you don't get out. Sometimes, when I feel a bit lazy,
I get out the car and I go for a quick drive round the worst possible
slum areas you can think of. I'll go into what we call in Liverpool,
cocoa rooms—that's where all the down-and-outs go for their cup
of tea for fourpence in a bloody great pot—and all the winos are
in there and the poor old men who have seen better days and I'll
go in there and have a look round and say to meself, "Now, take
your pick." Then I'm off home and I work like a bloody demon.

'Sometimes you put something down that you think is funny and
it doesn't mean a thing to anyone else. If everything you wrote got
big laughs, you would become very complacent. But occasionally

you do something you've got every confidence in and you think to yourself, "What a clever sod I am. I've written another belter." And nobody laughs. It reduces you to size. You think to yourself you're not so bloody clever after all, so get back to it and start again.

'It isn't money that you work for. You work so that you can look up and see your kids eating, so that you can tell your wife to go out and buy herself a coat. If I couldn't write comedy I'd probably be on the buses, and I wouldn't be a very good bus-conductor any-way—I'd always be giving wrong change. Thank God I can do it, that I've got this gift. I really am grateful for it. There are boys I went to school with and they're nothing. And I'm here. I still live in Liverpool, but I've moved out of The Dingle to West Derby. It's a nice area, very residential, but not snobbish. I would hate to live in a district where I had to wear my best suit every day, where I couldn't go in the back garden with the kids and kick a ball about. I don't want to change, I want to stay the working-class lad I've always been. Because I can't be anything else and it's no use kidding yourself.

'It's the greatest way to earn a living in the world. I sit there and think to myself—it's coming out of here (his head), down my arms, on to the typewriter, down to London and out of the telly and it will make an awful lot of people laugh. It gives you considerable satisfaction.

'The piece that gave me more satisfaction than anything I'd written for ages was an opening spot where Ernie thought he was going to receive a cup for being bloody marvellous. He honestly thought this and everybody else knew that he wasn't going to get the cup that Eric was holding. Everybody knew that Eric was going to drop him down a bloody big hole. And it built and built all the time. The odd thing about it was that although it was words it was marvellous television. Why, I don't know. People say it's got to be visual, but this defied that. If you can watch it and laugh, hear it and laugh, and read it and laugh, it's the test of any piece of humour.

'I've never been ambitious. I couldn't care less about writing films or novels. The only reason I left Ken Dodd was because I had a fear of television and had to face it out. It happened. Any-thing else that happens in the future will happen naturally, not because I want it to happen. There's nothing else I want to happen except that later on, when I want to take it easy a bit, I'd like to write children's books. I love *Wind in the Willows*. It's not so much Ratty or Mole as the big Badger, warm in his den, shuffling about in his carpet slippers, all snug under the snow. I love Badger.

'But where I am now will do me. I couldn't care less what happens. If I was to go down tomorrow—as far as I'm concerned, I've done it, I've reached the peak. I come down in the Pullman, first class, waiters all over the place, it's sir this and sir that and the compartment's full of executives and tycoons with their old-school ties and it's all a pink mass for the first half-hour with the *Financial Times*. Then after breakfast the cigars are lit and down come the brief-cases and out come the minutes of the last meeting. Super constructional engineers are drawing bloody complicated diagrams and working out mathematical problems that frighten the bloody life out of me and I'm sitting there with a little bag full of stupid bloody jokes probably earning five times more than any of them. This to me is funny. It sums up life, that life is bloody marvellous.'

The precise amount contributed by each member of a winning combination such as Morecambe, Wise and Braben is difficult to assess. Nothing can pin down on paper the total visual impact of a performer, the flicker of an eye, the wounded look of a suddenly pricked vanity, the dashed hope and the false sense of triumph, a tone of voice, an unexpected stress, an accent, a slight hesitancy, a note of impatience. But something can be learned by comparing the script as written and as performed after modifications in rehearsal, at the very moment of transmission.

Braben's script calls for Eric to enter wearing a wig which Ernie notices as he is telling the audience of the treats that are in store for them—'lots of laughs, music, a couple of songs, a special guest singing (he stops and points to the wig)—what's that ridiculous thing?'

(Script) Eric: 'What's that ridiculous thing. It's a great new song.'

(Transmission) Eric: 'What's that ridiculous thing called love. One of the finest songs ever written by Ian Carmichael.'

Ernie recalls all the insults, jibes and remarks he has suffered from Eric about his real hair.

'Real hair?' scoffs Eric in the script. 'Real hair? If it's real, how is it when it's a bit windy it moves up and down like badly fitted lino in a draughty kitchen?'

Morecambe had misgivings about this line and approached it carefully. Apart from its being difficult to say, it was, he thought, old-fashioned in its imagery and would not be understood by a lot of viewers. So on transmission he spoke it very carefully, very slowly.

'Real?' he said. 'If that's real hair—just excuse me one moment please—if that's real hair, how come when it's a bit windy it moves up and down like badly fitting lino in a draughty kitchen?' He then

Warren Mitchell as Alf Garnett
in *Till Death Us Do Part*

Marty Feldman

Eric Morecambe and Ernie Wise

buttressed the laugh which followed by adopting the 'aren't-I-a-bit-of-a-clever-dick?' look that he reserves for consciously clever or witty remarks. In short, he handled that line as if it were a crate marked 'fragile' and delivered it safely.

Eric explains that he cannot take off the wig because he is wearing it as an advertisement. Ernie is shocked. 'You can't advertise on the BBC,' he says. 'Nobody can advertise on the BBC. Even Lord Hill can't say what kind of pipe tobacco he smokes.'

The script merely called for Eric to say, 'No wonder, it's mine.'

What he did say was, 'And no wonder—it's mine. It is well known along the powers of corridor . . .'

Ernie : 'Corridors of power.'

Eric stops, baffled for a split second. Then : 'Ah, don't forget—he walks backwards.'

Ernie laughs and responds : 'Yes, he does.'

The audience, recognising the quickness of thought, laughed and applauded.

Eric recapped his line and finished it : '. . . the corridors of power . . . as quick fill Charlie.'

The script is momentarily lost.

Ernie : 'You ought to be ashamed of yourself.'

Eric : 'Well, you can't win 'em all. Anyway, what I thought—you looked worried there because you didn't think I was coming in . . .'

Ernie : 'No, I didn't think you were. Go on.'

It is the signal to return to the script and Eric does so.

A few sentences later, Ernie falters and nearly loses the thread. 'You see, the point is (pause)—what happens?'

Eric : 'You've got to be careful—the suit drops off as well. What happens is, if you do a commercial . . .'

The 'suit drops off as well' is almost a private joke and goes largely unrecognised by the audience. It is possibly a tag-line from some old story about a series of disasters and it taps the performer's nightmare of appearing on stage improperly dressed. In its way it is a reassurance, one of the verbal amulets they constantly exchange against a world that could turn hostile without warning.

F

8 | *Themselves and Others*

There are some comedians who, as Ken Dodd once put it, are visitors from another planet. They are strange creatures with indelible, unique personalities, who seem to grab their comedy out of some related but alien atmosphere. They do not impersonate or caricature any known human type except, possibly, children. They offer no comment on behaviour, and, like foreigners in a strange country, avoid criticism of the host society. Their justification and funniness lie in their being themselves—like Tommy Cooper.

There are others who watch the world with sharp and darting eyes, alert for signs of cupidity, lechery and the small panics of minor disasters. They relish them, not with the anger of the satirist who wants to shame people into changing, but with the acceptance of a fellow-in-frailty. They do not submerge themselves entirely in the portraits they present but filter them through their own personalities, part-owners of the very failings to which they are drawing attention—like Benny Hill.

'I am better,' says Hill, 'when I'm somebody else. But if I'm somebody else completely I'm not as good as if I let me come through and have a tiny chuckle and a little twinkle.'

His favourite stance is that of the simpleton who is not as green as he is cabbage-looking; his characteristic pose is the yokel with two eyes on a girl's cleavage and one hand ready to dart up her skirt. He is that most innocent of creatures, a stocking-top man, always ready for a stroll through the park on a warm summer's day.

He recalls with admiration the old revue comedians of his touring days during and just after the war. 'One of the joys about them,' he says, 'was that they would go on sometimes until they were seventy and they could still play sketches with girls of nineteen, dancing round the bed-springs with the oil-can and when the maid came in growling, "I'll 'ave 'er too". And they could get away with it! Look how Max Miller could still go on about girls when he was an old man! Perhaps that was part of their attraction —that they were young for ever. When I saw John Osborne's *The Entertainer* I thought, "You got it all wrong mate. That's not what it's about." '

With great tenderness he recollects his adventures as a boy of sixteen who had chucked in his Southampton milk-round in the early years of the war and found himself a job as assistant stage manager and small-part player in a revue called *Follow the Fun.*

'Can you imagine,' he says, 'a lad of that age suddenly flung in with twelve chorus girls? It was "Can I carry this for you, love" all the time. Oh, it was my initiation, it was lovely. Oh, those days'll never come back.'

At forty-five, his face bland, smooth and innocent, he is still able to play naughty lads and get away with it.

Hills's father was an ex-jockey, an ex-circus acrobat, an ex-soldier who managed a small surgical appliance shop in Southampton and hated it. Hill remembers that at school there was a constant cry of 'Hilly's dad sells French letters'. 'I didn't mind,' he says, 'but when I got on a bit my dad left that job and became my manager until he retired.'

His father played a one-string fiddle, and as a child Benny Hill sang 'Just a Little Love, a Little Kiss' whenever relatives called. He also did impersonations of the radio stars of the day—Gordon Harker, Claude Dampier, Jack Hulbert and Cicely Courtneidge. He joined a concert party soon after leaving school, did semi-pro dance-band work playing guitar or drums in the evenings, and comedy in the working men's clubs at week-ends.

'I pinched material from acts I saw at the local theatre. I had many acts. I had a cheeky-chappie act with a sports jacket with checks so big that the co-op salesman didn't want to sell it to me. In another act I wore an overcoat, a flat hat, a scarf and I kept saying "Eeeh, what a night!" because I'd seen someone do it years before. Then I got me mum to get me a collar I could turn back to front and did a vicar act: "Dearly beloved brethren, we are gathered here tonight to make money and by the looks of things we shan't make very much. . . . Will the ladies who want to be in the Young Mothers' League kindly come and see me in the vestry."

'It was ten bob or 7/6 a night, sometimes less. But eventually I was making more money than on the milk-round so I decided to turn pro, sold my drum kit and came to London where I slept on Streatham Common for three nights. It was early in the war and all the young lads had been called up. I was sixteen and was able to say a few lines so I got this job with *Follow the Fun.*'

There were pantomimes in the winter and summer shows in the

summer and touring revues in between. At eighteen he went into the army. For three years he was a soldier, then, fed up with guard duties and crawling under lorries, applied for a job with army entertainments as ASM and scriptwriter. He was told that army entertainers carted round and set up their own props and scenery and that Sergeant Charlie Chester did not want scriptwriters. However, there was a shortage of entertainers and he could audition as one if he wished.

That afternoon, Hill went to the Windmill Theatre where he saw a young comedian called Peter Waring. Waring, it will be recalled, was using material written for him by Frank Muir.

'Waring,' says Hill, 'was the biggest influence on my life. He was delicate, highly strung and sensitive. He always worked in tails and smoked a cigarette. He did throwaway stuff like "A bachelor is a man who's got no children . . . to speak of." When I saw him, I thought, "My God, it's so easy, you don't have to come on shouting, ' 'Ere, 'ere, missus, got the music 'arry? Now missus, don't get your knickers in a twist!' You can come on like Waring and say, 'Not many in tonight, there's enough room at the back to play rugby. My God, they *are* playing rugby.'" I only met him a couple of times and I was heart-broken when he died. When I saw him that day at the Windmill I didn't pinch his material but I went back to my aunty's in Bexley Heath and worked out an act which involved telling a shaggy-dog story about an Irishman, a Scotsman, a Welshman, a West Countryman and a Cockney, which gave me the chance to do all my accents. The next morning I did it for the audition and I was in army entertainments for the following two years.'

There was steady progress after his army service. He was straight man to Reg Varney for a time, did some early television, some radio and commanded a substantial place on the variety bills earning £80-£90 a week. It took the War Office to rocket him into the £1,000 a week class.

Hill was compèring a monthly television show from the Nuffield Centre. It was an unambitious venture—a 'mini-show', he calls it, a filler. On one transmission he picked up a piece of paper and said the following: 'A football pools coupon was lost last night in Chelsea. Will the finder please communicate at once with Scotland Yard, telephone number Whitehall Home Away, Home Away.' (For anyone unaware of the pools system, a home win was indicated by the figure 1 and an away win by the figure 2. Scotland Yard's number was Whitehall 1212.)

It was a simple, totally harmless little joke. A colonel at the War Office, however, misheard it as 'Whitehall, Homo Way, Homo

Way' and became incensed at the slur on the services. The War Office demanded the right to vet scripts of future transmissions from their property, the Nuffield Centre. The BBC refused. The headlines promoted the show from minor to major importance. The War Office said that unless they were allowed to censor scripts the BBC could not transmit the show from the Nuffield Centre. The BBC moved it to Shepherd's Bush Empire and called it *The Services Show*. A few weeks later, it became *The Benny Hill Show*.

Today, Hill writes all his own material. Much of it comes from television itself, which he watches avidly, a pad of paper beside him ready to receive notes. On *Tonight* he saw someone being interviewed in the street. A car went past and a word was lost. The result was a sketch in which a passer-by was talking about television programmes and expressing opinions which are no longer unprintable but, with certain exceptions, are still unbroadcastable. Every time he uttered a strong sentiment the passing traffic blocked it out.

Hill saw a toothpaste commercial in which a halo called 'the ring of confidence' surrounds the mouth of the girl who uses the product, while she tells her friend, who clearly suffers from severe halitosis, how to attract men. In Hill's version 'the ring of confidence' appeared around the girl's breast.

Hill is probably as permissive as he is permitted to be but, feeling doubtful about one sketch he did for a Thames Television programme, he asked an executive if it would be thought offensive. The executive thought not. 'The sketch,' says Hill, 'was based on the series *The Flying Nun* and I played a director of a television series about nuns. The actress who plays the nun gets pregnant and there are still thirty-six weeks to go. Her husband plays a small part in the series and I say things to him like, "How could you do a thing like that to me?" He replies : "I didn't do it to you." I say : "The first week you're here you put your feet through 10,000 dollars' worth of plate glass, and now this. Clumsy !"

'I'm telling them both off and crying, "What are we going to do? Look, if she was the flying nun, we could have got her a bigger habit and no one would have known. If she was the singing nun we could have got her a Mexican guitar and no one would have known. But you have to come up with a swimming nun. She swims from island to island helping the natives. On week twenty-six she's going to sink like a stone."

'The audience froze. It was Remembrance Night and maybe that had something to do with it. Maybe it was because the girl looked like a real nun and not an actress playing a nun. Whatever it was, it was a disaster.

'I really don't know how far you can go with comedy these days. I don't want to do filthy jokes, but I really would like to know how far I can go without offending.

'In general I like to compare my shows to a bag of liquorice all-sorts—I hope there's something for everybody's taste in them. To a great extent I'm guided by the studio audience. You say you are doing it for the people at home, but you are swayed a lot by the people in the studio. If you get coach parties who go "who-hoo" when you say "knickers" and who don't laugh at something a little more subtle, you find you are going that way—doing family entertainment hokum.'

Hill, by both writing and performing his shows, can afford to do as few as half a dozen a year. He spends much of the rest of the time travelling, always with a notebook. He is a keen observer of French, German and Spanish circus and variety acts.

'I once saw two clowns in Spain. They were very good, very strong. The straight man was elegant. It was fascinating because you could see that they knew they were playing to peasants and they were doing all the usual stuff like " 'ere missus, now get yourself comfy"—in Spanish of course—but you could see that they felt they were above the audience and would be off to the best restaurant in town immediately afterwards with a couple of birds. I had the feeling watching them, a feeling I've had frequently, that a lot of comedians could be gangsters. There's a touch of the Mafia about some of them. A lot of the comics I used to know had something of the villain about them—just a little touch.'

The comedian is, in fact, a licensed outlaw standing a little outside society and paid to be disrespectful to authority. He is someone who flouts the rules on our behalf. But, of course, there must never be any real threat. The gangster-comedian reconciles the paradox and creates a safe anarchy that abides by certain rules.

Tommy Cooper is totally free of menace. He comes bounding into our world shaking with laughter from some secret source, an affectionate and benevolent creature, bursting to share his joy and, for the most part, succeeding—often quite unaccountably, considering the joke and the way he delivers it.

Dick Vosburgh, script editor of a Cooper series, has noticed this. 'Tommy,' he says, 'comes on and says, "Man walked into a bar and went 'Ouch!' It was an iron *bar*." The way he says it is all wrong. The stress should be on *iron* not bar. But it doesn't matter with Tommy. He's funny. In fact, doing it that way somehow makes it more funny.'

Cooper is the kind who never really changes. Bob Monkhouse recalls how, when they were both in the revue *Sauce Piquante* in 1950, Cooper strode on to the stage, addressed the audience with 'Watch! Watch!' and then produced a giant pocket watch.

Cooper, an ex-guardsman standing six feet four inches and fiendishly dieting to keep his weight down to fifteen stone ten pounds, mixes the deftness of the skilled magician with the helpless appeal of a man who faces every inevitable disaster with the conviction that next time it will be all right. He has made a highly successful professional career out of appearing to be a clumsy amateur. Occasionally, just to keep the audience guessing, one of his tricks will go magically right, but for the most part he bungles them and so tops the bill and has his own television shows. Magic, in fact, is his hobby and his relaxation. He will practise for hours to perfect a piece of sleight-of-hand. He tours magic shops eager for new devices and tricks. Once after I met him by accident as he was entering the magic shop opposite the British Museum, I commented that it was convenient for him to have them so near each other, for he could get his tricks in the one place and his jokes in the other.

I make no apologies for repeating the crack. His jokes are often truly ancient. He tells the kind of story beloved by the undemanding.

'Do I look upset to you?' he asks the audience. "Cos I got home last night and found my car in the dining-room. I did. I said to my wife, "How did you get there?" She said, "It was easy, I made a left turn at the kitchen." '

It is easy to believe him when he says, 'You can hear a joke anywhere. Sometimes the barber tells me two or three and if I fancy one I use it.'

Clearly the barber could not stand in front of the camera and get paid for telling the joke, so it is not the joke itself that matters. It is the way Cooper delights in it, the way he truly and honestly believes that he has got this marvellous joke which he must share.

'I laugh at my own jokes,' Cooper admits, 'because I have never heard them before.' Certainly his laughter is not forced, is as much a part of him as his craggy moonscape of a face. He gives the impression that the joke is fresh and more surprising to him than it is to the audience.

'It's a good job I laugh,' he says. 'In the early days of the act there was many a time when I was the only one laughing. Some audiences thought I was just a lousy magician who couldn't get his tricks right. If I was playing in a theatre where that happened I daren't walk about in the daytime. You could hear 'em saying,

"Look at that big feller over there—can't do a trick. There's a little feller at work called Jim who can knock spots off him." '

The bumbling and bungling started unplanned when he was an apprentice shipwright in a Southampton boatyard before the war.

'My aunty gave me my first magic set when I was about eight and I loved it. I still love it. I was always giving little shows at school, but the first big one was in the canteen at work. There were a hundred people there and I had awful stage-fright. It's terrible. You can't talk and every trick went wrong. They were all laughing like mad and I was nearly in tears. Afterwards, though, I thought it wasn't such a bad idea and I started to do it on purpose.'

Cooper joined the Guards in 1939 and picked up his fez in Egypt. He did shows in NAAFIs and, after the war, tried to make a living out of it. For a time he half-starved but, gradually, he trained audiences to accept his brand of idiocy and they responded with gratitude.

Sketches for his television shows are supplied by writers but his stand-up, straight-to-the-audience patter and magic—where he is most effective—is all his own work. In this area, he operates purely by instinct, solely on what he himself finds funny. Mostly it works, but occasionally he has been wrong.

'Many years ago I was playing in Cumberland. I got this trick which is called the Duck Pan. It's a big round pan with a lid on it and I had a magical prop called eight spring chickens—funny-looking chickens, eight of them, on a rope. All the way up to Cumberland I was laughing to myself thinking how funny this was going to be. I laughed myself to sleep that night and I got up in the morning and thought, "Can't wait to do this trick." I started the act and kept thinking, "Shall I do it now?" but I kept putting it off until at last I thought—now! And I did it. I produced these eight spring chickens—very funny chickens, very scraggy—and there wasn't a titter. Not one titter! I never tried it again. If they don't laugh, it can't be funny can it?'

Probably his funniest piece is the one with the hats. He starts by announcing a serious dramatic poem :

> It was Saturday night in Joe's pub
> And a happy mob was there.
> The bars and tables were crowded
> And everyone was having a cheer.
> All of a sudden the door burst open
> And in walked a tramp . . .

Behind him is a prop basket full of hats and to illustrate the tramp's entry he grabs a tramp's hat and puts it on. After that, in quick succession, in walks a policeman, a bank manager, a fireman, a sailor, an old lady and several other hat-wearing habitués of Joe's pub. During the ensuing multi-sided conversation he grabs a different hat so that he can 'impersonate' each speaker. He becomes more and more frantic, more and more involved. I've been in the Palladium while he has had the whole theatre rocking with laughter at his total dedication to a ridiculous concept.

When writers provide him with material, Cooper, like Frankie Howerd, hates to see his own tricks of delivery and trademarks of presentation inserted into the script. It confuses him. Usually, he says things twice and once Dick Vosburgh and Barry Cryer started a script for him with 'Good evening, good evening'. 'What's this, what's this?' Cooper demanded. 'I don't say things twice.'

More often than any other comedian, Cooper is said to be able to triumph over material.

'You never,' says Dick Vosburgh with some force, 'ever read of a comedian not being up to his material.'

But, in truth, some of Cooper's sketches have been pretty dire. It may be, of course, that this is deliberately done in an effort to catch the schoolboy sense of comedy he favours. He appears, for instance, as Henry VIII being interviewed.

'Why did you have six wives?'

'Because I got married six times. The first time I was married I was a minor and had to get permission.'

'Who from?'

'The Coal Board. . . . Anne of Cleves was head over heels in love with me.'

'When did you first learn that?'

'When I saw her feet go past the window.'

'You have to give the writers the benefit of the doubt,' says Cooper. 'You might look at a sketch and think "Well, it's not all that funny", and sometimes it can read badly and play funny. Or it can read funny and play badly. But if you don't try you could be wrong. I know one thing—that long sketches are not right for me. To do a long sketch you have to be an actor.'

Cooper knows that he can never get far enough away from himself to act, knows that he is at his best in direct talk to the audience. But he seems to have a yearning for change. He speaks of Laurel and Hardy and W. C. Fields with total admiration, and the point he makes is that they themselves never take part in any plot setting but always blunder into existing situations and keep their personalities intact. He talks with relish of Peter Sellers' clumsy but dogged police inspector in *The Pink Panther*. It, or something similar, is a role he could play to perfection in a television series, for apparent clumsiness which conceals perfect timing is his gift. It would extend his range while allowing him to remain himself.

9 | Marty the Menace and the Cured Mr Took

Some comedians offer reassurances, others a threat. Some are victims and some are aggressors. Marty Feldman is a menace. It is a slogan that should be chalked on the walls of every film producer's office. Feldman's nature was clearly discerned at the BBC, but when this lord of misrule capered into the film studios he was cast as an inept, boss-dominated junior advertising executive. *Every Home Should Have One* was faulted for its frantic attempts to encompass every gag in cinematic history, yet its gravest error was in an almost total failure to project the nature of its star. There were some Walter Mitty-like sequences, but Feldman is not the stuff that dreams are made on; nightmares, perhaps.

A man stands at a bus stop and is joined by this little creature with the broken nose and the wild, bulging eyes. 'Evening,' says the little man. The greeting is reluctantly acknowledged. Feldman presses on :

> 'Nice evening.'
> 'Yes, thank God.'
> 'You're welcome.'

The man at the bus stop cannot understand. 'Sorry?' he says.

> 'You said "Thank God" and I said, "You're welcome." '
> 'Yes, but . . .'
> 'Of course, you wouldn't be expected to recognise me in my present form, could you?'
> 'Who are you then?'
> 'God. Ronald J. God.'
> 'Oh, I see, your name is God.'
> 'My name is God, yes. Because I am God.'
> 'I beg your pardon.'
> 'Don't be frightened—I shan't hurt you. I am a merciful God. I could smite you with a plague of frogs if I wanted to. But I don't want to.'

171

'That's very kind of you.'

'I am a kind God. Would you like to worship me?'

'Not really. I'm waiting for a bus.'

'You could have a quick worship while you're waiting. You sure you wouldn't like to worship me? You could sacrifice a goat to me if you've got one about you. Or a virgin. Goat or virgin, I'm not a choosy God.'

'Blast, I seem to have left my virgin in my other suit.'

'Well, you wasn't expecting to meet me, was you? No. See, I thought I'd pop down to earth in man's own image and have a shufti about—see how things were getting on as it were. I created all this, you know.'

'Yes, I believe you.'

'I made it all. In my infinite mercy I created the whole world. See that number 73 bus—I created that too in my infinite mercy. And you. I made you an' all. I am omnipotent. I have power over everything. I am all-powerful. Lend me five bob.'

'What!'

'I am God and I'm ordering you to lend me five bob.'

'Certainly not. Go away.'

'I shall smite you with a plague of frogs.'

'Go on then.'

'I shall cause the earth to open up and swallow you.'

'Go on then.'

'I don't want to. Not just now. Half a crown?'

'No.'

'I can cause you unbearable suffering and exquisite pain.'

'Go on then.'

(Feldman kicks him.)

'And lo, it came to pass, even as I said.'

'All right—all right—here's your half a crown.'

(Feldman looks at his watch.)

'Oh dear, I'm afraid it'll have to be five bob.'

'Why?'

'It's ten past twelve—Sunday—my day of rest—double time.'

'Oh, all right.'

'Thank you and, lo, you shall be rewarded.'

(Feldman leaps on to the man's back.)

'God will go with you—even into your house—yea—even unto your very spare bed. Go with God.'

'All right, all right.'

'God is tired. Can we take a taxi? No doubt about it, I work in mysterious ways.'

Now that's the real Marty Feldman. He is shattering, disrupting and menacing, the cause of shivers of apprehension.

The things that go to make up Marty Feldman are easily explained but do not add up to an explanation. His nose was broken in Manchester while boxing for the London company of the Jewish Lads' Brigade. He always had a lazy eye and this, plus a thyroid defect, gave him his bizarre appearance.

'It bothered me, of course,' he says, 'but there are very few comedians who look like normal human beings. If they did they wouldn't be comedians. Frankie Howerd is too big, Charlie Drake is too small. The traditional court jester had a hump on his back. Comedy is the way to approval. You can't get the approval that is given to perfect specimens, so you get it another way. The appearance is obviously of great initial importance but it's like when you go into a shop—you'll buy the package which looks most interesting but when you get home and open it, if the goods ain't any good, you won't buy it again. So initially it's a great help to look like I do if you are a comic. However, if the audience don't find you funny, they won't switch on again. A freak only has novelty value. They are not interested in freaks the second time. Comics, if they haven't got deficiencies or inadequacies, create them. Jack Benny created a myth of meanness and Harpo Marx, who was a normal-looking guy, made himself abnormal with a wig and played dumb on top of it. I probably wouldn't have been a comedian at all if I didn't look the way I do. You use what you have. Given a different set of equipment I would probably have made a good footballer or musician. Comedy is what I do, not what I am. I'm a writer and performer—it comes out comically. Vocationally, one might want to be a tightrope-walker but have a bad sense of balance. I didn't have any ability for playing the trumpet, though I thought at one time I had the vocation. It's rotten if you have a vocation and no ability. I have another vocation as a professional footballer, but I have no ability at that either. You get to love your chains, I suppose, and then call it a vocation. I like doing comedy. It's cathartic and I enjoy it. At the same time it is an agonising thing because I'm always frightened, always living on the edge of a precipice. But I don't know what else I would do. I'm frightened of the audience not laughing—I don't mean the audience there, in the studio, I mean the ten million people watching a television show or the audience for a film, because if there's no response it doesn't work.

'Being on television is a bit like being a court jester. In place of the King you have the audience, but they could have your head chopped off just the same if they wanted to. The audience are anarchists by proxy and they allow us to do all sorts of things—break laws, kick policemen up the arse, throw bricks through windows—up to a point. If you go too far they'll have your head off. It's happened to a lot of comedians. It's a precarious existence. You have to know when to stop before the King stops laughing or the laugh turns icy. It's the reason I want to get out of television as a permanent place because your head is on that chopping block all the time. Nowhere else, neither the theatre nor the films, gets the same intensity of reaction.

'A comedian is a man who makes people laugh. If you don't make people laugh you are not a comedian. You thrive on laughter, you need it. When it doesn't come you get into the state that has happened to others—and maybe it will to me one day—a terrible fear of doing anything new. You rely on what you know because it works, because you want the sound of the laugh. Comedy is a kind of *voyeurism* from the audience's point of view. They are watching you being embarrassed, humiliated. It implies a kind of sadistic streak in the audience and, of course, it exists in them because it exists in life and it is always there when you perform something funny. They laugh at your discomfiture and they laugh at your humiliation. The fact that you are only pretending to be discomfited or humiliated is beside the point. You don't want to exhibit yourself in a ridiculous light any more than you want to exhibit yourself during copulation. It is like pornography, like watching through a keyhole. You are allowing them to watch things you don't want to show really. The audience is privy to private happenings.'

Feldman is, of course, aware that he is a comedian of menace.

'The immediate reaction to anything you are afraid of is to laugh, like the children laugh at the bogeyman though they know it is not real. Kids love it and audiences revert to childhood when they watch comedy. In a way comedy's about children. All art is. Gauguin said you must learn to paint like a child. He didn't mean childishly but with a child's fresh vision. We all had it once but we forget. Children like to be threatened and menaced and they like to join in the game. Comedians play out fantasies, but the audience know they are fantasies. They don't really believe it any more than they think it is the end of the cartoon when Tom and Jerry are blown up. They know it is not real violence. I did a sketch once in which I smashed a lot of supposedly valuable antiques. If the audience had thought they were real antiques they would have been horrified and shaken.

'There are as many kinds of comedy as there are comedians. The only common denominator is insecurity. Comedians are not on top of life. They feel threatened in some way and they work out their fears in comedy. Even so, not all comedians are like that—the way Bob Hope works, implies that he is very much on top of life. Comedians are either totally vulnerable or totally invulnerable.'

Feldman was born in East Ham, London, in 1934. His father worked the markets and when he later went into the army, young Feldman was sent to a boarding school from which he ran away several times.

'It was a kind of Jewish Dotheboys Hall, full of rather sadistic masters. But there was one who was great. He had worked with ENSA and he put on school shows and cast me for the comic parts. They were very professional routines, a bit corny but great for kids. I got hooked on comedy then and started collecting photographs. My heroes were Sid Field, Harpo Marx, Stan Laurel, Buster Keaton—and still are. I was taken to see Sid Field in *Strike a New Note* and I've never been quite so bowled over. Nobody else ever had that effect on me except Danny Kaye, the first time I saw him live at the Palladium.'

Feldman eventually went to a grammar school in Finchley and left when he was fifteen after making school history by getting nought for maths. This was very difficult, as they gave five marks for putting your name on top of the paper. He just scribbled 'Can't do it'. But he got 98 per cent for English.

'I think,' he reflects, 'most comedians were pretty poor at school. They probably found like I did that if you could make the kids laugh and defy authority at the same time you became a small-time hero. It's a feeling you get hooked on, something you want to perpetuate. I looked more or less the same as the other kids, but at one of the schools I was at I was the only Jewish kid and it gives you a sense of separation. If you are going to be a court jester you need a hump on your back and my hump was two thousand years of Judaism.

'I was badly treated at school and I found that if I couldn't compete on equal terms I could be accepted as being separate and equal as a one-man minority. It would have been the same if I had been the only Catholic kid at a Protestant school or the only kid with ginger hair in a school full of spades. I've always thought of the so-called Jewish sense of humour as European rather than Jewish. The people I like—Keaton, Stan Laurel, Oliver Hardy,

Harold Langton, Jacques Tati—aren't Jewish. Harpo is. I don't know what kind of conclusion is to be drawn. Perelman is very Jewish and as a writer he has influenced me tremendously. But as Lenny Bruce said, you don't have to be Jewish to be Jewish. Barry Took and Frank Muir are "Jewish" in that sense. Tony Hancock was very "Jewish"—his whole attitude was, "My God, what are they doing to me?" I found my father very funny and he was Jewish. If he hadn't been in business he could have been a brilliant comedian. He had a Grouchoesque sense of humour—vaguely insulting but not really meaning it.'

Feldman was a sort of early hippy in the London of the early 'fifties. He bummed around Soho, played a trumpet after a fashion, was briefly at Hornsey College of Art and was sacked from his job as office boy in an advertising agency. At one time he thought he was a painter.

'I used to write poems at the bottom of my paintings, and John Minton, the artist, thought the paintings were rotten but the poems were good. He showed them to Dylan Thomas. Thomas encouraged me and I got a couple of poems published. I still write poetry, but it's for private consumption only, for my wife.

'At the same time I got hooked on *Take It From Here* and wanted to write comedy scripts. Like all my generation, I'm a child of the union between *Take It From Here* and the Goons. Denis Norden and Frank Muir are my spiritual fathers, which makes Spike Milligan my spiritual mother, I suppose. There is no writer of my generation who was not influenced by Frankie Howerd, Tony Hancock, Spike and Denis and Frank. I wanted to be part of comedy writing, but somehow it wasn't something that anyone did for a living. I felt it was some kind of great club that these people belonged to and I wanted to be a member and didn't know how to get in. The awful thing is that there is no way in. Nobody elects you. You just find one day that you are a member. One of the great moments of my life was when Spike Milligan came over and said "Hello Marty", and another one was when Denis Norden knew who I was. You do these television shows and you never think of anyone really watching them. You can't really conceive of ten or twelve million people watching.

'I wrote scripts but I didn't sell any. Instead, I got involved with various music-hall speciality acts. I did one in Dreamland, Margate, where I was an assistant to a man who called himself "Tayowana from the Rolling Plains of North America". Actually, he came from Peterborough. I had to fire arrows into his stomach and beat him with burning clubs. At the end of the act he put himself into a great big trunk with dragons painted on it and blew himself up while the band played "Land of Hope and Glory". The other genuine Red Indians in the act were Joe Moe who was a Hawaiian, Johnny Myers, a Jew from Stamford Hill, his wife who was from Jamaica, and me.

'I played bongoes as well. I couldn't really, but they mustered every ability you had. If I could have whistled "In a Monastery Garden" I would have been the only Red Indian ever to whistle "In a Monastery Garden". Joe did a Hawaiian war dance and nobody ever questioned its authenticity. We got about seven quid a week between five of us. After Margate we toured the lesser halls and when the act finally folded I teamed up with Joe Moe and we did an act in the Leicester working men's clubs.

'Eventually, I did another act with Joe and another guy and we ended up in *Saucy Girls of 1952.* And *1953.* We called ourselves Morris, Marty and Mitch and we did a couple of *Showcases* on television. Ernest Maxin discovered us and swears that it was a good act, but in my memory it was the worst act I ever saw. Mitch stood at the microphone and sang things like "Tenderly" and we'd do cross-over gags—pathetic ones. I'd come on wearing a solar topee and carrying a gun but without my trousers. He would say : "Where are you going?" "I'm going hunting." "What are you hunting for?" "My trousers." We used to end up by doing "Crazy Rhythm" on two trumpets and drums. We did remarkably well, considering what we had to offer. We used to do impressions of Laurel and Hardy and once, when they were appearing at Finsbury Park Empire, Mitch and I went to see them. They were very touched that any young comedians cared about them because they were going through a terrible period of decline and they were knocked out that we did an impression of them. They invited us round to their dressing-room and put some stuff on tape to help us with the impressions, but it was destroyed when I had a fire at home. Laurel said that Oliver Hardy was the great talent and Hardy, in his dressing-room, said that Stan Laurel was the guv'nor, and though they never saw each other off stage they still, after all those years together, loved each other.'

Feldman was writing all the time and eventually joined the team that was then producing *Educating Archie.* Eventually, he found a permanent—or so it seemed—partner in Barry Took. They had first met at York Empire while touring.

'We had argued about the billing,' says Feldman. 'Neither of us wanted to go on in the second spot after the interval so we rang our respective agents. We were enemies the first day and friends by the end of the week. It was rare to meet anybody under the age of seventy in variety. Barry and I talked about Perelman and the

Marx Brothers and Keaton and found that we had a lot in common. We became friends, though we didn't write together for three or four years. After *Archie* ended we wrote the last series of *Take It From Here* and then we wrote for Frankie Howerd, a couple of radio shows and then moved on to write *Bootsie and Snudge*.'

Later, they were to write *Round the Horne*, one of the most successful radio shows ever to happen during the age of television and, for television, *Marty* itself. Their last collaboration was on the screenplay of *Every Home Should Have One*.

Strains, tensions and dissensions ended their partnership, quite apart from Took's new job as Head of Light Entertainment for London Weekend Television.

Took remembers his meeting with Feldman in a slightly different way. 'He got on to his agent,' he says, 'because we were arguing about who was bottom of the bill. I really couldn't care less. He was a very slender, pale, frightened-looking boy with a wispy beard. I could see that he was the talented one of the three as a performer and we became friendly. He was intelligent about seeing what was wrong with my act. I was dressed in the smart, pseudo-American way, wearing the poor man's variation of the silk suit. He said I should dress as I did for the street, as it was much funnier. So I went on in checks and a cheese-cutter cap and carried an umbrella and I got a Moss Empires tour soon afterwards.'

'I felt much safer writing with Barry,' says Feldman. 'I'm one of nature's collaborators. Barry and I were a good balance to each other. He's also a marvellous editor. Any time Barry wants to write with me I'd love to write with him.'

By the time John Cleese asked Feldman to join the television programme called *At Last the 1948 Show* he was so securely established as a writer that it never occurred to him that he was wanted as a performer.

'In ten years writing,' says Feldman, 'I used to suffer a lot as I watched people doing the stuff and think that I would like to be at it again. But an eminent agent had told me that I wasn't very good. I thought, when John Cleese put it up to me, that I must have another go and it came off. I've never set out to do anything, really. I've accidentally come across something and fallen on my feet. Or other people's.

'I don't like anything I've ever done. I can only see mistakes. I like ideas because an idea is pure when it comes to you and it's never going to be that good again. It's not sullied by the inadequacies of the writer, the performer, the director or anybody else. It never works quite as well as it does in your mind.

'I can only see where I've been, not where I'm going. I see

myself as part of the mainstream of comedy, not as an iconoclast or innovator. Comment is not the job of the comedian. His purpose is to make people laugh, but through his comedy he comments on the mores and behaviour of the times in which he lives. Think of the number of silent films made about cars. They told you a hell of a lot about what was happening to America at that time. The car has become the symbol of America. Harold Lloyd says more about the America of the 'twenties—be a booster, not a knocker—than any novelist. He does in one two-reeler more than Sinclair Lewis did in a whole series of books. Nowadays people aren't reading Sinclair Lewis, they'd far rather see Harold Lloyd.

'Chaplin said more about automation in *Modern Times* than any-one else has done since. People who invent machines expect you to take them very seriously and comics don't. That's good. Comics bring life into proportion rather well. I'm not talking about my own work. *Till Death Us Do Part* reduced the whole racial thing in England down to this ridiculous bigot. Obviously, if you laugh at something menacing you don't remove it, but you can remove your fear of it. You couldn't laugh Hitler out of existence, but you could make *The Great Dictator* which helped us to understand what Hitler was.

'Some of the stuff I do contains implicit attitudes about life or behaviour but they are not conscious. You don't set out to write or perform a political pamphlet. But what you are and what you believe in will come through in whatever you do. I don't feel it is necessary to hammer my political feelings or religious beliefs into an audience but they will come out in what I believe to be funny, even if I don't write it myself. The act of choosing means that I endorse the values inherent in the piece. If that piece is an anti-established Church piece, which a lot of pieces I do are, then the implication is that I'm anti the established Church, which indeed I am. But I don't do them for that reason. It depends on the kind of comedian you are—whether you are concerned with doing the things you believe are funny or the things that you think the audience will approve of.

'My first need is to do the things that I find funny. Secondly, I want the audience to like them, but it is second. If your first need is to make the audiences like it, you will go to the majority, and if majority opinion happens to be that the blacks should be kept out, then you will do lots of anti-black jokes. There are comics who will go with every wind of change. You have to be liked to be successful, but you can't set out to be liked. You do what you do and people either like it or they don't and if they don't like it you get out and do something else for a living.'

Took is tall and burly and after his early adventures in variety, which led to West End revue, he chose to write only and leave the performing to others.

'Tall people,' he says, 'become writers because nobody is sympathetic to a tall man. He feels rotten and inferior and nobody will believe him when he tells them. So he writes it down and puts it into the mouth of the small man who says it for him. He projects his own feeling of inferiority on to somebody else. Ray Galton and Alan Simpson feel as frightened and insecure as any of the comedians they have ever written for, but they can't show it because they are huge, rich men, physically massive and very well organised in most aspects of their lives. How can they say that they are frightened? At some point in the past they banded together as a sort of little league of comfort. Short men find it easy to trade on their peculiarities and become self-consciously grotesque after a time. This is very destructive to their personalities. It's very sad that people will destroy their personalities in order to get glory. It's like a general saying, "Send more men, I have to win a victory, keep on sending more men." You go on destroying men to get some spurious thing that doesn't exist. The victory doesn't really exist and the next day it's forgotten. The comedian's glory is forgotten. They become a myth like Sid Field. Field was a very good comedian and a drunk and thank God he died before anybody twigged it. It was the same with Hancock only, unfortunately, people twigged before he snuffed it.'

Took was born in North London and grew up in sight of the Alexandra Palace television masts. He had a brilliant physicist brother who was a student until he was twenty-five. Took himself left school at fifteen.

'I couldn't be the clever one in the family,' he says, 'so I had to be the funny one. That was how I survived in the family environment, the way I contributed. I wanted to be a musician but I wasn't good enough.'

It was a similar ambition to Feldman's.

'Comedy teams,' Took continues, 'are usually made up of people who have similar backgrounds and different approaches. Look at Muir and Norden, Galton and Simpson. A musician's ear is useful because you hear word sounds and word shapes. There's not one top comedy writing group that didn't come out of radio.

'You cannot categorise the act of creation but you can say that a joke is constructed on known factors. Name those factors and you will eventually get a joke out of them. This is more or less the American system. In *The Laugh-In* set-up (in which Took worked for a couple of months) you are given certain materials with which to work, certain people for whom to write. They have known characteristics and you construct jokes about these people in relation to other people and *their* known characteristics. Pure inspiration usually comes from the mildly and controllably insane like Spike Milligan and Peter Sellers—both tremendously inventive but slightly mad—Harry Secombe, Marty, Ron Moody. Ron Moody inspired is tremendous. I've seen him leaping about the streets of Liverpool with inspired lunacy, producing wonderful, inventive, visual comedy in those dark, wet streets.'

One of the most successful sketches he did with and for Marty Feldman was about a maniac golfer. Feldman himself considers it one of the best things he has ever done. The golfer (played by Feldman) drives and his shot lands in the back of a stationary lorry which then drives off. The golfer follows, determined to play the ball from wherever it lands.

'I was sitting thinking and got the idea and wrote a page about it,' says Took. 'I put it in a drawer, my piece of material against hard times. When we needed a sketch for Marty I brought it out, as it would never make a half-hour on its own and there's no better comedian to play it. We fooled around with it together but it all started from "What would happen if?"'

Though he was a comedian himself and, in a sense, has devoted his whole professional life to comedians, a great disenchantment descends on Took whenever he considers them.

'When I started I just wanted to make people laugh, but ideas change over the years. Comedians don't impress me; I can take them or leave them alone. To go on and on doing nothing but make people laugh indicates that there's something wrong.* I believe that they need to make people laugh because they feel so angry, and if they showed their anger they would really kill people. This is an adolescent attitude, a child's way of getting its revenge on the world. It wants to kill its parents and it can't, so it makes them laugh. I don't like comedians very much because I don't like neurotic people very much. I think they should go and get cured. I think people with colds shouldn't sneeze on me. The comedy writer hasn't got the disease so badly, he doesn't have to posture. I'm mad too, but I'm as cured as I can get.'

---

* Dr Sidney Crown, a psychoanalyst who. has taken a special interest in comedy: 'Wanting people to laugh at you can either be a healthy outlet or the product of conflict, in which case it can be a neurotic outlet. But being a comedian is no more unnatural than being a psychoanalyst, a writer or a television producer. It is natural to be all these things; they express the uniqueness of the individual. Humour is no different from any other skill and comedy may be a very healthy sublimation for a comedian which stops him from breaking down.'

10 | *M. Python's Flying Breakthrough*

Towards the end of 1968 a programme called *Monty Python's Flying Circus* appeared spasmodically and erratically on BBC 1. Its transmission times varied but were always late on Sunday night. Sometimes it overlapped with the *Laugh-In* on BBC 2 and, once or twice, it did not appear at all. The programme was distinctive in a number of ways. It showed animated cartoons of people who looked like something out of a Victorian anatomist's sketch-book and the acting material was unpunctuated by music or by the literary and theatrical device known as the tag or punchline. The sketches merged into each other, coalescing like a series of dream images, or were discarded like half-eaten fruits in a rich harvest. Sometimes characters from early sketches would pop up later, mumbling and grumbling about their roles or the quality of their lines. The animated cartoons showed sliced-open heads from which objects, people and other animals would pour in cornucopian profusion.

The chief performer was John Cleese, a stone-faced young man who looks like a slightly mad subaltern, the kind who in the face of danger can be relied upon either to desert his men or lead them into a stupid attack which will decimate them and gain him the V.C., preferably posthumously. For all the lack of expression in his face, Cleese's head is remarkably transparent, rather like one of those clocks where all the gears and cogs can be seen whirring away under a glass dome. Sometimes the wheels appear to stick and he has to give the casing a good thwack with the heel of his hand to get them going again.

Two of the others, Michael Palin and Terry Jones, are deft young performers, though they are not instantly identifiable like Cleese. These three, with Graham Chapman and Eric Idle, write the show. The animation is by Terry Gilliam, an American.

Initially, *Monty Python's Flying Circus* attracted some attention, though even when put out at an earlier hour—10 p.m. on one occasion—it never gained more than four million viewers and its average was two and a half million. It would be more accurate— if less dramatic—to call it an advance rather than a breakthrough. It clearly derives from the Goons, and though other television shows have groped towards what has been described as its 'manic flow'—and if someone did not use that phrase about the Goons it was an oversight—none has quite succeeded.

Monty Python's cleverness lies in the way it has put to work new television techniques, electronic advances which have at last enabled the medium to attain the non-stop flow of images which, paradoxically enough, only radio could provide in the past.

Cleese pinpoints himself with objectivity. 'Lower middle with pretensions to middle-middle' is how he describes his background. He was born in Weston-super-Mare in the second month of the war and his immediate ancestry is replete with solicitors, insurance men and auctioneers. 'It is funny,' he says, 'how the whole of the *Monty Python* crew came from exactly the same strata. I have a feeling it's a sort of floating group without any affiliations to any other class.'

He has the demeanour of an ex-public schoolboy without any of the arrogance, though he can assume that when the occasion demands.

'I had five years of Clifton College,' he says, 'from which I hope I have now escaped, though probably not in certain aspects. Looking back I see a whole set of values being imposed on me which I must have absorbed and not questioned for at least another three or four years. I sometimes wonder if some of the comedy in *Monty Python* doesn't come from a reaction against these values.

'The public school is valuable in some respects.* Eighty per cent of the people I know—including me—are all ridden with self-doubt and are really very vulnerable. It's just a question of who's got the best façade. I thought it would be interesting to pursue some sort of analysis, though I wasn't desperately unhappy or thought that I had any unsolvable problems. An American analyst said, "Your defences are good, don't mess with them." The moment he said that I thought, "What defences?" '

After Clifton he taught at his old prep school for a time while waiting to go to Cambridge, where he studied physics, maths and chemistry.

Cleese writes in partnership with Graham Chapman, another

---

* 'They (the public schools) should be preserved in order to provide a constant source of amusement for the educated classes, such as meself.'— Brendan Behan

scientist, a qualified doctor. Marty Feldman believes that they work through a comic idea far more rigorously and scientifically than he himself does.

Despite his preoccupation with weights and measures, Cleese entered upon the new world of the artistic and creative side of university life—and joined the Footlights Revue—at the end of his first year.

'I was rather frightened,' he recalls. 'I had had next to nothing to do with anything artistic or dramatic and was terribly overawed at meeting actors, directors and people who wrote criticism for *Varsity*. The way they thought was so different from the way I thought that I was really out of my depth. They would tear to shreds a film I had seen and thought jolly good and I used to get really worried. I had to get them to explain what they meant. The artistic or creative way of thinking was completely alien and I was very insecure. After two years in the Footlights I gradually began to gain a little confidence in my judgment.'

He wrote and performed for Footlights, lifting ideas and rewriting them from such sources as *Punch* and the Peter Simple column in the *Daily Telegraph*. Until a month before the end of his final term, his destiny was to be a solicitor. Then came the Footlights Revue called *Cambridge Circus* which transferred to London. It did not make a sensational impact but 'a couple of very nice people from sound radio came around making inquiries and I suddenly realised that getting into the business was actually a feasible proposition,' says Cleese. 'It was,' he adds, 'a great help that it was the BBC because from the parents' point of view the BBC was very respectable and very establishment and had a pension scheme. Three of us took jobs there.'

The BBC guaranteed him £1,500 a year and said they would find him things to write. He wrote, in fact, for Dick Emery and was responsible for a Christmas treat starring Brian Rix and Terry Scott. It was called *Yule Be Surprised* and Cleese, mildly aggrieved, recalls that some people still mention it when they want to get at him.

'Radio is a very quiet world,' he says, 'rather like a public school common room. There's not a great deal of pressure, not very much rivalry. Nobody is ever really dismissed unless they set the building on fire.'

He rejoined the cast of *Cambridge Circus* when it was revived and taken to New Zealand and then America in 1964. When it closed, Cleese stayed on and joined the American production of *Half a Sixpence* in which he played the cad who embezzles Tommy Steele's money. There followed two bizarre months on *Newsweek*, the American magazine, and a stretch with the American Establishment Revue.

Cleese had writen a few sketches for *That Was the Week That Was* and David Frost had kept in touch. Frost asked him if he would like to join the cast of his new show, *The Frost Report*, and Cleese was happy to return to England. It was then that the impassive Cleese face first registered with the public.

'I was nothing,' he says, 'in *Cambridge Circus*. Other people had more life and movement. But it worked for me on television because people could see what was going on in my mind. I think the straight face came originally from fear. The first time I saw myself on the box I thought it was a ventriloquist act. My lips were hardly moving. Visually, I'm quite underdeveloped. But I really do work out what I'm thinking when I'm performing and somehow it shows. I always reckon that I think with my ears. I'm not very good at observing people but at the end of a conversation I can remember a great deal of what they have said and probably know to some extent how their mind works. But I don't think I know what kind of person they are.'

At Last the 1948 Show followed for Cleese. Another television show about the same time was *Do Not Adjust Your Set*, a superior kind of children's show written by Eric Idle, Terry Jones and Michael Palin, with cartoons by Terry Gilliam. When Cleese was offered his own show he did not want to take the full writing burden upon himself and asked Chapman, Idle, Palin, Jones and Gilliam to join him.

'We didn't really know what we wanted to do,' says Cleese, 'but instinctively felt that the group could produce something. I suppose the crucial thought was that Terry Gilliam had done one particular animation for *Do Not Adjust Your Set* in which a series of things had happened which had no real relationship to anything else except by way of a sort of visual association. We thought it would be much better to do that than to keep on stopping everything with that dreadful business of the punchline with the camera zooming on a fellow who holds a startled expression or scratches the top of his head for eight seconds, applause, fade to black, come up on the next item. Listening to a studio audience applaud is the most boring thing in the world. Studio audiences ought to be entirely ignored, which is what we try to do.'

A lot of people have suggested dispensing with studio audiences, but they are necessary for the stand-up comedian and as a human punctuation mark for the more traditional sketches. There is nothing more dismal than a sketch which finishes in silence or with the forced full-stop of a musical chord.

'We had a studio audience,' says Cleese, 'and were polite to it, but it was ignored. The incredible thing about a lot of television shows is that the directors are more concerned about the three hundred people in the studio than the ten million people watching. It stems from a lack of confidence and the belief that if you can make the studio audience laugh it is a successful show, no matter if it looks absolute rubbish on the box.

'I think one must have a lot of arrogance. You write something and read it out to three or four people. They react and you make alterations, read it again, decide that it's funny and go through a week's rehearsal when you think it is the unfunniest thing in the world. If you don't have that basic belief that it is funny and that you are doing it the right way, if you keep changing it because people aren't laughing at rehearsal, you finish up with nothing. In a terrible phrase, it is an act of faith.'

Monty Python was heralded by the *Radio Times* as a new venture in satire, which aroused the anger of its creators without whetting the appetite of the public. All the same, it has lampooned certain institutions—the army, the police, certain groups such as 'upper-class twits' and certain individuals such as David Hemmings who was compared to a block of wood and was said to have appeared (he didn't, of course) by kind permission of the Forestry Commission.

'The army is something of a communal obsession,' says Cleese. 'If you go along with Bergsonian theory that the human who becomes mechanical is a source of humour, then military people are an advantage in comedy. We use police and army a lot in any case because they are authority figures. If you want to make a fool of anyone it is obviously much better if he is a cabinet minister, a merchant banker, a clergyman, a policeman or an army officer rather than a plumber or a plasterer's mate.'

Cleese believes that the trend of the *Monty Python* show will be to more relevance, which is not the same as more reality.

'People put too much importance on "real" comedy in its social sense,' he says. 'I'm probably a very small minority, but I always thought that *Till Death Us Do Part* was a comedy show and I remember thinking it was pretty good professional writing. Laughs were being got with certain standard tricks. Then I would read that it was immensely significant. You don't have to be "real" when dealing with ideas. You can often say more with a cartoon with enormous exaggeration than with "real" people.'

Cleese himself believes that the amount of 'breakthrough' achieved by *Monty Python* has been exaggerated. 'Shows prepare the way for other shows, and sometimes shows that make genuine breakthroughs are missed. Spike Milligan's Q5 was missed. Milligan is the great God to all of us. *The Goon Show* influenced us enormously. When we first saw Q5 we were very depressed because we thought it was what we wanted to do and Milligan was doing it brilliantly. But nobody really noticed Q5.'

'Watching Q5,' says Terry Jones with (to give him the benefit of the doubt) an unconscious pun, 'we felt almost as if our guns had been spiked! We had been writing quickies or sketches for some three years and they always had a beginning, a middle and a tag-line. Suddenly, watching Spike Milligan, we realised that they didn't have to be like that.'

'When we first thought about *Monty Python*'s form,' says his partner, Michael Palin, 'we wanted something different, but for a week or two we couldn't think of anything.'

The key to the style, they said, was in a cartoon done by Gilliam for *Do Not Adjust Your Set*. It started with Enoch Powell doing a commercial for Daz. A cannon-ball hits the Daz packet, which explodes, covering the countryside with detergent like snow. It becomes a snow scene with a coach and horses. Then along comes a cowboy who holds up the coach. There was another animation which showed a man felled by a falling elephant. 'It was,' says Jones, 'a chain-of-consciousness thing.'

A typical *Monty Python* sequence starts with a stock film of the army showing rolling tanks and troops moving forward, accompanied by stirring military music. After five seconds a roller caption is superimposed. The roller reads : 'In 1945 a group of British Army officers, working deep behind enemy lines, carried out one of the most dangerous and heroic raids in the history of warfare.' There is a gap on the roller, followed by : 'But that's as maybe.' There is a wider gap. The stock film is now of a peacetime parade-ground army, marching and drilling. The roller starts again with : 'And now . . . Unoccupied Britain, 1970.'

Scene : a colonel's office.

COLONEL : Come in, what is it?
PRIVATE WATKINS : I want to leave the army sir.
COLONEL : Good heavens man, why?
WATKINS : It's dangerous.
COLONEL : What!
WATKINS : There are people with guns out there.
COLONEL : What!
WATKINS : Proper guns, real ones, not toy ones. Proper ones. A bloke tried to give me one, but I wouldn't take it. He said

they've all got guns, all of 'em. All of the army. And some of
'em have got tanks. On the far side.
COLONEL : Watkins, they're on our side.
WATKINS : And grenades. And machine-guns. Somebody's going
to get killed. So I'd like to leave.
COLONEL : Watkins, you've only been in a day.

Two Italian gangsters enter, demanding 15/- a week, else they
will set fire to the army. The Colonel refuses, saying, 'No, this is
silly. The whole premise is silly and it's not well written. I'm the
senior officer here and I haven't had a funny line yet. I'm stopping
it.'
Several sketches later the Colonel reappears and once more
criticises the show for being silly.
Later there is a sketch in which a man tries to persuade a petshop
keeper that the parrot he bought half an hour earlier is dead, which
it undeniably is. 'It's resting,' says the shopkeeper.
The purchaser has, however, taken the liberty of examining the
parrot and has discovered that the only reason it was sitting on its
perch in the first place was because it was nailed there.
'Course it was nailed there,' says the shopkeeper. 'Otherwise it
would have been through those bars like a flash of lightning.'
The final line of this sketch is : 'I'm not prepared to pursue my
line of inquiry at the moment as I think this is getting too silly.'
This is another cue for the Colonel who pops up to say : 'Quite
agree, quite agree. Too silly, too silly. . . . Well, get on with it. Get
on! Get on!'
Clearly, the *Monty Python* writers tend to be impressed or, at
least, keenly aware of their own unorthodoxy and experimental
daring. I doubt if the several references to the fact that there are,
indeed, sketches in progress and that they have been written in a
certain manner is due to any Brechtian concern over the nature
and danger of theatrical—or, in this case, televisual—illusion.
There must eventually come a point where the constant drawing of
attention to the absence of a punchline becomes twice as tiresome
as the old-style revue writer's concern to get one in at all costs, and
statements that the general public won't understand something are,
if true, a cop-out and if untrue, well—silly.
Monty Python's Flying Circus is funny because of its attitudes,
its lines and its visual effects; it is funny because it constantly
changes direction and never slackens its pace. The methods it
employs in achieving this funniness are of no more general interest
than technical details about the camera lenses, and for its creators
to draw so much attention to its form can be boringly self-indulgent.

It was noticeable that in the 1970 winter series *Monty Python*, still transmitted at late and erratic hours, though now shifted to Tuesday evenings, tended to get more 'relevant' and, on one occasion, did a notable caricature of David Frost. Since Frost was largely instrumental in promoting the cast's individual and collective careers, this indicated a healthy ingratitude.

II | *Francis Howerd, Esquire*

'Some faces seem to be always engaged in
weeping, others in laughing or whistling, others,
again, in eternally blowing an imaginary
trumpet, and these are the most comic faces of
all.'

—HENRI BERGSON

His voice is rich and fruity, swooping down with relish on a sudden,
sly thought, cracking high in mock indignation and outrage, flab-
bergasted—never has his flabber been so gasted!—at the interpretation we 'filthy minded people' are placing on his innocent—in-no-
cent—words. He grimaces, the folds on that large, mournful face
sagging as he sighs his eyes skywards in supplication, begging that
someone up there should forgive us for the depth of our depravity.
He himself is guiltless. He launches on some anecdote and immediately fears misunderstanding. He tries to explain, he fluffs and
flounders, starts again and makes a worse mess of it. He goes 'ooh'
and 'aah', despairing of ever disentangling himself. Somehow he
claws himself back to safety with a triumphant, groan-inspiring pun
or a gossip-girdled story which he punctuates with swift backward
glances to ensure that no one is eavesdropping on the confidences he
is whispering to a thousand-seater theatre or ten million viewers. But
his dignity is slipping and he clutches it about him, remembering
that he is a thespian—*thes*pian, he said—an ac-*tor* who can dismem-
ber words into syllables with the best of them. He too, has taken
elocution lessons, even if they were cut-rate and by correspondence
course.

Frankie Howerd's floundering is intentional, the 'oohs' and 'ahs'
rehearsed to the last gasp. The performance may seem rough and
unready, the work of a man who relies on personality only, but it
is highly polished and thoroughly professional, hewn out of years
of success and failure, honed on thousands of audiences.

Frankie Howerd, wrote J. B. Priestley in 1955, 'does not need witty material. Either you find his stage personality very funny itself, as I do, or you do not like him at all'.

Howerd himself finds this a doubtful proposition. He remembers a critic who praised him one week by saying he would be funny if he just stood there and read the telephone directory and the next week chided him for using poor material. Howerd does not believe that he could be at all funny reading the telephone directory. His personality can make old jokes shine like new, but he is far too insecure and clever to rest on it.

Fifteen years after Priestley, Bernard Levin wrote: 'Let whichever television service has the wit and the nerve, go to Mr Frankie Howerd (to Whom Be Praise) and ask him, for a suitable fee, to spend the whole of election night in the studio, filling in the inevitable dead ground between results with his inimitable and memorable ad-libbing.'

Mr Levin (to Whom Be Praise) has got it quite wrong. What Mr Howerd says on the subject is this:

'I know exactly what I'm going to say. If I don't know, it becomes very obvious. There's a vast difference between me waffling deliberately and me waffling when I don't know what I'm going to say. I got into a muddle and started to waffle in a Royal Variety Show. The camera showed how amateur it looked, my eyes went. So they cut it out for the transmission. I don't ad-lib at all, but the more times I say I don't, the more people are convinced that I do. Obviously, if you are playing in a theatre and the roof falls in you've got to make some remark. You are forced to ad-lib and practically anything you say would be funny—provided nobody is hurt. If you said "Heads or tails?" people would shriek with laughter. But it doesn't really call for great wit to make an observation like that.

'I once made a spontaneous speech which was worked to the last second. I may have been suddenly called upon to make it, but I knew it was coming all right.'

Francis Howerd was born in 1921 in York, but the family moved shortly afterwards to Eltham. At the age of thirteen he joined a church dramatic society where he played the part of Tilly's father in *Tilly of Bloomsbury*. From that day he decided he would be an actor. He failed his attempt to get into the Royal Academy of Dramatic Art, for which he auditioned with selected readings from Shakespeare and Shaw. 'I was very nervous,' he says. 'I went home and cried my eyes out for about two hours and then I thought that as I was obviously not meant to be a straight actor I must try something else.'

He joined an Eltham concert party which toured church- and

scout-halls charging sixpence per seat and giving the proceeds to charity. Howerd eventually produced it, partially wrote it and did the comedy pieces. 'When I say I wrote it,' he confides, 'I mean that it was mainly a question of stealing things I'd seen other people do and twisting them slightly.'

In his spare time he was an insurance clerk until he went into the army, where he developed his act. 'I took music-hall jokes and in order to make them sound different I tried to think up ways of disguising them, spinning them out into long stories full of *non sequiturs*. In a way, desperation forced me into some small measure of originality. Stealing jokes is one thing, but some try to steal style as well. I can see quite a lot of me in comedians who were looking at me or listening to me on the radio twenty years ago and who have now reached the top. They obviously founded themselves partly on me, partly on the Goons. Obviously, my own style developed from the music-hall acts I saw, though I didn't consciously found it on anyone in particular. I was a great fan of the straight theatre as well, and passionately fond of symphony concerts, so I wasn't just stuck in a kind of music-hall groove.

'And I saw a tremendous number of films. I had very catholic tastes, I really did enjoy opera, symphonies, light music, concert party, music-hall, pantomimes and straight theatre. Comedians tended to look at other comedians and not to be so interested in the straight side of the profession. I think that watching a lot of plays which built up to a good third act—which was the old way of doing it—gave me a sense of climax which I tried—and still try—to work into my performance. There should always be an element of surprise. Most of my work developed from an awareness that people do ramble on, that they very rarely finish sentences and that they interrupt each other all the time. If you do a monologue and say, "Well, of course, um-um, I met this man—funny man—yes, I quite agree, well, you know the sort of man I mean", this is how people talk. Norman Evans used to do this kind of thing in *Over the Garden Wall*. He was a great artist who, like all great artists, comedians or actors, had beauty in his performance, rhythm. He had a kind of poetic quality. Jimmy James had it, so did Sid Field and Max Miller. There was a beauty of delivery, a beauty of rhythm and timing—like a piece of music. Even though Norman Evans was talking to an imaginary person you could always hear the replies he was getting from his phrasing. He produced a personality on the other side of that garden wall without you ever seeing the person.

'I try to paint a picture of a situation with me in it and with people around me who the audience can't see. Very often it's much better that they don't see the other people, they visualise them.

The regular cast of *Monty Python's Flying Circus*: Michael Palin (foreground) with (left to right) John Cleese, Graham Chapman, Terry Jones and Eric Idle

Ray Galton (right)
and Alan Simpson,
creators of *Steptoe and Son*

(below) Wilfrid Brambell as Albert and Harry H. Corbett as Harold in the comedy
series *Steptoe and Son*

I always had a comedy lady sitting at a piano and it was most important that she never spoke. She must be a sort of empty canvas and I fill in the portrait with what I say about her. People are never sure whether she's there or not. When I did radio she often sat there, never played the piano and was never heard. She was just somebody to talk at. I still use her.'

Howerd went right through the army trying to get into *Stars in Battledress* and never made it. He was also turned down by Carroll Levis, the great Discoverer himself. He went in for talent competitions which he never won. Eventually, he joined—unofficially—an army concert party and, after the war ended, was officially placed in a minor concert party in Germany. 'They were,' he says apologetically, 'short of entertainment.'

When he left the army he trudged round the agents, most of whom wouldn't even see him. 'I was a very shy, very nervy boy. It was only by chance, playing a free show for troops at the *Stage Door Canteen*, that an agent heard the soldiers laughing and wandered in to see what they were laughing at. He was from Jack Payne's office.'

Payne put him into a touring show called *For the Fun of It* in which he shared bottom place with Max Bygraves. Top of the bill was Donald Peers. It was 1947 and the job lasted ten weeks.

Radio was then the key to a career.

'The BBC were desperate,' says Howerd, 'to find another comedian to alternate with Derek Roy on the weekly *Variety Bandbox*. They auditioned a lot of people, including me, stuttering away in a cold studio.'

Howerd opened in *Variety Bandbox* ten weeks after he had entered show business as a professional.

'The first three or four months were disastrous,' he admits. 'I wrote my own scripts and the audience appreciation figures were very poor. The BBC said that unless I bucked my ideas up in some way I would have to go. I thought it was the end of my career. I sat down and thought, "Well, there's obviously something wrong, so what is it—the script or me?" And I thought, "It's you. You are being too visual. You are doing what you did on music-hall, you are forgetting that people can't see you. Your timing, your tricks are geared to a visual audience." So I started thinking in terms of vocal tricks only and forgot face-pulling. I also tightened up the scripts. My appreciation figures went up very quickly. Then, after I'd written scripts for eighteen months—I'd never thought of myself as a writer—Eric Sykes wrote to me. He wrote some bits and pieces and I thought some of it was right. Then he came up and saw me and trotted round writing with me. He was brilliant

G

but inexperienced to start with. I was able to help him, I think. He had great ideas for lines and I knew something about construction.

'My popularity on radio shot up enormously. Within a year I went round the halls again, but this time I was top of the bill. In those days this was considered unusual. It brought problems. I wasn't prepared for it emotionally. Other artists had acquired their technique over years. Suddenly, I was a star without the background of experience in the theatre. It wasn't that I was getting too much money—I was, in fact, still on the same money I had got under the original contract which was harsh. The problems were to do with what was expected of me as a performer. I was successful on radio but, like a lot of radio stars, I wasn't necessarily good on the stage. I hadn't had much experience but I was top of the bill and a top of the bill performance was expected. And top of the bill ability to handle crowds, top of the bill ability to handle off-stage appearances and open things. I was a bag of nerves and terribly, frightfully shy.

'The great paradox of show-business is that you have one of the most insecure professions in the world attracting the most insecure people. In my case I was a nervous wreck with tremendous determination. Determination of that kind suggests a certain amount of arrogance. Because, however nervous one is, the very fact that one goes on and does it assumes a belief that one can do it. So how do the two things match up? Nevertheless, they do go together very often—this extraordinary nervous fear that you can't do it and this arrogance to suppose that you can.

'There is an emotional need, the feeling that you have something in you that you need to express. It isn't all negative, it's not all seeking for compensation. A writer doesn't necessarily write in order to compensate. He can partially feel that he has something to say, that he has some talent. Talent cannot be explained by feelings of inferiority. I thought I had some talent because I could make people laugh, and because I thought I had something, I was determined. I didn't know whether the talent was big or small. I was also driven to do it because I was a lonely boy. A lot of people are lonely, are neurotic, but they don't turn into comedians. People tend to generalise that all comedians are tragedy figures off stage. I would have thought that on the whole actors in general and comedians in particular are rather resilient. Their suicide-rate is very low and few have nervous breakdowns or go into mental hospitals. Loneliness and feelings of inferiority will contribute to anybody's drive but it doesn't account for talent. At the same time, I don't think softness in childhood is the best way to bring out any talent that is there. I don't mean as far as money is concerned. Rich children can be just as unhappy as poor children. Whatever class you are, a certain pressure, a certain measure, even of suffering, tends to bring out a talent.

'I was oversensitive and frightened of failure. This is good. It means that I'm sensitive to audiences. But it can work both ways, depending on what the audience is like. A measure of toughness is essential. You must be able to ride over bad patches and bad audiences. I learned the hard way. I learned through failure. I came face to face with failure in a big way in the 'fifties when the music-hall was going out. I was told, in fact, by a number of managements, that I was finished, that I'd had it. I was told that I must consider myself a closed book by a lot of people in the business— people who put on television shows. Towards the end of the period I was obviously tempted to do so, to accept what I thought was the reality of the situation.'

But the closure of the variety theatres in the 'fifties coincided with the rise of television and many people managed to transfer their talent from one medium to the other.

'And a lot didn't,' says Howerd. 'The number of people I appeared with week after week in *Variety Bandbox* who didn't survive is horrifying. It's quite staggering. There were hundreds and hundreds of artists I knew who fizzled out. Tony Hancock was extremely fortunate in being guided and helped in those days by Galton and Simpson. I didn't have a Galton and Simpson. I'm not saying it was anybody's fault. Failure, to a large extent, is one's own fault. At the same time, one has to be realistic and say that there was a watershed, a change in the kind of entertainment. I had been a very successful music-hall artist and the music-hall as we knew it died. I was a big star in radio and radio died. And I hadn't been able to find my feet in television. There was nobody else to blame but me for that. Also my health was very bad at this time. I had a nasty fall from a horse and it affected my nervous system very badly. And I had a lot of troubles in my private life. At the same time I discovered my financial position wasn't what I thought it was. It never rains but it pours and it poured for four years. In 1961, for instance, I worked four months out of the year. My agents put me up for seaside shows but there was only one management who would give me employment—in Yarmouth, where I was second on the bill to Tommy Steele. That lasted for ten weeks and in the winter I got a pantomime, but that was for only six weeks. And I wasn't getting much money. Of course I got into a deep, deep trough of despair and I thought, "I must be realistic. I'm not wanted and that's it." I can say with a certain amount of truth that whenever things have gone wrong, when I was not discovered, when I couldn't get work, when I was told that I'd have to get out of radio if I didn't improve, I have come to the conclusion that the fault was in me. So I started to think what else I could do, what kind of job I could do. There was no great conspiracy against me. There weren't a lot of big fat men sitting back and saying, "Ha ha, we're going to destroy Frankie Howerd." It was rather interesting that during this time Galton and Simpson split with Hancock and asked the BBC if they could write a pilot show for me. The three of us said we would do it for nothing but the BBC didn't think I was right.

'Then, half-way through 1962, my mother died. She'd been very ill for three years and had slowly got worse and worse. My father had died when I was a teenager and my mother had always been a tremendously staunch supporter. My mother had been a rock to me. Her death was a terrific shock. When she died I experienced death. I thought to myself, what does it matter, all this striving? It's people that matter, people that one loves or ought to love. If you are fond of someone who dies, part of you dies with them and your mind dulls and I didn't care. And the funny thing was that as soon as I didn't care I started to get offers. For four years I had been struggling to get with a new management. I couldn't get any change out of them, no help, nothing. The day after my mother died they were on the phone asking me to do something. I laughed. It seemed to me to be very funny. I didn't care then but I didn't feel bitter either. Not really. You couldn't blame anyone else. But obviously luck can be against you sometimes and one can't blame oneself for everything that happens—a car breakdown, getting stuck in a traffic jam. At the same time, you can't blame anyone else for it either. Looking back, I'm really more concerned that the people around me were so worried. They probably suffered. One can bear one's own trouble sometimes. If a man's married with four children and he's out of work, the worry is not for himself, it's for his family.'

The reinstatement of Frankie Howerd, star of variety theatre and radio, both of which were moving into history alongside the silent screen, came out of the new, trendy satire boom. It is another point at which the divisions between kinds of comedy break down and they are seen to be dependent upon each other for sustenance.

He was asked, as he would put it, to do a turn at the Establishment Club. It happened because Howerd went to a show-business dinner, the kind where there is usually more competing than eating. He nearly turned down the invitation, as 'they were all stars and I thought, "How dare I go there? I shouldn't really be among them." '

Among them were Peter Cook and Jonathan Miller.

Howerd made a short speech. That evening Cook, who had never seen him before, asked him to go to the Establishment.

'Having had two glasses of whisky at the time,' says Howerd, 'I would have agreed to go to the moon and it seemed about just as likely. He reminded me later that I had promised, but I thought I would have to get out of it somehow. It was crazy, a music-hall comedian at the Establishment, which was one of the most extraordinary things that had happened in London show-business! Tremendous publicity surrounded this little club; everything that happened there was written about. But I thought that as I have promised I had better do it, though God knows what I'm going to do. I got to the typewriter with Johnny Speight and we thought out some things and knocked out a sort of act. At the end of it I tacked on some of my music-hall stuff by asking the audience to imagine they were at a summer seaside show and I did my stuff with the pianist. It was a piece of impertinence really, because the two things obviously didn't go together. Anyway, I got away with it, it was very successful.'

Howerd went to the Establishment shortly after the appearance there of American satirist Lenny Bruce and talked about the problems of following him.

'They said, you know,' he told the audience, 'that they wanted someone controversial to keep the club in the newspapers. I'm not that kind of comedian. I'm more the lovable kind. I don't do that kind of material. I'm very sorry if you feel you've been cheated. If you've come along expecting controversy and vulgarity and filth, you won't get it from me so you may as well piss off now.'

'If,' says Howerd, 'I had done that act in any other club, nobody would have taken any notice of it. But it brought me back to the press, which is valuable. Ned Sherrin kept coming along to see it and asked me to do a little piece in *That Was the Week That Was* which I also did reluctantly. It wasn't me, really. Johnny and I knocked out a script in about ten minutes or so and I went along thinking, "Well, it's late at night and I don't suppose many people will be watching. You can't win 'em all." It was a tremendous success. Where I was fortunate was that I was in two controversial shows, shows that were news. People still refer to the TW3 thing and say that was my finest hour, which is something I can never see. To me, we just wrote an act to fit the show like I would have done for pantomime. It was as simple as that. I did a thing about the budget, about Harold and Dot (Harold Macmillan and his wife, Dorothy) and about how it was her, not him who was behind it all.

'While I was doing this satirical stint at the Establishment, I dashed into pantomime, *Puss in Boots*, in Coventry. That's typical of my life really.'

In 1963, Howerd played a Roman slave in *A Funny Thing Happened on the Way to the Forum*. Seven years later the role was to be reflected on television in *Up Pompeii!* Between them lie many television shows and a revue, which, though tarted down to West End standards, recaptured some of the old variety vigour. There have been many occasions when he could have fulfilled his early ambitions to be an ac-*tor*. He had, in fact, already played Bottom in an Old Vic production of *A Midsummer-Night's Dream* but that, he says, is very much a music-hall part anyway. More recently he has been invited to the National Theatre and the Chichester Festival Theatre and has been offered innumerable parts in straight plays.

'It's most extraordinary what people see in me,' he says. 'I've had extraordinary parts sent to me. I'm inundated with plays and some musicals, all of which—often I just don't know what people see in me because I can't—it's really quite extraordinary. I mean they are highly sophisticated things sometimes and tremendously intellectual things. You'd be surprised—and it sounds terribly pompous this and I don't mean it to be, 'cos I find it amusing actually—you'd be surprised at the number of West End shows that I have turned down. I mean—I'm sure if I told you the titles—I mean you'd say you couldn't really see me doing that—well, maybe. I've just been sent a Zen Buddhist musical! Extraordinary!'

Clearly he was simply amazed—I mean, well, yes, we-ell, who wouldn't be at the thought of doing something like that?

'Why do it? Why not do what one is really able to do—what one is best at? One of my reasons for my period of decline was that I was getting a bit adventuresome and I really don't think—you see, it's an interesting thing that familiarity doesn't necessarily breed contempt. If I go and see Jack Benny, who I admire very much, I want to see Jack Benny being Jack Benny with his meanness, his vanity and his struggle against the world. I don't want to see Jack Benny in Shakespeare or Restoration comedy. I think it is very dangerous to jettison one's own personality. A lot of established artists do it. They get bored with their own success and want to change. I enjoy doing cabaret work, club work, things which put me into immediate contact with an audience. I enjoy doing television when it's good. The problem with television and films is that you've got no second chance. If I open in a play or I'm doing an act and it doesn't go well I can say let's re-rehearse it and get it right. If you're on tour and things don't go well there's time to alter them. But with films and television, it's done, finished by the time it gets to an audience. That's why they are much more dangerous. At the same time, because one's doing something new all the time, I enjoy it. Funnily enough, it's in this area that I'm not asked to do the adventuresome things. To some extent one can play a way-out part in a film or even a character part that would not be accepted in a club, in the theatre or on television. Maybe it's because there is a very strict story-line and the cinema is a more remote thing. It's not a problem confined to me. Most comedians find this, particularly in Britain where the film industry has never been geared to catering for them. Unlike America. On the stage I stick to my own—I hate the word, but it's the only one I can think of—image.

'Material is different. I'm not shy about trying new stuff, but the old stuff gives a sense of security. When I first do something new it's usually awful. I have to mould myself into it, wrap it round me like an overcoat. It's like a bit of rough clay; I need to shape it, make a face out of it. The problem isn't so much doing new material as getting it. I get through a tremendous amount on television, but to get the right stuff for a stage act which will go in London and the North, for sophisticated and unsophisticated audiences, is very difficult.

'What makes people laugh depends to some extent on their intellectual ability and how sophisticated they are. It has nothing to do with wealth. A lot of poor people have, in fact, a very sophisticated sense of humour. A sense of subtlety, an aesthetic sense, even spiritual and artistic feelings are not the prerogative of one class or monied group. But on the whole, the majority sense of humour tends to be simple, and successful comedians are those who appeal to a majority. A majority gives you a living.

'They want simple humour—done well. You must remember that you are providing a service, dealing with a commodity. People pay you, and often pay you very well—overpay you in fact—for this service. You tend to some extent to say, "Well, I don't think this is all that funny, but experience has taught me that a lot of people will think it is." One's got to gear oneself to other people. The things that I do are *likely* to make people laugh. Likely to. It doesn't always work. I do things I *think* will probably make people laugh, therefore I probably tend to be less sophisticated than in fact I am. If you're oversophisticated people just don't like it, you don't appeal to the majority. So one has to rein oneself in a bit, one has to give what is demanded of one. There are a number of artists who wouldn't agree with this. They say, "I do what I believe in and if they don't like it, it's just too bad." I don't take this attitude. My attitude is that I'm providing a service and there-fore, within reason—within reason, within some reason—I give them what they want. If I wanted to do Hamlet and they don't want to see me do Hamlet then I'd say to myself, "No, don't do Hamlet, they don't want to see me do it, they want to see Laurence Olivier do it."

'The things that amuse me are little throwaway lines, trivial things which don't often appeal to others. For instance, on tele-vision I was going to announce that I would sing a song—this isn't funny but it amused me—and I said, "Now ladies and gentle-men, I'd like to tap-dance the whole of the second act of *Aida* by Verdi.' It didn't receive more than a titter in the studio but it amused me. You see, nobody will laugh at that. Another thing I liked was a piece I did on radio as a Professor Challenger type of explorer who says, "Ten miles out of Liverpool there was a collision between the ship and an iceberg. Very luckily we were travelling by the iceberg. But of course, when we got out into the Mediterranean we felt right Charlies." Now that didn't get a titter either, but it amused me.

'When someone writes me a script I don't want all the "oohs" and "ahs". What I want are funny lines. Often the shape of the lines, the twisting of the lines round, I do a fair amount of. I twist lines around a lot to make them more conversational, to make them flow from me as thoughts I just happen to be thinking at the time. So the "oohs" and the "ahs" which, incidentally, I do very little of as a matter of fact—I give the impression of doing a lot but I don't —are put in by me. When I first started, the technique I used was this kind of stuttery, colloquial, untheatrical language with half-sentences. Ten years later, the Americans discovered the Method. It was exactly what I'd been doing—mumbling and saying, "Well, now, ah. . . ." I was about ten years before my time. Technically, in a kind of way I suppose—in a *kind* of way—if I was being pompous, one could say that I did a kind of Method humour.

'It's partly one's fantasies that come out on the stage, not necess-arily one's real character. If an actor is playing a villain he is not necessarily villainous off the stage. But you cannot play what you don't understand. How can you play love scenes if you have never been in love? How can you show jealousy if you have never been jealous? A good actor has all these components in him, he under-stands them. One takes little bits of one's mind, bits of one's experience and magnifies them, makes them into tremendous eccen-tricities. I don't think my stage image is the same as me in private life. Not at all. On the stage I'm acting. In private life I don't act so much. You often act on the stage when you don't feel like acting. It is false, deliberately contrived. It is false for a reason, false as much advertising is false, false as much as the assembly of anything for a specific reason is always false to some extent. I go on with a headache and I say "Thank you very much" and it's not real. If I was being real, I'd go on and say "I don't feel like it tonight" and go home. It involves acting, but what you act can touch and spring from streams of something within yourself. What I portray on stage are, in some cases, minor facets of myself, of my experience of life, maybe of childhood, which I then magnify into comicalities and eccentricities, little desperations. My attitude to people in real life is not the same as the attitude I show on the stage, but at the same time I've had those feelings in a minor way and I extend them and make a caricature of them. A lot of peculiarities and neuroses can be got rid of on the stage. Comedians epitomise the weaknesses of human nature, never the strengths.'

Howerd's most recent and extensive exposure to the public was as the slave Lurcio in *Up Pompeii!*, a weekly BBC TV forum held, it almost seemed, for the purpose of proving the one belief held in common by all comedians : that in the right place and with the right timing there is no such thing as an old joke. Here were venerable puns, ancient lines, hallowed gags and any number of ripe and fruity references to such time-honoured ambiguities as the relationship between slave and mistress and the purpose, to say nothing of the scarcity, of vestal virgins. Week by week, at an hour when the well-behaved children of BBC executives are safely tucked into bed, the antics of such eminent Pompeiians as Ludicrus Sextus, the Senator, his wife Ammonia, his son Nausius, his daughter Erotica and other characters characterised as Senna, Odius, Cuspidor and Hernia, were released amid a cascade of cleavage and a forest of thighs.

But the sole purpose of it all was to provide a frantic moving frieze against which Howerd commented with twentieth-century knowingness on his randy Roman contemporaries.

Ostensibly he was the cause of all the scurryings and hurryings, the comings and goings, the cooings and billings and the leapings and larkings following such plot hinges as the general consumption of a potent love potion, but he himself was never wholly involved. He was there, the bridge between B.C. and BBC looking back on all those distant and dirty-minded ancestors linked to us by common desires and shared dottiness.

'Greetings,' he would announce straight to the camera. 'Greetings, noble plebeians, crafty artisans and arty courtesans. The bit I'm going to do now is called the prologue and—er—you see, not only is this a quick way to get into the fruity part of the plot, but also it helps me to fill you in with who is who, who does what to whom and to whom they does what to, you see, and, in addition, how, which brings me back to the fruity part. . . .

'I'm absolutely indispensable, that's why they made me the Major Domo. I said *Domo*. Let us have no misunderstandings at the commencement.'

He not only knows who's who, he knows what's what.

'So delightfully chaste,' murmurs Erotica's dim-witted father. 'And so easily caught up with,' observes Lurcio. Erotica wants to borrow the chariot to pick flowers for her mother. Lurcio knows she is going to meet a lusty young gladiator. 'Believe me,' he tells the camera, 'they'll flatten more flowers than they'll pick.'

There are constant references to the way the audience are responding. 'Oh, I'm flogging a dead horse with this lot,' he grumbles.

The format allows him the freedom he needs to step out of the frame and make direct contact with the audience, whom he chides and protects. It is the pure one-foot-on-the-footlights music-hall technique adapted for television. He is knowing and shockable, but on our account, not his. He becomes pained and protective about his viewers—dirty-minded lot, wanting to peep through the key-hole, with him—to see what his mistress is up to with the soldier. He will stop it at once, for our sakes, not his. He is, as Priestley said, fussy. 'There is about him an almost feminine fussiness,' he wrote. 'He reminds us of some despairing hostess.'

The formula has now moved over to films. The first one keeps the title of the television series, but if it is as successful as the signs indicate there will follow a whole series of 'Up' films set in different periods. *Up the Chastity Belt*, written by Sid Colin and Galton and Simpson, deals with the Crusades. If that makes money it will soon be 'Up' with practically everything.

Vulgar? Of course it's vulgar,' says Howerd. 'And corny. I can be vulgar on television, but I'm not any more vulgar when I go into clubs. People often expect me to be. People, in fact, very often ask me to be more vulgar. But the thing about vulgarity is that it is not corrupting. It is not like sadism, violence or perversion. Vulgarity is an integral part of life. The most vulgar people, generally speaking, are children. Children accept functions of the body very readily. They are vulgar animals who don't find anything wrong with vulgarity. I don't think any child watching a vulgar show is corrupted by it. He may say "bleeding" if he hears it twenty times in a show, and if you think that is disgraceful then it is. But I'm not talking about swearing and I don't think the stuff I do is corrupting. Some things can be. I believe in a certain amount of discipline, in personal discipline and discipline in art.

I don't believe that anybody should be allowed to say anything anywhere, because that doesn't make any sense. A measure of self-control is necessary. Drivers are not allowed to drive on either side of the road or at what speed they like. Whether we like it or not there is a certain amount of censorship which we call law. You can't break into somebody else's house and take their money. We don't consider it the right thing to do—it's anti-social. This goes right through art as well. Or should do. So there is a degree of what one could call "taste". The point is not to hurt. Shock occasionally, if you want to get a message over, but this is a vastly different thing. Vulgarity is not shocking or tasteless depending (a) on how vulgar it is and (b) how it's done. That's important. Very often the skill with which you do it can take away the offence. I find a good joke shockingly told offensive. I find bad art offensive —at least what I consider to be bad art. We can only go on our judgment.'

Howerd has reached eminence. He is still insecure, but he is no longer afraid.

'I'm not a bag of nerves any more,' he says. 'Of course, you can't go on in a complacent haze and I'm nervous about the reaction to a new show or a new film. But I accept ups and downs. Nobody's consistently successful and the fact that I have failures occasionally doesn't worry me particularly. It must happen.'

12 | *Loners*

The stand-up comic stands alone, nothing between him and his audience but his wit, his personality and his ego. He offers himself as he is, without support from writers in the background, from feeds standing beside him or from props, though a violin, a pair of spectacles or a newspaper can all be turned into armour at the drop of a decibel in the volume of laughter. The stand-up comedian can be brash or gentle, but the brashest is often vulnerable and the gentlest shows his strength by the manner in which he controls his shakes.

Usually, the older he is the better he is. A young comedian remembering someone else's jokes is never as funny as an old comedian remembering his own, even if he stole them himself in the first place. They reflect him, his personality, his uniqueness. What he is doing, standing up there all by himself, is saying two seemingly contradictory things. One is: 'Look at me, I'm an ordinary chap, a likeable bloke. I like doing the same things as you, eating, drinking and the other, and I've got the same weaknesses—more, in fact, than you have.' And the other is: 'Look at me, I'm unique. I'm different. I'm sharper and cleverer than you and if you start anything with me I'll shoot you down with a line straight between the eyes. You may be able to tell the odd joke or two in the pub but I'm funny and, what's more, I get paid for it.'

TED RAY

His real name is Charlie Olden. He once worked as Nedlo, the Gipsy Violinist. His professional name came from the British golfer who won the United States Open Championship in 1920.

'My father,' says Ted Ray, 'was what you might call an unsuccessful comedian. He came from a puritanical family. His father made stained-glass windows and violins. To the old man's horror my father started going round with a little concert party and eventually worked in the pubs, playing the piano, singing and telling jokes. But when he got married and had a couple of kids he had to settle down.' He took a pub in Wigan, Ray's birthplace, but the brewery failed and the family moved to Liverpool where his father became a ship's steward.

'I was destined,' says Ray, 'for a respectable job. They didn't want me running round the country like a gipsy or a mountebank. I worked for a time as a clerk and eked out my twelve bob a week salary by playing the violin at dances in the evenings.'

He started to sing a little and tell jokes. 'Once, I thought I had broken through to success. I went on in a little place in Liverpool and told a joke. I'd never heard a joke go so well in my whole life —nor since. I worked for twelve minutes and it was marvellous. The audience were falling about laughing. Of course, I came off delighted. The manager came round and said, "Would you mind fastening your flies the next time you go on?" I think it was the most humiliating experience of my life. I thought of sewing them up for the next performance and saying, "There are no flies on me", but I didn't. I just went back to the hard way of getting laughs.'

He toured for a few weeks in a third-rate revue and found himself in Birmingham. 'In those days, pros could get into any theatre on matinées on presentation of their card. It had gilt edges and said ON TOUR and it was very impressive. You may not have worked for six months but it got you in. I went into the Prince of Wales in Birmingham about a quarter of an hour before the curtain went up. Across the stage was an iron safety curtain and written on it, in large letters, was : THIS THEATRE CAN BE CLEARED IN THREE MINUTES.'

A few weeks later, Ray replied to an advertisement in a stage paper asking aspiring amateurs to go to the Shoreditch Music Hall in the East End. He travelled to London by bus with his violin and little else and found his way to Shoreditch. There were twenty-four acts waiting to go on. Some were successful, others got the bird. When it came to his turn, Ray walked on in his grey suit, his violin in his hand.

'Fearless, I was,' he says, 'completely fearless. I played my opening music and I just stood there for a moment looking at the audience. Then I put the fiddle under my chin and said, "This theatre can be cleared in three minutes." I murdered 'em, I knocked 'em stiff. It was like a bomb going off. I don't suppose it would get get a titter today.'

The following day he was approached by an agent and asked to sign six contracts starting at £15 a week. He has been in work ever since.

'I'd hear jokes, like anyone else. It wasn't exactly stealing, but it's remarkable how many scruples you find when you're affluent. You took the jokes and built them up. I also wrote parodies of popular songs. Then there was a bit of violin playing and I picked up a few dance steps. Eventually, I had a pot-pourri of an act.'

Ray snatches his material from the headlines and rapidly scrutinises the subject with the photo-electric cell of his memory. He then links it to an instantly recognisable image, contrasting the most illustrious subject with the most mundane object, forming a picture of apposite opposites. For instance, when John Lennon confessed that he smoked marijuana at a Royal investiture, Ray came up with: 'Nobody can use the loo at Buckingham Palace because John Lennon's taken the pot away.'

Are beatniks in the news? Ray says: 'We have a beatnik maid— she comes in once a week and dirties the place up a bit.'

Ray on mini-skirts: 'I found a lost kid in a big store. "You should have held on to your mummy's skirt," I said. "I couldn't reach," said the kid.'

'A joke,' says Ray, 'is something you kick around in your mind until you get the tag-line.'

In *Jokers Wild* he and other comedians are faced with challenges to do jokes on particular subjects or finish off a line.

'Of course memory comes into it an awful lot,' says Ray. 'Half the time you don't know whether you're getting it out of the pigeon-hole or creating it from experience. We were given the line—"I wouldn't say the film was old . . ." and challenged to finish it. So you say, "I wouldn't say the film was old, but Napoleon had his hand in his trouser pocket." Now I'd never said that before in my life, but what I'm working on is a mental picture of Napoleon with his hand inside his tunic and the old gag that he stood like that to protect his wallet. Or you could say, "The film was so old that the projectionist was Friese-Greene." Now that's a bit subtle for most of them. They'd ask who Friese-Greene was, so you try to make it a little more obvious and say, "I wouldn't say the film was old, but the projector fell over and the candle fell out."

'I always had a good memory. When I was at school doing the school certificate exams every day for a week I went out of that classroom an hour before the other kids. On the last day the form-master came to me and said, "You'll never pass, you've been too hasty." When the results came out I had the third highest marks in Liverpool.

'No comic should ever admit that he's stuck, and if you can't remember one, twisting an old one about is a way of avoiding defeat. Say someone challenges you to tell a joke about a banana and there's a sudden blockage. So you say, "Well, I was in the greengrocer's the other day to buy some bananas and I came out and there was a feller on a bike—no, it was a tandem—and I saw a girl had fallen off the back so I shouted to this feller—as I was eating one of my bananas—"Hey mate, your tart's fell off the tray."

'The joke's not funny. What's funny is that the audience is in on the struggle and they find that funnier than if you had a banana joke up your sleeve.

'There was one time when I was completely stopped, though. I was in Eastbourne in a summer show and, as I'm playing the violin, a very old gentleman gets up in the stalls, walks right past the centre and up the aisle. He is followed by a very old lady, very slowly. The audience notice them and they are looking and tittering, so I stop playing and say, "Pardon me, sir. Do you know there's a woman following you?" The old man stops in his tracks, turns round and slowly walks back to the orchestra rail. My heart sinks. I think he's upset. There's dead silence. Then he looks up at me and says, "Ay, and she's been following me for fifty bloody years." For once I couldn't find a topper. I let him have it.'

After Shoreditch, Ray worked places like Shepherd's Bush Empire, the Metropolitan, Edgware Road, and the Holborn Empire, all number one variety halls. At last, in 1933, he got his chance at the Palladium.

'George Black put me on second turn and gave me seven minutes. Seven minutes! I told them I bowed for five, but they didn't think it was funny. It was a quiet audience. People laughed politely but it wasn't the bomb I'd been expecting. Unknown to me, though, the rest of the bill had died and during the interval I was told I was to go on next to closing for a further twelve minutes. I stopped the show.

'The most important thing is to keep it simple. When they came into the theatres they'd all done a day's work and they didn't want to sit there analysing, they just wanted to laugh. You don't have to be more sophisticated if you move from the provinces to the Palladium. People are the same. Can anything be more simple than Jack Benny's "My grandfather made this violin and my father sold it to me"?

'I've often started with something as simple as "A terrible thing happened to me on the way to the theatre. I drove down a one-way street and there was a bus coming one way and a lorry coming the other. Does anyone want to buy a tall, thin Austin?"

'But you can keep it simple and clever at the same time. What it comes down to—for a stand-up comic at least—is the picture you create : "I used to be a female impersonator till a sailor chased men up an alley." You've got a picture of this feller in drag being chased by a sailor, and if you're a good audience, an audience that's seeing the picture, you'll laugh. But if you get in front of a sticky audience who are not seeing the picture, only hearing the words, you've got to start thinking ahead and deleting, or you try self-deprecation. You tell a joke that falls flat and you say, "That's the last time I'll buy jokes from Enoch Powell." Now they begin to think, "Well, he's a decent feller, he can take it", and you've got them off their guard.

'It's an awful thing when you don't get any kind of response, especially if you are the star of the show. It hasn't happened to me too often, but you can never find a reason for it. I once did a marvellous fortnight at the Palladium. I'd been working with Carmen Miranda and we had no script—we just went on and started talking. She was a great ad-libber. Then I went to Derby. It was a fair bill and there I was, Ted Ray, direct from his success at the London Palladium, and I died twelve times that week. A few months ago I went to Derby for a one-night stand and killed 'em. So either I've improved or they have.

'I don't think it's possible for an audience to laugh at you without liking you. But it's got to come naturally. To go on and plead to be liked is sick-making. The only time they'll laugh at someone they don't like is when he's very blue. Then they will laugh and come out and say, "That was terrible!"

'I could never be blue, even if I wanted to. For ten years I was in *Ray's a Laugh* on radio, the ordinary family man. When I went into the theatres, people brought their children to see me.'

The decade of *Ray's a Laugh* roughly coincided with the decline of the variety theatre.

'I never really thought they would close, but when the closures came you could see why. They were giving up the ghost. Instead of having eight different acts, they'd put on one star and three acts doing two appearances each. The variety had gone. The final blow came when they put on the strip and drag shows. They brought in a few people who liked that sort of thing, but when they tried to get back their family audiences they found they had lost them.

'The quality of humour today has deteriorated immensely. Even twenty years ago you'd get four comedians on a bill and on a Monday night you were never in your dressing-room. You were watching all the other comics to see if they would use "bloody". It was the way you pointed your strongest gag and if it was used once it couldn't be used again.'

Ray, like most comedians, loves the lore of the stage, loves recalling stories like the one about the old pro who was asked 'Is variety
dead?' and sighed 'Shouldn't be surprised. It was very ill when I
was in Barnsley last week.' Or the time when Robb Wilton slipped
across to the pub for a drink between houses and was recognised by
the landlord. 'Robb Wilton, isn't it?' Wilton was pleased at being
recognised and nodded. 'Seen 'em all,' said the landlord, 'George
Robey, Harry Tate, Little Titch, the White-Eyed Kaffir—none of
'em made me laugh and I'm damned sure you won't either.'

'It's when you get an audience made up of landlords like that,'
says Ray, 'that the job of the stand-up comic becomes the hardest
in the world. And I don't say that because I am one. Sometimes it
gets very lonely up there. That's why I always take the fiddle with
me. It's been a great prop for me, it lets me retire with dignity.'

But the real stand-up comic, whether in full, fearless flush or
battling against a cold, hard audience, could never leave it like
that, could not end on a note that seemed to suggest that dignity is
the most important thing. It would be the wrong picture. The joke
was clearly there, being 'kicked around in the mind' waiting for
the right, rueful tag-line to swim up out of the past, to arrive, by
some kind of natural selection, out of the long experience.

'Sometimes,' says Ray, 'you don't want applause, you want a
ten-yard start.'

TOMMY TRINDER

You let Tommy Trinder speak for himself. You have little option.

'Sometimes,' he says, 'my wife says, "Don't you ever stop talking?"
And I say, "If I stop talking, we stop eating." The strange thing
is that when I'm working to an audience I have no idea why I say
a certain thing. I can really talk without thinking. Something comes
to me and I say it. Some of the ad-libs have been good so I try to
keep them in. I've got a quantity of stock ad-libs. The thing that
gets me is when I hear my own ad-libs being cracked by somebody
else. I say it's a wise crack that knows its own father. Years ago,
when I was a lot thinner in the face, my chin protruded a lot more
than it does now and I used to crack a gag about going to a race
meeting and a woman looked at me side-faced and said, "Didn't I
back you at Newmarket?" I would thrust my chin out and show
the profile. I heard it used by a comic who had a face as round as
Oliver Hardy's. I thought, "Stupid man, why crack a gag that
doesn't fit you?"

'I have a very active mind, inasmuch as what I'm saying now I
thought of seconds ago and my mind is active on the next subject.

That is one of the reasons I find it difficult to learn a song. I cannot concentrate long enough to say "Now what's the next line" because I'm thinking that somebody has moved, somebody has opened a box of chocolates. You think of a gag you could have cracked and then you think "Oh my goodness, what's the next line of the song?" Otherwise I might have been in opera. And starved.

'I read the papers. I do not read books. I read autobiographies if Trinder is mentioned in the index. But I'm a great newspaper reader. I've discovered that audiences do not assimilate the news. I tried an experiment in a club once. I read the morning newspaper and cracked gags that night about the news. They didn't mean anything. Two nights later I cracked a gag about something that was in the papers two days before and it got a big laugh. You can be more topical than your audience. I was playing the Embassy Club in Bond Street and I read in the paper that evening that Rita Hayworth had divorced Orson Welles. When I got to the club Orson Welles is in, sitting right at the ringside, being very noisy, making a bit of a nuisance of himself. Most of the people in the show were complaining. Now, in cabaret, when I go on I say "Good evening, my name is Trinder" and I hand out photographs to various people. I got to Orson Welles and said, "Good evening, my name is Trinder", and Welles said, "Why don't you change it?" I said, "You proposing marriage already?" It's not the quality of the ad-lib as much as the speed with which it is said.

'When the late King and present Queen Mother were Duke and Duchess of York she received the Freedom of the City of Edinburgh. I was invited with Max Wall and Larry Adler to the show as part of the festivities. The following year Edward abdicated and the Duke of York became King. Years later, during the war, I'm invited to Windsor to do a show for the Royal Family. They didn't live in the castle but a place called Adelaide Cottage. Cottage! If you built a cottage like that you'd be pinched for ribbon development! Anyway, I'm out on the lawn there and I do the show. Afterwards, I'm presented to the King. He puts his arm round my shoulder. His manner was so familiar, his face was so familiar that I felt that here was somebody I've known all my life. And he said, "Tommy"—he called me by my first name which, let's face it, pleases your ego a little—he said, "Tommy, you know it's wonderful to be able to laugh in times such as these." And I said, "Well, sir, the last time I had the honour to entertain you was eight years ago in Edinburgh." He said, "Yes, I remember it very well. You've climbed very high since those days, haven't you?" I said, "Well, you ain't done so bad yourself."

'Now I'd no idea I'd said it. It was just a retort. I thought he was going to have hysterics. Buckingham Palace put out the story to the newspapers and two weeks later I was invited back.

'I was the first man ever in show-business to have my own posters all round London. There were huge hoardings saying: IF IT'S LAUGHTER YOU'RE AFTER, TRINDER'S THE NAME. YOU LUCKY PEOPLE! Then I was offered a site opposite Aldgate Station. I thought that if I was going to put one up there it ought to be in Hebrew, so I asked the *Jewish Chronicle* for help and they sent along someone who translated it for me.

'On June 5th, 1971, I'll have been on the stage for fifty years. I always say I'm the youngest veteran in show-business. I was born in 1909 and I had to get a magistrate's licence to leave school and go on the stage. I was twelve. I was a boy singer. I was an extrovert. I always wanted to be the best. As a kid I played football and if I couldn't be captain I'd take the ball back. I was in the wolf cubs and had to be a sixer. There's always been that drive. Today, the business is still a challenge. I don't want the money and I don't· want the work. But I see someone and I feel "I can do better than that, why aren't I doing it?" I'm driving myself all the time because I feel that once I let it go, I'm gone, I'm sunk.

'I won a singing competition at the Collins Music Hall, Islington. Across the road at the Islington Empire was a juvenile show called *Casey's Court*, run by Will Murray. He asked me if I'd like to join his show and arranged with my mother and father that I would get 7/-6 a week and my keep. That was a godsend to my people and they couldn't get me packed off quick enough. 7/-6 was the rent of the house. My father was a tram-driver. I opened at the Palace Theatre, Oldham, all clogs, shawls and cobblestones. My mother stitched a pound note into the lining of my jacket so that I would have the fare home if things went wrong. That jacket was ripped open before I got to Crewe. My job was to cut bread for the boys and we slept four in a bed. I was about sixteen before I realised that people slept longways. I was one of the first mammy singers. One of my songs was "What is a Mammy, Daddy? Everyone's Got One But Me". Later I joined an act called Phil Rees's Stable Lads and we worked the *Folies Bergère* in Paris for a year. There was a gag I cracked privately: I had to leave because I used to get so hungry—I was breast-fed. We didn't have a permissive society in those days and it was quite a novelty. At my height I used to brush past them in the corridors. I started building up the comedy when I left and I did a lot of working men's clubs on my own. I worked with all the top variety acts and took the best laugh out of each of them. They were always the dirty ones. Every comic

had one dirty gag that he used to punch them between the eyes
with, so I had a right collection. I had the filthiest act in show-
business and I wore more make-up than Grock. I was fifteen or
sixteen at the time and I had to look older to suit the type of
material I was using.

'I was a Jack of all trades. I never decided to be a comedian, it
was just that comedy became predominant.

'There are two essentials in comedy : timing and confidence. You
walk out there and you must prove to the audience that, irrespec-
tive of what they think or what happens, you are the guv'nor. I have
seen comedians entertaining a hard audience. They crack their gag
and nothing happens. Their timing goes and they start pressing.
It's a lesson you learn from golf. Once you start pressing, your
game goes. So you say to yourself "All right, you'll come round in
a minute" and you try different things. They say the Savoy Hotel's
the comics' graveyard. I go there twice a year. You see a dowager
duchess looking at you as if to say "What's this?" You look back
and say, "Hello, madam. And the food's no good either, is it?" You
see someone who seems to be intrigued with the act and you tell
them, "You'd better get on with your food, you can't expect them
to warm it up twice." Of course, you get complaints from the
management, but who cares about that? I'm always getting complaints from managements. One thing about it, the complaints are
universal. I get them from the customers and the waiters as well. I
went on one night and said, "I've just got back from Australia. I love
Australia. With the Australian accent, it's the only place in the
world where I sound refined." So four Australians complain. One
night during the Cyprus crisis a waiter dropped a tray. I said, "Any
more of that and I'll report you to Makarios." He said, "I'm not
Cypriot, I'm Greek." He got into trouble and to save his job I had
to say I had arranged for him to say it.

'I try to encourage chat from the audience. I say, 'Well, now,
before I declare the meeting closed are there any questions?" And
you get them at you. I always get the last word. Except once. I'm
playing the Palladium, and at the Empire, Leicester Square, is one
of my films called *The Bells Go Down,* in which I was a London
fireman in the Blitz who gets killed at the end of the picture. A
man and woman walk in late at the Palladium and I say, "You're
very late, sir. This is a live show, not a cinema. But if you want to
go and see a good film, you want to go to the Empire, Leicester
Square." The man said, "No thanks, I prefer to see you die here."
I had to turn round to the audience and say "Take no notice, it's
Max Miller made up to look like a gentleman", but I must admit
my retort wasn't as good as his. That was the best ever pulled on

me. Obviously he had seen the picture, obviously he was a fan and obviously he had a great sense of humour.

'Everything that you see, everything that happens to you can be used. I fell off the stage once in Australia, so I'm giving my performance in evening dress on crutches and you can see that I've got a foot in plaster with a pad underneath it. The compère introduces me and on I walk. After a while, I find I can stand on one crutch so, quite accidentally, I say to the compère, "Hey, would you hold my crutch!" Now this gets a laugh and I say, "I took a chance there. By the way, I did this the first week I was here—can you imagine?—broke my leg in Australia! That's after paying national health insurance for thirty years in England!" This gets a laugh. It's really a statement of fact and it's a thing you think of.

'One night I pull up my trouser-leg to show the plaster right up to my knee and I say, "What do you think of this?" And a woman out of the blue said, "I think it's beautiful." I said, "You think that's beautiful? You must be having an affair with a wicket-keeper." But why I said it I don't know except that, to me, it looked like a cricket pad.

'Then I cracked a gag where I said, "Well, it's a status symbol, really. I came out as a single act and look, I've got a full supporting cast." Now the audience reacts by groaning like they always do with a pun, so I turn round and say, "Do you think I broke my bloody leg just to crack that?" Which gets a bigger laugh than the original.

'These are mostly statements of fact. I say the thing the other feller would've said if he had thought of it in time. I've often said to an audience, "What sort of a mentality must a man have to think of a joke like that?" I see the funny side of most things. When I was in South Africa recently, I opened at Kimberley and the locals took us to the showplace, the diamond mine which they call the Big Hole. That night, with this very fresh in my mind, I walk on the stage and said, "I've had a look round Kimberley, saw the Big Hole. Tried to buy it. Wanted to take it back to England. Put the Labour Government in it." Well, I was amazed at the reaction. They cheered me and this became a permanent part of the act. I had found a little jewel in this opening gag. I cracked it at every performance in South Africa and it never failed.

'Well, I got to Cape Town and we played in a theatre exclusively for coloured people. I've never let known my feelings on the apartheid question in South Africa, inasmuch as I feel I'm a guest in a country. Well, I wouldn't go to a man's house and criticise the cooking. It's the same when I go abroad. I see things I approve of and things I disapprove of. The thing that amused me there was that the South Africans classify a Chinaman as coloured and a Japanese as white. I used to ask, "How do you tell a Chinaman from a Jap?" and I said, "It's easy. You throw him a pair of socks—if he washes them he's Chinese and if he juggles them he's Japanese." Anyway, we played this coloured theatre and, I must say, the audience was fantastic, very demonstrative, I think one of the things that helped was that as I was compèring the show I would come on after the overture, introduce myself and, as usual, talk to the latecomers with "Good evening, sir", "Good evening, madam, you're very late. We started without you. Is that all right?" This is purely habit. What I didn't realise was that a European standing on the stage and calling coloured people "sir" and 'madam" was something they weren't used to and they thought it was wonderful. So I got to my opening gag about putting the British Government in the Big Hole. And there was a stony silence. I suddenly realised that the coloured people loved the Labour Government. They are the only people in South Africa who did. So I thought, "Oh, my goodness, this has flopped", and very quickly I said—I mean, self-preservation is the first law of nature—I quickly said, "Oh, ha ha, I'm sorry. That's the gag I crack for the white trash." That went bigger than the original gag ever went.

'Back here you've got to be careful about coloured gags. One gag isn't too bad, but you suddenly find you are using four or five and unconsciously you're becoming a bit racialistic. You'll go on and say to the musical director, "How are you?" Then turn to the audience and say, "He wasn't too good, he had a blackout last night. He's taking her out again tonight." Then a couple of minutes later you say, "Twenty-five Pakistanis came in to Felixstowe today —disguised as an oil-slick." Now these gags are not dirty and you are using them because they're topical, but you suddenly start thinking, "I mustn't do this." People could object and they'd be perfectly justified in thinking you're a bit racialistic. If there's one coloured person out there I'm going to upset him. And while any of the gags are not objectionable by themselves, collectively they are.

'Gags pile up without you noticing. I'm talking about a man going to a psychiatrist and I'm doing all the shakes and bumps and I say, "I hope nobody walks in late, they'll think I'm Tom Jones." And, then I say, "You know, this is very difficult, particularly when you've got a second-hand truss." It gets a laugh so I go on to say, "Well, of course I can never do this gag on a rainy night. It squeaks." Before you know where you are, you are doing a routine about a truss and you think, "What the hell did I start that for?" You've added one to another. Whilst they're laughing—naturally, you don't talk on a laugh—your mind's active and you're thinking. You're not taking any notice of the laugh, it's breathing space.

'I never write anything down, but people don't believe that I work like this. I'm playing Rangoon during the war and every light in the city goes out. I start off by striking a match, then get a hurricane lamp and do a routine about the lights going out. When I've finished a colonel comes up to me and says, "I say, Trinder, that was a funny gag when you got them to turn all the lights out."

'When I started I always said I'd do the kind of act they would book at the Palladium. So I always wore a lounge suit. At some of the provincial places I played they'd say "The show's got no comic" because they thought the only kind of comic was a man in funny clothes. The format in those days was that you did three songs. My act consisted of a verse and chorus of a song, then some patter, then a chorus to finish the first number on. Then I came on and did an Egyptian burlesque. I'm double-jointed and I used to do all this Egyptian dancing with two saucepan lids. Then I'd change and come back and do an eccentric dance. In those days I was one of the fastest Charleston and eccentric dancers in the country.

'I was second turn on after the knife-throwers or jugglers, did twelve minutes, got £12. Nobody knew who Tommy Trinder was, nobody knew what I did, so I used to walk on and say, "Good evening. My name is Trinder. I'm going to sing for you. Ha, you lucky people!" That was typical of the next twelve minutes, brash, cheeky, self-confident. It was purely through trying to establish in the first thirty seconds what you were going to do. Then came the latecomers and that started me off ad-libbing. I used to show people to their seats and chase around trying to build up an act. We didn't have any scriptwriters. I used to eat, sleep and drink show-business.

'I don't want to offend anybody. If I see a clergyman sitting in the audience it throws me. I don't even want to say "blimey" in case it upsets him. And I'm an agnostic!

'I do quite a few Jewish gags and I speak a bit of Yiddish. I always tell the people, though, that I'm a yock. And I never say anything detrimental. Dr Herz once said that if people tried to understand Jewish people as much as Tommy Trinder did, there'd be no anti-Semitism in the world. So I'm doing a show for Ajex, the Jewish Ex-Servicemen's outfit at the Empress Hall, Earls Court. It seats about twenty thousand people and I've got limes all round.

One of the limes keeps going off me and I say, "You know his trouble, he's anti-yock." A couple of days later I got a letter from a rabbi who said : "I was amazed at your knowledge of Yiddish. But I would like to point out one mistake you made. You referred to yourself as a yock. The term 'yock' is used in a derogatory manner about non-Jews. You are a goy and, if I may say so, a good goy." I wrote back : "Thank you very much. I would like to point out that my knowledge of Yiddish has been picked up from my many Jewish friends. They always refer to me as a yock and as they know me a lot better than you do, I am a yock and not a goy."

'There's a strange thing that's happened only recently. In the days of the theatre the audiences were strangers to each other. Someone would heckle and you'd come back at him and he was always the butt of your joke. The audience were on your side. But now you've got the clubs. Charlie is the club comic and Charlie heckles you and you beat him down in flames. But the audience object to this. "That's our Charlie," they say. "He can't do that to him." It's become a different technique now. You mustn't insult Charlie. Some of these clubs are unbelievable. You've got no standards any more. The only one I've got is when an agent rings me up and I say "How much?" If they can afford to pay my price it's a club worth going to. There was a girl, a famous singer I'm very fond of, singing in one club and there was a bit of noise at the back. The chairman says, "Quiet, why don't you give the poor old cow a chance." This is soul-destroying. I was in a club once where I asked "Am I on next?" and they said, "No, we gotta game of bingo first." So I'm standing on the side and the caller starts : "Eyes down, All the Jews, 22, All the fours, 44. Fuck me! All the eights, 88."

'And I've got to follow this. I couldn't resist it. I poked my head round and said, "Will you keep that child quiet please."

'I worked a beautiful club once and there's a girl singer on the bill. One night I took the trouble of counting. She said seventeen bloodies, six buggers and four fucks. This is a woman! With a mixed audience! How do you follow that?

'The clubs book quantity. They book an artist, pay him a lot of money and tell him to do an hour. The singers can't sing for an hour so they crack jokes and crack them badly and they kill them for the man who's coming in next week who relies on jokes. The clubs are getting dirtier. It's a question less of humour than of shock. It's like a stag-party where someone starts off in a mild way and then each one will try to top the other. I was sitting in a club with the proprietor when a woman came on and she cracked material that would have disgusted me if a man had cracked it. "Good gracious, listen to this," I said to the proprietor. He said, "They like it, don't they?" I said, "They're more shocked than amused." But he couldn't make out what the objection was. Me, I'll compete with anybody, but not in an offensive way.

'The only time I was knocked speechless was when I was President of the Lords Taverners and I had to go to Buckingham Palace to talk to the Duke of Edinburgh and Mike Parker about a cabaret. The Duke always takes part. And I go down to see them and we sit and talk and I'm pattering away, never stopping, and the Duke of Edinburgh says, "Look, I've got some work to do, you'll have to be going." So they take me out and I'm just going to leave when I say, "Oh, I must tell you . . ." And the Duke of Edinburgh says, "Why don't you piss off?" I said, "It's a nice way to be shown out of Buckingham Palace." But it was the one time I was really speechless.'

And it hasn't happened since.

BOB MONKHOUSE

Bob Monkhouse has no discernible hump. He is neither fat nor thin, neither tall nor short. His nose is straight and his chin is irreproachable. No folds of flesh droop under mournful eyes and he has neither the defiant cockiness of a Rolls-Royce-owning sprig of the working classes, nor the doom-haunted aura of one to whom everyone and everything is actively hostile. He bears no memories of racial oppression or economic exploitation, looks younger than his years and is darkly handsome. In short, as a comedian, he has everything against him.

He is a dedicated pursuer of the pun, the quip, the gag, the crack, the one-liner. He seems more self-confident than a High Court judge. 'Yet,' observes a friend, 'Bob can walk into a room where thirty people are sitting, twenty-nine of them actively liking and admiring him, and spend the whole evening trying to win over the thirtieth.'

'That *was* a shrewd observation,' says Monkhouse, hammering heavily at the past tense. 'It stopped quite recently, within the last four or five years. There is some point of maturity when you enter a room and think not "Will these people like me?" but "Will I like these people?" I think I crossed that invisible line when I found the authority to go on stage to an audience that didn't like me, do everything I knew to win them and, having failed, leave the stage thinking we were ill-met—but that's all. To know, without the slightest shadow of doubt in my mind, that it was purely a bad engagement for both of us—as much a shame for them as it was for me.

'But every comedian has a feeling of insecurity—and therefore aggression—to some extent, or there wouldn't be the endless search for love and approval as evidenced by applause and money.'

Monkhouse's father was chairman of the family firm of Monk and Glass, custard-makers. 'I was brought up in an atmosphere of "Some day, son, all this custard will be yours." I suppose I didn't like the feeling of so much security and the prospect of so much corn-flour.'

He was born in Beckenham, Kent—not, as he says, the usual comedian's background. 'My deep feelings of insecurity,' he says, 'go back as far as I can remember. I wonder whether I was animated by my mother's tremendous coolness? She was never a demonstrative woman and was always very stoical in the face of pain or worry. She and my father seemed to have reached an agreement—almost, I would have thought, before I was born—that they would demonstrate very little to each other by way of affection but would get on extremely well. My brother, who is an accountant and with whom I'm not close, is rather like my father and mother in that he is not a demonstrative man. So, plumped down in the middle of this, with a very emotional nature and attempting to keep it within the strait-jacket of Beckenham, where you didn't shout or laugh out loud—it was vulgar—I always had great difficulty in expressing my emotions.

'I got a terrific flash of parallel when I was reading *Catch 22* and Yossarian is trying to shout that someone in the bomber has his guts coming out and the louder he shouts the less he seems to be heard. It's rather like Lewis Carroll—you must run twice as fast to stay still. I didn't seem to be able to get their attention and the more I did the more distant they became, until I got to a point where I actually wondered if they knew I was there. It's textbook stuff.'

Monkhouse was sent to Dulwich as a day boy—'I hated it'—and wanted to be a writer. He worked as a reporter in Beckenham but found he was writing jokes.

'I was fifteen and I liked puns. It was all based on observation of what was making other people laugh, not on what made me laugh. Puns seemed to be tremendously witty. I was sending jokes to Tommy Handley, Ronald Frankau, Bonar Colleano, jokes like: "Ma, he's mechanising me." The odd thing is that audiences always applaud the sweatier sort of joke, either because it is one that has taken a moment for them to understand or they want to convince the performer that they have perceived it.'

At fifteen, he also wanted to paint and act and he joined the

Young Conservatives and Youth for Labour in order to organise
their drama groups.

'My mother was quite a good painter and sculptress and she
wanted me to be a portrait painter in oils, but I preferred doing a
quick sketch in pen and ink. That way I got an immediate reaction.'

Monkhouse started sending strip cartoons to *Beano, Dandy, The
Knockout* and *Radio Fun.* 'I liked the formality of the humour,'
he says. 'The fact that if you were very rich, you always lit a cigar
with a £5 note in the last frame, and if you were even richer you
went to the Hotel de Posh and had a completely spherical plum
pudding with custard on top like snow and a piece of holly. I loved
the phrasing in the balloons and the hangovers from Victoriana
that were in *Chips and Jingle.* If you were a tramp you had a
stick with a spotted handkerchief and carefully ragged ends to your
trousers. It seemed to me to be a world in which I could operate
quite successfully, so I wrote and drew a great deal for these
comics and also started my own little publishing outfit. Children's
papers were in short supply during the war and I took an office in
Penge and started commissioning other writers and artists. I used
a deep voice on the phone and paid them in postal orders. I
assembled the stuff, sent it to printers in Gloucester Road and
then to distributors in London. I was a hustler. Looking back at it
I'm agape. I don't understand it now. I must have had such a
hunger. . . .'

He even sold a cartoon to *Punch.* It showed an old man dozing
off in the British Museum with his beard inserted as a marker in a
book.

Monkhouse joined the R.A.F.—'a fair dash of the younger Bilko
still in me at that stage'. He got himself posted to London and
continued publishing his comics from an office in Bishopsgate. In
the final stages of his R.A.F. service he also appeared in a Notting
Hill Gate revue which included the young Benny Hill. 'Benny kept
telling me, "Until you've been round the halls, me dear, you don't
know what you're doing." He had a perfectly awful act. He wore
a red tie in order to open with "Oops, me tie. Thank goodness. I
thought my tongue was hanging out".'

Monkhouse started broadcasting and later appeared in the revue
Sauce Piquante.

'By that time, it was quite clear that I had no talent. What I
had was a certain facility, but that's all. The other people around
me in that show with really exciting personalities and originality
were Norman Wisdom and Tommy Cooper. I'm quite sincere. I
really was untalented. I had no more than the perky mind of the
average compère presenting cabaret in a northern club, the bright

boy who sings a little song, tells a little joke, works very hard and hasn't yet got the measure of his job. I was doing formula stuff, learned by listening to American radio shows.

'I thought that if it was funny to say "I was so scared that even my goose-pimples had goose-pimples", it would be equally funny to say "She was so ugly that even the bags under her eyes had bags". It was that derivative. Except that every now and then I'd have a little flash of inspiration and find that I could come up with amusing and fresh notions. But very few of them were based on character. I wasn't aware of the fact that warmth was more important than veneer. I thought that by acquiring the patina and displaying the panache I would be putting forward such an immediately attractive and interesting persona that the audience would be prepared to listen to me for ten or fifteen minutes because of my sheer professionalism and the number of witty things I had at my finger-tips. I didn't understand then—I do now, I think—that an audience only enjoys a comedian when they feel a genuine warmth from him. But, fortunately, there were so few good people about and so many rotten ones that I was able to survive.

'I realised that I didn't want to go round the music-halls so I took up scriptwriting with another ex-Dulwich schoolboy, Denis Goodwin.'

They wrote a lot of shows for a lot of comedians and frequently performed themselves, both as a double-act and as soloists.

Monkhouse is fascinated by the mechanics of comedy. Some years ago he was a guest at a New York benefit concert and discussed comic theory and formulas with Milton Berle. Berle asked him to say any two words and Monkhouse said 'Last Thursday'. Then Berle said, 'Give me any joke you've heard me do.'

The joke was, 'This suit is made from virgin wool. It comes from the sheep that runs the fastest.'

'Right,' said Berle, 'I'll now go on and tell the joke but instead of saying, "It comes from the sheep that runs the fastest" I'll say "It came from a sheep last Thursday" and I'll get the laugh.'

Monkhouse, still marvelling twelve years later, describes how Berle did it. 'He cracked a series of one-liners, progressively shorter, one after the other, doing about ten, till the audience was laughing in pulse, till he got them into an absolutely neurotic state with laughter. Then he said, "How about this suit? That's virgin wool. Came from a sheep last Thursday!" And they roared. He was completely the master, he had them hypnotised. I've known such moments occasionally when you've suddenly got the audience and you're riding them like a jockey rides a horse. And it's very much like a race, because you must then tell yourself that they're going

too hard and they'll tire. You must pull them up. They have had
three sexual jokes, so now cool it for three minutes and do non-
sexual jokes!'

Monkhouse is aware that he is vulnerable because of his apparent
non-vulnerability.

'I try to compensate for it by being so highly polished and professional that the audiences say he is so able and he parades such
a number of comic thoughts before us that there is a place for him
in the business. But where professionalism becomes too obvious,
the British public resent it so much that quite a number of performers, among them Harry Secombe and Bruce Forsythe, have had
to disguise their ability under a kind of gaucherie. I don't think
the public has ever quite forgiven Roy Castle for being able to
do so many things so well.'

Monkhouse has been accused of having a mid-Atlantic accent.
'Either because it is unoriginal or because it reflects an unoriginal
attitude. I'm quite unable to detect it myself but, in any case, the
whole of show-business is permeated with American accents and
every singer sings in the voice of the Deep South—except Ruby
Murray. I don't think it matters any more.'

13 | *If You Don't Shut Up, I'll Bring the Comic Back*

For a time it looked as if the clubs were going to take the place of the old music-hall. There are certain superficial resemblances between them. The audience sit at tables and drink and eat while the performers battle against a high noise-level and occasional barracking. But the music-halls were devoted to the show, were there specifically for the purpose of providing live entertainment. Individuals might have been given the bird, yet the performer in general was admired and respected. Certainly, the best of them were undisputed masters of their environment. In many of the clubs the performer is treated with little respect and sometimes with contempt. The club is there for other purposes and could exist without him. 'If you don't shut up,' threatened one bingo caller, 'I'll bring the comic back.'

Bingo, bar sales, hot pies, lottery tickets and gaming tables take precedence in many places. New, curtailing gambling laws may yet bring the performer back into prominence, though the most likely effect is further closures and fewer places where he can work.

There are two kinds of clubs: the night-club, run usually by someone who knows the business and is a professional showman—or, at least, caterer; and the working men's or social club which, though it can vie with the night-club in the splendour of its appointments, is controlled by a committee under a chairman and secretary. These may be highly competent coalminers or lathe-operators, but as a rule know as much about the entertainment business as the entertainer knows about coalmining or lathe-operating. Even when they appreciate the nature of the artistic temperament, small as its permitted bounds are in clubland, they have a rare way of showing it. Roy Douglas, the last comedian to appear at the Windmill Theatre before it closed, was working in a club in the North East and received neither laughs for his jokes nor appreciation for his singing. 'You noisy buggers,' remonstrated the chairman. 'A feller gans up y'eer and sings his balls off and ye didn't listen.'

Certain basic performing requirements are just not understood. Many thousands of pounds may be spent on décor and the provision of respectable dressing-rooms, while the sound equipment is bought on the cheap, the musical backing is provided by semi-pros, some of whom cannot read music, and the lighting would be inadequate in the street outside. I have heard singers and comedians battling against ferociously bad microphones that would make Sir John Gielgud sound like Louis Armstrong—on a 1927 record.

Yet the clubs are important. The best of them pay huge sums and attract international stars such as Gracie Fields, Eartha Kitt and Tom Jones. In drab, grey towns and in cities created for the sole purpose of manufacturing and selling articles that can be weighed or measured, the unquantifiable products of the entertainment industry are a new commodity, or at least one that has not been seen live and locally for a generation or more. The atmosphere is cheerful and relaxed. Value is given for money that was hard-earned, and, having paid out anything between £1,000 and £4,000 for a performer, the management are not inclined to let anything distract from the performance.

The worst of them are a rigorous obstacle course for new talent, though in many cases the talent is so coarsened and blunted by the experience that it is unfit to appear anywhere else and will spend the rest of its time being at best tolerated, at worst jeered at, as a prelude to the Sunday noon strip-show or as an interim between the drag acts which seem to exercise a peculiar fascination among the brawnier and beefier customers. And their menfolk as well.

For, as Freddie Davies, who started in the clubs and now returns to them from pantomimes, summer shows and television appearances as a £1,250 a week comedian points out : 'If the comics who use real filth are spotted by someone who wants to give them a break, they have no material they can use anywhere but in a club.'

Davies is an old-fashioned droll as befits a man whose grandfather was a music-hall comedian and whose great-great-grandparents worked the Paris music-halls. He calls himself 'Parrot Face' and pulls a funny hat down over his head so that his ears stick out, crunches up his face so that his eyes bulge and affects a spluttering, splashing lisp. He specialises in budgerigar jokes in which sexual innuendo is rare and anal implications are few.

He knows the rougher places from personal experience, remembering the concert chairman who rose to announce : 'Before turn comes on tonight, I'd like to tell you that new lavatories 'ave just been completed. So will you please refrain from pissing in car parks.' He has been in the middle of his act when the club secretary has taken the microphone from his hand, announced a winning lottery ticket number and said, 'Right, lad, carry on.'

'You can't call yourself a comic unless you get laughs,' says Davies, 'and if you get no reaction you must give it up. This is the main reason why the club comics use very blue material. If you do a clever blue act like Bob Monkhouse it's different. He does it from choice, using a studied formula. He does double entendres and blue rhymes and blue jokes and it is all brilliant. People go to see him, knowing what he is going to do. But to go on and do a first gag which finishes up with "arseholes" is filth. I object to it, but I can understand why they use it because it gets a shock reaction. I was lucky, I did six years with Butlins and daren't utter a blue joke. When I started working the clubs I must have been the only comic using clean material. This was a novelty. I started in them at the end of 1963 and died a lot of deaths, had a lot of hard times. I knew I had to find something that was a bit different. I'd been doing a lisping song and an impression of Leonard Swindley (a *Coronation Street* character) who wore a Homburg hat. One night a woman shouted out, for no reason at all, "Tell us a joke about a budgie." So I gave them the old one about the feller who bought a budgie in a petshop and it wouldn't talk. He goes back to the shop to complain and is told to buy a ladder. The following day he's back again, still complaining that the bird just sat there, staring. The petshop owner advises a mirror, then a little ball and a lot of other budgie gear. Eventually, the man comes back with the news that the budgie is dead. "Did it say anything before it died?" asks the shopkeeper. "Oh, yes," said the man, "it said, 'Didn't that feller sell you any birdseed?' "

'It's a super joke,' says Davies, 'and it always gets a laugh. As it involves two people I gave the lisp, the funny hat and face to the feller who was complaining, and the shopkeeper was me as I normally am. It worked and after about three weeks, I thought "My God, this could be a very funny gimmick." It was getting yells in the clubs and it was very clean. I kept at it and one night, me, as the feller behind the counter, gets exasperated with me, as the feller who is complaining, and calls him "Parrot Face". It caught on. I did some radio work, but they wouldn't let me do the lisp because they said it was an affliction—and they were quite right, I suppose it is.'

Davies was working at the Candlelight Club, Oldham, in 1964 and knew that he was about to be visited by a representative from Hughie Green's show, *Opportunity Knocks*. Beforehand, Davies told him, 'I'm going to do a lot of rubbish to start with, but when I put the hat on to do this particular joke, this is what I want you to see.'

The following night opportunity knocked. Davies didn't win but he was put into the final all the same. He was already heavily booked up, so he cannot say whether it got him more work, but it pulled a few extra people into the clubs and eventually put his fees up.

'It wasn't the jokes that were getting the laughs,' he says, 'it was the character. So I kept plugging Parrot Face. I didn't do it all the time but where, after a string of gags I would need a whoofing big tag—the place the big blue gag usually goes—I'd stick my hat on and finish up with Parrot Face. It helped me tremendously against the blue machine.'

Davies recalls the story of a friend who was just starting and was approached by the secretary of a club with the offer of a one-night booking. 'What's the fee?' asked the secretary. 'A fiver,' said the comic, hesitantly. The secretary snapped his book shut. 'But you only tell bloody jokes,' he snorted.

For all that, a good pro club comic can make from between £75 to £100 a week, sometimes for a full week's engagement, at others split up by doubling—that is, working two clubs in one evening— or by doing a Sunday lunchtime and night for £25, a Thursday and Friday for £15 and a Saturday for £18.

'The main fault of a large majority of working men's clubs,' says Davies, 'is that they run their shows like a meeting, a council meeting. That's why they have a chairman and his job is to keep order. They are in the Dark Ages. A lot of the trouble is caused by the fact that the performer may be on £50 a week and the guy who has engaged him or is introducing him might work all week in the pit for £30 and work bloody hard too. How can they expect someone who works all day in a factory or pit to run a business in the evening? There should be some sort of organisation, not only to protect the artist, but the clubs as well. They waste such a lot of money.'

Duggie Brown is a clubland star. At thirty, he is already an old pro. At fifteen, he bought himself a guitar, joined a group and was on television's *6.5 Special*, the Saturday evening rock programme, before he knew how to hold it properly. The group had an unusually long life, staying together for eleven years. They worked a summer show in Perth during which Brown, a bricklayer's son from Rotherham, acted as feed and straight man to the comic. 'I

H

thought it was a waste of time then,' he says. 'Now I know the experience was invaluable.'

He is watchful and stands sentry over himself, on permanent guard against any outbreak of foolish optimism or self-delusion.

'People say it's a bad club or a good club, but it doesn't matter really. What matters is yourself, how you fit there, and if you don't fit there something's wrong with you. You should be able to bend yourself. I can't afford to buy topical material so the laughs are based on the attitude, the approach. I depend more on how I'm doing it than what I'm doing. When I've been doubling I've found out later that I've done a gag that's been cracked earlier in the evening by someone else. It's still got laughs. So it doesn't matter about changing the material as far as the public's concerned. But it matters to yourself. I do silly, slapstick stuff, but it's not me when I walk out on that stage. It's nothing of me, really. There's no part of me there. I switch on when I walk on and I switch off as soon as I come off. I'm a morose person. I love to sit in cocktail bars with a gin and tonic. Just watching. People come up and say, "You're a comedian, tell us a joke." And I say, "What job are you in?" And if they say they're a miner I say, "All right, you give me a bag of coal and I'll tell you a joke." It's a job. But it's a job I enjoy once I'm doing it. I like to see people laughing, more so than applauding at the end of a song. I still do the odd song, but I don't finish it as I don't like to see them applauding it.

'My attitude is that I'm just the lad from the next table who's got up to have a bash, that I'm no better than anybody else. I make a point of doing things wrong. I pretend to forget the end of a joke. It's like when I played the guitar—I got a lot more work and money by playing it wrong than I would have done by playing it right. If you know your weaknesses you're a step ahead of everybody. You've got to have ambition and I have a lot. But I wouldn't like to get on if I'm just going to be in between. There are so many people who are half-way up the ladder and they live as if they're right on the top.'

Mopheaded Duggie Brown leaps on to the stage after the build-up, hand-mike to his lips, his public voice higher, stronger and with more of a laugh in it than his private voice. He works at tremendous speed, his eyes darting around the huge Batley Variety Club where, later, Cliff Richard will draw out the 'oohs' and 'ahs' and be listened to respectfully as he talks lightly about what it means to be a Christian pop singer.

Brown spots two women returning to their tables. 'Hey,' he calls out, 'do you write on the walls same as us?' He gets his first laugh and reassures his audience : 'I'm not going to do anything

exciting. Later on I'm going to do one or two impressions—I've
got some good bird impressions, I eat worms. And I might tell one
or two jokes like this Scots bloke running down the road and this
little woman is running behind him and she put her hand right
up his kilt and she said, "Eh, what are these for?" And he said
"Four?" '

The women shriek but he pretends that they haven't understood
the joke, starts to repeat it but gives it up saying, 'Never mind,
nobody's perfect.'

The place is packed and the waitresses scurry round with the
scampi and chips and drinks and Brown bounces about the stage,
gurgling and laughing between his jokes, waiting for the right
moment to hit them with another, his timing as accurate as a quartz
clock. He tells a Pakistani joke and the response seems good-
humoured enough. There'll be more later, but first he bangs home
another blue gag. 'Did you hear about the honeymoon couple? On
the first night she said, "Darling, I've got a confession to make,
I've been to bed with other men." He said, "So have I, turn over."
He gets a big laugh. He is not considered blue by club standards.
He keeps asking the musicians for a chord as if he was about to
start on a song, but every time he suddenly remembers something
which he must tell the audience, something he must share like a
small boy bursting with news.

'A woman walks into a police station. She says, "Constable, I've
just been assaulted by an idiot." The policeman said, "How do
you know he was an idiot?" She said, "I had to show him what
to do." A quick one : Speedy Gonzalez took a girl into the woods.
He said : "Can I?" She said : "Will it hurt?" He said : "Did
it?" '

He tells them that if they'd like to have a gamble they can try
one of the meals. And that he believes there'll be a game of brag
later on in the gents.

He asks for the chord again and immediately says, 'Did you
hear about the two Jewish fellers and one's crying his eyes out, you
see, and his friend says, "Abie, wha' are ye creein' for?" ' He stops,
ponders : 'That sounds like a Scotsman doesn't it?' The audience
agree. He thinks some more and starts again. 'There's these two
Scots fellers and one's crying his eyes out and his friend says, "Jock,
wha' are ye creein' for?" He said, "I'm creein' because I've just
found a wage packet on the floor." He said, "You've found a wage
packet and you're creein'?" He said, "Yes, you ought to see the tax
they've stopped off it." '

The jokes cascade out of him in a torrent. He is lavish with
them, a joke millionaire convulsed with conscience and wanting to

give them all away. The audience respond with warmth, generous with their laughter.

Towards the end of his act he launches into his big story, the hit-'em-between-the-eyes, the whoofing big tag that, if there were any aisles, would have 'em rolling in them.

'This chap's got this little parrot, you see, and he's teaching it how to speak. And all it'll say is "Who is it?" ' (The last three words are uttered in a high, parrotlike shriek.)

'Well, he goes out to work at 8 o'clock one morning and at half past nine there's a knock on the door. And the parrot says: "Who is it?" He said: "It's the plumber, I've come to mend your pipes, will you let me in please?" '

The plumber's voice is gentle and inoffensive.

'And the parrot says: "Who is it?" He said: "It's the plumber, I've come to mend your pipes, will you let me in please?" And the parrot says . . .'

A woman in the audience shouts out 'Who is it?'

'Who is it?' echoes Brown with a shriek.

'He said: "It's the plumber, I've come to mend your pipes, will you let me in please?" And the parrot says: "Who is it?" '

The parrot's voice fades, the story-teller becomes uncertain. Clearly, he has realised that he is in a rut. He mutters the next line: 'It's the plumber, I've come to mend your pipes, will you let me in please?'

Brown laughs nervously. 'I've forgot the end,' he confesses. 'Er, oh dear, I know the characters like. Oh, and I was going right well, as well. The parrot was in the cage and I know what he said. He said "Who is it?" you see. And this chap's outside and he's got this bag with some spanners and some lead piping and, er . . .'

By this time his voice is nearly in tears.

'And he says: "It's the plumber, I've come to mend your pipes, will you let me in please?" And the parrot answered him and it said, er: "Who is it?" . . .'

He abandons the story entirely. 'Two coloured chaps,' he announces, 'in the middle of Birmingham—Alabama. And one said: "Rastus!" ' It is the same sound as the parrot's voice. Brown recognises it. 'That sounds like the parrot, doesn't it?' he asks. 'Must be a blackbird.'

The parrot story seems to have been forgotten. There are other jokes and a total change of mood as he announces, 'Tonight is the grand opening of—Tony's wallet.' Then he remembers the parrot joke.

'The parrot's in the cage. I know what he said. He said "Who is it?", you see, and there's this chap outside and he didn't say "It's the plumber, I've come to mend your pipes, will you let me in please?" He said, *"It's the plumber, I've come to mend your pipes, will you let me in please?" Angrily.*

'Well, it went on for four and a half hours, not quite as long as I make it last. In the end, the blood-pressure got the better of him and he collapsed in a heap on the stairs. And at 5 o'clock the man came home from work and he fell right over this body and he looked down at it and he said : "Who is it?"'

And the voice is exactly the same screech as the parrot's.

'And the parrot says, "It's the plumber, he's come to mend your pipes. . . ."'

The parrot's voice is exactly the same as the plumber's, and the rest is drowned in laughter.The act is over and the whoofing big tag is as clean as a rhubarb-scoured saucepan.

What dirt there was in the act seems to be there because it is expected by the audience. Freud says : 'It is curious that common people so thoroughly enjoy smutty talk and it is a never-lacking activity of cheerful humour.' Clearly, Freud either did not know any stockbrokers or he classed them as 'common people' along with everyone else. The only class divisions in smut appear to be in the quality of the joke rather than the depth of the dirt and this is a factor that is common to all humour, cutting across economic or social differences and having, as Jonathan Miller and Frankie Howerd say, much more to do with degrees of intelligence.

All the same, Freud makes some pertinent remarks on the subject.

The smutty joke was originally directed against the woman and is comparable to an attempt at seduction. If a man tells or listens to obscene jokes in male society, the original situation, which cannot be realised on account of social inhibitions, is thereby also represented. Whoever laughs at a smutty joke does the same as the spectator who laughs at a sexual aggression. . . .

The smutty joke is like the denudation of the person of the opposite sex towards whom the joke is directed. Through the utterance of obscene words, the person attacked is forced to picture the parts of the body in question or the sexual act and is shown that the aggressor pictures the same thing. There is no doubt that the original motive of the smutty joke was the pleasure of seeing the sexual displayed. . . .

One of the primitive components of our libido is the desire to see the sexual exposed. Perhaps this itself is a development— a substitution—for the desire to touch which is assumed to be the primary pleasure. . . .

In all obscene jokes we succumb to striking mistakes of judgment about the 'goodness' of the joke as far as it depends upon
formal conditions; the technique of these jokes is very often very
poor while their laughing effect is enormous.*

There is not a club comic who would not agree with Freud's
conclusions.

The clubs and pubs are full of drag acts and most of them have
little or nothing to do with the business of comedy. Their appeal
seems to lie solely in the extent to which they can impersonate
women and some of them undergo hormone treatment as an aid
to achieving the desired cleavage effect. This is clearly interesting,
even fascinating to certain audiences and may, indeed, give rise
to a lot of nervous laughter.

Many comedians dress as women as *part* of their repertoire, either
to play pantomime dames or to parody certain female types. Others
choose drag as their sole means of expressing comedy. It was always
a slightly disreputable end of the trade until Danny La Rue (real
name : David Patrick Carroll) achieved fame, fortune and a place
in the Royal Variety Show, because of the larky way in which he
approached a basically steamy aspect of show-business, and through
a quite remarkable degree of glamour which outshines many of
the women he either works with or has in his audience. There is
no doubting his immense popularity, but his humour is essentially
drag humour—that is, it feeds upon and draws constant attention
to the ambiguity of his performance. A great deal of it is created
very simply by reference to the fact that beneath all the female
finery hangs a male appendage.

On a television show with Max Bygraves he explains how he
has travelled from the North and has driven down the M1.

' "Dan," they said—they always call me Dan for want of a better
word—"Dan," they said, "it's very dodgy on the road so you'd
better travel in the gear." What a drag! "Travel in the gear?" I
said. They said : "Nobody will know." So off I go and somehow I
got a bad tear—see the rent in the back?—so I thought I'd pop
into a transport caff for a needle and thread. Well, Fred wasn't
there, so I thought, right mate . . .'

'Did you feel a fool?' interrupts Bygraves.

'No, there wasn't one handy,' rejoins La Rue. 'I sort of stood
there, when suddenly this geezer comes up and says "Ay, ay." Of

* Freud, *Wit and Its Relation to the Unconscious* (Unwin, 1916).

course, I didn't take any notice, I never do. Then he said, "My goodness, if you came out on my lorry girl you'd get a big surprise." I said, "If I came out in your lorry, mate, you'd get a big surprise." '

Bygraves says he can understand it. 'That hair, that dress, that figure—take it all away and what have you got left?'

La Rue assumes a deep, gruff voice and sings 'Oh Danny boy. . . .'

Clever as the performance is, costly as the *couture* may be, the comedy is almost entirely restricted to the fact of impersonation. When he does slide into character—Lady Cynthia Grope of the Conservative Party, a teenage rocker, a geisha girl, a stripper—it is never sustained for long and is still full of out-of-character references to the anomaly of a male form beneath a female appearance.

When Rex Jamieson walks on as Mrs Shufflewick the fact that he is a male impersonating a female is quite irrelevant. Mrs Shufflewick, in fact, could be a woman and possibly many people in the audience believe that she is. The act stands or falls entirely on the character and comedy presented on the stage and owes nothing to a knowledge by the audience of a dressing-room transformation scene.

Mrs Shufflewick, wearing a scraggy fur and a three-stringed pearl necklace, dangling ear-rings and little hat, her skirts a modest length, stands with her eyebrows raised, the wide thin mouth curling slightly at the ends, and recounts the shocking adventures of a night out remembered through a haze of gin, stout and double Drambuies with a cheerful matter-of-fact Cockney acceptance that treats disaster as routine and frailty as a welcome distraction.

Rex Jamieson, rootless in a room in Bristol, shuffles about in a baggy yellow sweater hunting for old scripts in bulging suitcases. He is visibly a martyr to dyspepsia and is depressed over the imminence of bankruptcy proceedings. 'Yes,' he acknowledges, 'I think you could say I'm blue. I've got some pretty blue gags that I start straight off with. I know if they go down well I can do the rest. If they are a bit dodgy on those, then I switch and go into the cleaner version.

Mrs Shufflewick, in a London dockside pub, finds no reason for self-censorship :

'Like this fur? It cost £200, this fur did. I didn't pay for it meself, I met two hundred fellers with £1 each. So I was all right. I wasn't done, was I? I don't think so anyway. I can't remember meself now, to tell you the truth. It's the gin and tonic, you see, it fogs the brain—I'm happy to say. This is very rare, this fur. It is known in the trade as untouched pussy—which is unobtainable in London at the moment. And there's very little knocking about elsewhere. But I'm lucky to be here at all tonight. I tell you for why. As you know, I'm weak-willed and easily led, and I went out last night. I was the first one in the pub—two minutes after opening time. I forget what I'd been hanging about for to make me so late, but still I was sitting in there with a glass of beer minding me own business, doing no harm to anyone and, all of a sudden, the door opened and this sailor walked in. I'd never seen him before and he came over and he plonked himself down beside me, not so much as please may I, or share my lettuce or anything, and he pulled out a packet of picture postcards he'd brought back from the Middle East and, quite honestly, I had never seen anything so disgust . . . I mean, I am broad-minded to the point of obscenity, I mean, I know how many beans make five and I've been about in me tea half-hour, but my God, if you'd seen these—and they were in Agfacolour, I mean there was nothing left to the old imagination. How they get themselves in those posi . . . I couldn't do it. So I gave them back to him after twenty-five minutes. I said I've no wish to look at this type of literature, thank you very much. I said as far as I'm concerned you can get behind me, Satan. And those were the worst few words. . . .'

There is no need to finish the sentence, for the words are drowned in the laughter. Jamieson has probably the best sense of timing in the whole comedy business. He will hold a pause for as long as eight seconds and then intuitively drop in the crudest line with the delicacy and deftness of an expert fisherman casting a fly.

'I was at the Windmill for three years,' says Jamieson, 'and I had to type out my act and submit it to the Lord Chamberlain. When it's typed out on paper it doesn't sound anything, just a load of rubbish. It always came back stamped with approval. I've had one or two concert secretaries who said they thought the act was a bit near the knuckle, but I don't think I've ever had any complaints from the audience. Only once or twice in Wales, where you get a lot of those chapel people. Women respond even more than men. They laugh louder and applaud longer. I never look at an audience. I always look above their heads into space. I think if you were looking at their faces and they were a bit glum it would put you off.

'London is the best place for me because Mrs Shufflewick is basically a Cockney character. But I've done it all over the place and it's usually gone well. Lancashire's very difficult. I don't think they like southern comics. I was top of the bill at the Hippodrome,

Wigan, and I didn't get a titter from Monday to Saturday. They just didn't know what I was talking about. It was awful. I tried changing the stuff, I tried everything. Thank God I was staying in a pub.'

'I don't remember leaving the pub. I know I had my head on his shoulder. I forget who was holding me feet. We got outside. Now I don't know if any of you have ever been out with a sailor. . . .'

'I was brought up in Southend,' continues Jamieson, 'by a foster mother. I never had any theatrical experience until I went into the air force. I was in *The Gang Show* for two years and that's when I first started doing this drag-act business. When I came out of the air force I thought I'd stick to show-business and I got an audition at the BBC. I did a vicar act as well in those days. They said : "Oh, no, we can't have that, we'll have all those religious maniacs ringing us up. Can you do anything else?" So I said : "I've got a charlady act and I can do that if you like." So they said come back next week and we'll give you another audition and see what this charlady is all about. So I wrote a script which, looking back now, must have been pretty awful, and I went up and did it.

'The producer said he would give me a broadcast but that we'd have to think up a name as he couldn't put me on as Rex Jamieson and then have me talking about me old man and that. So he told me to go home and write down about a dozen different names as stupid as I could think of and ring him with them. That's what I did and he picked Shufflewick. I had an aunt who was very much like Mrs Shufflewick, so I suppose I got a bit of it off her. She was raving mad.'

'. . . I'd got no money in me bag, so I 'ad to walk all the way home, 2½ hours. Oh, my poor old feet when I got there. I got to my road and I thought, it's no good me charging in and having a scene with the old boy because all he's going to say is where have you been, who have you been with and how much have you managed to—spend. So I thought, what I'll do, I'll take all me clothes off downstairs and I'll just sort of slide up and creep in and if he says anything at all I shall just say "I was watching the Epilogue and I nodded off", to which there is no answer. So I got there. I took all me clothes off, I hadn't got a stitch on, all in a bundle under me arm, and I was up the staircase and everything in the garden was lovely, not a sound and I got to the bit where it bends round the corner at the top and I got the shock

234 | *The Laughtermakers*

of me life—I'm on top of a 29 bus. And all these people turned round, you know—all sober. Oh, I could have hit 'em. As if they'd never seen a woman with no clothes on, on top of a bus before—they're so narrow-minded. So I just stood there, you know, I thought I'd stare 'em out. And I thought, let one of them make the first move and one feller did—dirty, filthy beast, bless 'im. I came downstairs with as much dignity as I could muster 'cos I still had me hairnet on, you know. And I must say, the conductor wouldn't take any fare—he just kicked me off. . . .'

'I did a television in 1950 and Vivian Van Dam of the Windmill saw me and sent for me. Then there were variety dates and a television series with Ralph Reader that bumped my money up quite a bit. And another TV series with Norman Evans. With the BBC I knew very well what to do and what not to do, what they would accept and what they wouldn't. But there again, you see, I got away with a lot of things because of the timing. I used to do a lot of radio—*London Lights, Midday Music Hall, Saturday Night Variety*—about ten a year. Then they stopped all the radio variety and put on these record shows so they wouldn't have to pay the artists. Now I've fallen on bad times. I'm such a shocking business person. Whenever I get any money, bills come in and I have to pay it all out again. I enjoyed the life until the last year or so. Now there's so much work gone that'll never come back—variety theatres and BBC. When you're doing odd nights in clubs you have to travel all the time. In variety you only travelled week-ends. But I get plenty of work. I did two weeks at the Royal Court Theatre Upstairs last Christmas. A very good audience, a little higher class than the usual club audience, but better if anything. They laughed just as much as the lower classes at the blue bits.'

14 | *Spike — the Cosmic Comic*

One of the great mysteries of comedy is how so apparently shallow and transient an entertainment can create an impression so deep and lasting. We look back on the great clowns of the past—on Keaton, Chaplin, W. C. Fields, Sid Field and Tony Hancock—with more affection than on their more heroic contemporaries, for it now appears that they were more representative of their times and, on the whole, more likeable. I believe that the same will happen of the present crop of comedians and that the restless, unquiet spirit of Spike Milligan, the most creative of them all, will be recalled by people who will be hard put to it to name the prime ministers of his day. But Milligan is not yet ready for posterity.

One of his projects is a clown's-eye-view of the Bible as a feature film. 'God knows,' he says, 'whether it will come off or not, but Peter Sellers and I are going to try and do it. I thought, "Why should all the serious writers have charge of God? Why can't the clowns have some of Him?" I've written the first joke. You have this great echoing sound like timpani being played through an iron tube. Then there's a rush of wind and the screen is black, swirling black. Then a voice says, "In the beginning, God said. . . ." And another voice thunders out, "LET THERE BE LIGHT!" And a 40-watt bulb goes on and there's a bloke in a nightshirt lying in bed underneath it. He sits up and says, "Who put that light on?"

'I'm going to have God coming down to earth in the body of a First World War soldier who used to pray to him a lot. He arrives at the barrier at Waterloo and is asked why he hasn't got a ticket. He says, "I . . . er . . . they don't give tickets where I come from." "Where do you come from?" "Heaven." "Heaven! What are you talking about. What's your name?" "God."

'The ticket collector calls a copper and says, "This chap hasn't paid his fare." When God tells the copper that he's God, the copper says, "You bin drinkin', sir? You don't look like God." "Well," says God, "I'm a ball of light, you see, and I can't come to the barrier at Waterloo like a ball of light. It would put the fear of . . . er . . God into you."

'There are other things. Japhet falling over backwards when he's drunk and the neighbours, very shocked, saying, "You're supposed to be in the Bible." And Joseph in his coat of many colours being lowered down a well—ha ha—down a well! A lot of lunacy goes on in the Bible. And the sea not opening for Moses and when the Jews dance round the Golden Calf it's to Victor Silvester-type music and they've all got numbers on their backs and there's a cry of "Stop this sinful Mecca dancing!" And have you thought of the problem of getting two bloody chickens up a gangplank together?

'And Christ. He must have done tricks, I think. He did tricks with the bread and fishes : "Now, I 'ave heah, six fishes in my left hand, and a few loaves in my right. I shall now do this extraordinary trick of making them go all the way round."

'I'll do the Crucifixion in a launderette. I see launderettes as the end of the world and the only thing that could possibly move anybody there is a Crucifixion. They are all there, those awful late people who go in about eleven or twelve at night with plastic bags —cripples, dwarfs, whores. And while they're putting all this crap into the machines, the soldiers come in and put the Cross up at the other end of the launderette and they nail Christ to it. And the people take no notice at all. They look at him with this dead look and they pretend not to see anything, like you get when somebody dies on the pavement. And there are whispers of "Shouldn't let those kind of people come in here, long-haired louts, trouble-makers". And when the Roman soldier sticks his spear into His side all the blood comes out and goes over his uniform and one of the watchers says, "There, there, dear. I'll put that in with me smalls."

'Whatever else it will do, it'll kill old Huston's version of the Bible.'

And whatever else it will be, it will also be the seven-year-old boy clown in Poona being forbidden to approach the crib in the nativity play, but going there all the same and sweeping off his hat and hearing—and never forgetting—the sound of applause. For comedy is a search for the childhood state of virtue in which purity, smut, vulgarity and impudence are all enfolded in the same innocence, where laughter happens unprompted by comedian, writer or joke. The quest is the same for both the laughtermaker and the laugher.

Index